Balancing Environment and Development

Costs, Revenues, and Benefits of the Western Riverside County Multiple Species Habitat Conservation Plan

Lloyd Dixon, Paul Sorensen, Martin Wachs, Myles Collins,

Mark Hanson, Aaron Kofner, Thomas Light,

Michael Madsen, Lindell Marsh, Adrian Overton,

Howard J. Shatz, Brian A. Weatherford

Sponsored by the Western Riverside County Regional Conservation Authority

Transportation, Space, and Technology

A RAND INFRASTRUCTURE, SAFETY, AND ENVIRONMENT PROGRAM

The research described in this monograph was supported by the Western Riverside County Regional Conservation Authority and was conducted under the auspices of the Transportation, Space, and Technology Program within RAND Infrastructure, Safety, and Environment.

Library of Congress Cataloging-in-Publication Data is available for this publication.

ISBN: 978-0-8330-4609-3

The RAND Corporation is a nonprofit research organization providing objective analysis and effective solutions that address the challenges facing the public and private sectors around the world. RAND's publications do not necessarily reflect the opinions of its research clients and sponsors.

RAND® is a registered trademark.

Published 2008 by the RAND Corporation
1776 Main Street, P.O. Box 2138, Santa Monica, CA 90407-2138
1200 South Hayes Street, Arlington, VA 22202-5050
4570 Fifth Avenue, Suite 600, Pittsburgh, PA 15213-2665
RAND URL: http://www.rand.org/
To order RAND documents or to obtain additional information, contact
Distribution Services: Telephone: (310) 451-7002;
Fax: (310) 451-6915; Email: order@rand.org

Preface

Population growth and economic development are increasingly colliding with environmental goals and regulations that protect threatened and endangered species. Perhaps nowhere is the clash more evident than in the western part of Riverside County, California, which is one of the fastest-growing regions in the United States. In response, federal, state, and local government agencies adopted the Multiple Species Habitat Conservation Plan (MSHCP) in June 2004. The MSHCP sets up a large habitat reserve and allows continued development outside the reserve area.

This monograph examines the cost of assembling and operating the reserve, the adequacy of revenue sources, the prospect for achieving the habitat-conservation goals specified in the MSHCP, and whether the MSHCP has streamlined the permitting processes for transportation and development projects. This research was sponsored by the Western Riverside County Regional Conservation Authority.

This monograph should be of interest to policymakers who address environmental and economic-development issues at all levels of government, environmental groups, and private developers. The MSHCP is an ambitious effort that is a potential model for other parts of the country; thus, the findings should be of interest both regionally and nationally.

The RAND Transportation, Space, and Technology Program

This research was conducted under the auspices of the Transportation, Space, and Technology (TST) Program within RAND Infrastructure, Safety, and Environment (ISE). The mission of ISE is to improve the development, operation, use, and protection of society's essential physical assets and natural resources and to enhance the related social assets of safety and security of individuals in transit and in their workplaces and communities. The TST research portfolio encompasses policy areas including transportation systems, space exploration, information and telecommunication technologies, nano- and biotechnologies, and other aspects of science and technology policy.

Questions or comments about this monograph should be sent to the project leader, Lloyd Dixon (Lloyd_Dixon@rand.org). Information about the TST Program is available online (http://www.rand.org/ise/tech). Inquiries about TST research should be sent to the following address:

Martin Wachs, Director
Transportation, Space, and Technology Program, ISE
RAND Corporation
1776 Main Street
P. O. Box 2138
Santa Monica, CA 90401-2138
310-393-0411, x7720
Martin_Wachs@rand.org

Contents

Figures

Tables

Summary

With increasing frequency across the country, population growth and development interests are colliding with environmental goals and regulations that protect the habitat of threatened and endangered species. Perhaps nowhere is this clash more evident than in western Riverside County—one of the fastest-growing metropolitan areas in the United States and the home of a diverse array of increasingly rare species. Policymakers in Riverside County in the 1990s found the regulatory process for reconciling environmental and development interests both ineffective and inefficient. Regulatory requirements and litigation slowed development projects and increased their costs. And required project-by-project mitigation for endangered-species impacts resulted in a patchwork assembly of uncoordinated habitats. There was legitimate concern that these problems would only grow worse over time.

Responding to this challenge, in 1999, the Riverside County Board of Supervisors and the Riverside County Transportation Commission (RCTC) initiated a comprehensive regional-planning effort called the Riverside County Integrated Project (RCIP). A key element of the RCIP is the Multiple Species Habitat Conservation Plan (MSHCP), a plan to conserve 500,000 acres of the 1.26 million acres in the western part of the county. In return for establishing the conservation reserve, the U.S. Fish and Wildlife Service (USFWS) and the California Department of Fish and Game (CDFG) issued the county and 14 cities in western Riverside County a 75-year "take" permit for endangered species. Finalized in June 2004, the take permit allows the cities and county to approve development projects outside the reserve that may negatively affect sensitive plant and animal species, thus allowing for continued growth and development outside of the reserve area. The agreement vested responsibility for acquiring and managing the reserve with the Western Riverside County Regional Conservation Authority (RCA).

The MSHCP is an ambitious effort, mitigating development impact on 146 plant and animal species. While it is a potential model for other areas in the county, questions remain about the cost of assembling and operating the reserve, the adequacy of revenue sources, the prospect for achieving the habitat-conservation goals specified in the MSHCP, and whether the MSHCP has, in fact, streamlined the permitting processes for transportation and development projects. This monograph examines a series of issues that address these questions. Specifically, we examine the

- extent to which the MSHCP has shortened the permitting processes for transportation and development projects and reduced the frequency and scope of lawsuits that attempt to stop or modify projects
- effect on average travel speeds of faster completion of four major transportation corridors in western Riverside County and the monetary value of higher travel speeds
- market value as of mid-2007 of the land already acquired for the reserve and of the land needed to complete it
- advantages and disadvantages of land-acquisition strategies that vary in the period during which the reserve is assembled and whether annual acquisition goals are set in terms of acres or annual outlays
- costs to administer the plan and operate the reserve over the 75-year planning period
- adequacy of revenue for the plan and options for raising additional revenue
- prospects for achieving the plan's habitat-conservation goals, using USFWS's conceptual design for the reserve.

Our analysis examines the MSCHP's benefits for the permitting process. The MSHCP is also expected to have important ecological benefits—namely, the assembly of a well-planned reserve area rather than the patchwork of uncoordinated habitats that could result without the MSHCP. Assessing the MSHCP's ecological benefits, however, is beyond the scope of this analysis.

After providing some background on the MSHCP, we summarize our findings in each area that the study addressed and identify issues that our analysis raised and that the RCA Board of Directors, RCA staff, and stakeholders should address moving forward.

The Multiple Species Habitat Conservation Plan

The plan area for the MSHCP encompasses the unincorporated lands within Riverside County west of the crest of the San Jacinto Mountains as well as the cities of Banning, Beaumont, Calimesa, Corona, Hemet, Lake Elsinore, Moreno Valley, Murrieta, Norco, Perris, Riverside, San Jacinto, and Temecula. Under the arrangement, these jurisdictions share responsibility for assembling and managing the reserve area, and each in turn gains greater local control over land-use and development decisions consistent with the plan.

Figure S.1 provides an overview of the MSHCP area within western Riverside County, including existing public land as well as the additional area from which the reserve will be drawn. The 500,000 acres to be conserved include about 350,000 acres already held in public trust, along with 153,000 additional acres that will be conserved under the MSHCP agreement. The 153,000 acres will be drawn from approximately 300,000 acres that constitute the potential MSCHP conservation area in Figure S.1.

Of the land still required when the plan was adopted, federal and state agencies are obligated to fund the acquisition of about 56,000 acres (see Table S.1). Local governments, in turn, are expected to purchase an additional 56,000 acres from willing sellers. It is anticipated that an additional 41,000 acres will be conserved though the entitlement and authorization processes for private development, relying on incentives as well as existing local, state, and federal development regulations.

According to RCA staff, 35,526 acres were acquired as of October 2007 (see rightmost column of Table S.1). To date, very little acreage has been conserved through the development-review process because developers have, by and large, avoided projects that would require contributions, as opposed to sales, of land to the reserve. As density increases and development options decrease, contributions through the

Figure S.1
Location of the MSHCP and Targeted Areas for Conservation

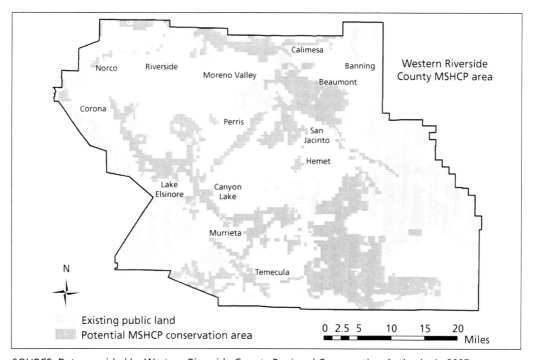

SOURCE: Data provided by Western Riverside County Regional Conservation Authority in 2007.
RAND *MG816-S.1*

Table S.1
Responsibility for Assembling the Reserve

Resource	Target Acreage	Acreage Acquired as of October 2007
Existing public or quasipublic (PQP) open space		
Federal	248,000	248,000
State	34,000	34,000
Local	65,000	65,000
Subtotal	347,000	347,000
Land for RCA to assemble		
Federal and state acquisition	56,000	14,677
Purchases by local government	56,000	20,192
Contributions by private developers through development-authorization process	41,000	657
Subtotal	153,000	35,526
Total	500,000	382,526

SOURCE: Data on target acreage from TLMA (2003, pp. 4-3–4-13). Data on acquired acreage provided by RCA in 2007.
NOTE: There are 1.26 million acres in western Riverside County.

development process may accelerate. If they do not, however, local government will likely need to fund the purchase of much of the 41,000 acres in addition to the 56,000 acres for which it is already responsible.

Benefits of the Multiple Species Habitat Conservation Plan for Constructing Infrastructure

Our analysis of the MSHCP's effects on permitting transportation and development projects is based on (1) interviews with organization representatives who have substantial experience with and insights into the MSHCP and its implementation and (2) a detailed questionnaire completed by most of those interviewed and other knowledgeable stakeholders. The number of organizations involved in the process of seeking or issuing permits is limited. The questionnaire was sent to the 38 such organizations we could identify and completed by 19, representing the perspectives of cities, transportation agencies, wildlife agencies, consultants, lawyers, environmental organizations, and developers. We also interviewed 22 individuals. While the number of completed questionnaires and interviews is not particularly large, it reflects a substantial proportion of organizations experienced with the permitting process under the MSHCP, and we believe that it provides a reasonably accurate overall picture of the plan's perceived impact on the permitting process.

Considerable care was taken to design the questionnaire so that responses would accurately reflect reality. For example, respondents were asked to identify specific road projects that have been active in the planning process since the MSHCP was adopted and to answer detailed questions about each project. In spite of these precautions, stakeholder perceptions of the MSHCP's impact on the permitting process are subject to error and should be interpreted only as an initial indication of the MSHCP's impact. Further work is warranted exploring the feasibility and cost of using administrative data on the time needed to complete the permitting process with and without the MSHCP.

Overall, the findings on the MSHCP's impact on the permitting process for road-transportation projects are encouraging. Projects that affect federally listed species appear to benefit the most from the MSHCP. Stakeholders indicated that the MSHCP had accelerated the permitting process for all such projects with which they were familiar that had completed major steps in the permitting process since the MSHCP was adopted. Examples include Clinton Keith Road in the southern part of western Riverside County and the River Road bridge over the Santa Ana River. Savings in time ranged from one to five years, and, in some cases, the MSHCP was perceived to have allowed a project to proceed that would not have proceeded otherwise. The perceived benefits were also substantial for projects affecting federally listed species that had not yet completed a major step in the permitting process: Stakeholders believed that the MSHCP has increased the chance that the project would receive all the required authorizations and has accelerated the permitting process in a substantial majority of the projects identified. Examples cited include the Mid County Parkway and the realignment of State Route (SR) 79.

The MSHCP's effects on road-transportation projects that do not affect federally listed species were seen as positive overall, but the effects do not appear to be large; in some cases, the effects were seen as negative. For example, for projects that have not completed major steps in the permitting process, stakeholders reported roughly equal numbers of cases in which the MSHCP had (1) accelerated the permitting process, (2) slowed the process, and (3) had no effect on the process.

The MSHCP's perceived benefits also extend to road-safety and maintenance projects. While the amount of time saved was not thought to be great for such projects (typically six months to one year), the large number of such projects can cause the aggregate time savings across all safety and maintenance projects to be substantial.

A sizable majority of stakeholders believed that, since its adoption, the MSHCP has reduced the number or scope of lawsuits that have sought to stop or modify road projects. While the consequences of this reduction may be reflected, to some extent, in stakeholder estimates of the degree to which the MSHCP has accelerated the permitting process, the perceived reduction in litigation may also add to the quantitative estimates of time savings.

On the downside, our findings suggest that the MSHCP has increased the cost of the permitting process, at least in some cases. Stakeholders reported that the MSHCP increased the cost of the permitting process more frequently than it decreased the cost for road projects that have not yet completed major steps in the permitting process. The MSHCP presumably reduces the cost of obtaining the required authorizations for road-safety and maintenance projects because it exempts such projects from review for consistency with the MSHCP; however, we could not investigate the magnitude of such savings or whether the MSHCP adds to or reduces project-permitting costs across all projects.

Stakeholders generally expect the MSHCP's benefits to continue for road projects over the next 10 years. The acceleration of the permitting process and the reduction in lawsuits are, by and large, expected to be somewhat greater than have been observed to date. Time savings are frequently expected to run from one to five years, and expected time savings of greater than five years were reported.

While the MSHCP appears to provide benefits for many road projects, findings on the impact for commercial, industrial, and residential development projects are mixed. Stakeholders reported that the MSHCP has increased the time needed to obtain required permits as often as it has reduced it for development projects on more than five acres and expected similar outcomes for development projects over the next 10 years. The findings suggest that the MSHCP has, on the whole, reduced the frequency and scope of lawsuits about development projects, but the magnitude of the effect is lower than for road projects.

The MSHCP is still relatively new, and our findings provide an early look at its impact on the permitting process. The extent to which the MSHCP actually facilitates placing infrastructure will be much clearer over the next three or four years as major infrastructure projects, such as the Mid County Parkway, work their way through the permitting process. The plan's benefits may also change over time, for a number of reasons. First, stakeholders will become more familiar with the permitting process, potentially accelerating it. Second, there may be fewer points of contention between the resource agencies and permittees as the habitat-conservation goals for the plan are achieved. Finally, the plan's benefits may grow as economic growth continues in western Riverside County over the long term. The permitting process without the plan in place would likely become increasingly onerous as the amount of open space declines. The findings in this monograph can serve as a baseline against which future assessments of MSHCP benefits can be compared.

So far, we have presented our findings on the MSHCP's perceived benefits for the permitting process. But this analysis can be turned around to assess what would happen if the plan were to disappear (e.g., be abandoned). If the plan were revoked, the permitting process for many roadway projects would likely lengthen—our research suggests by up to five years. There would also be increased delays in the many road-safety and maintenance projects that are planned for the coming years. If the plan were abandoned, the habitat-conservation process in western Riverside County would also revert to the uncoordinated, project-by-project system that existed before the MSHCP.

Delaying the placement of transportation infrastructure in western Riverside County will reduce mobility in the area. To better understand how large these reductions might be, we used a detailed computer model of the transportation network to quantify the mobility impacts of delays in completing four major transportation corridors that resulted from the Community and Environmental Transportation Acceptability Process (CETAP) in western Riverside County. Our analysis suggests that delaying the four CETAP corridors will cause travel speeds in western Riverside County to decline more rapidly than they would otherwise. The effects on individual trips may not be large, but they can add up when aggregated across all trips taken in a year. Average speeds do not change by more than 1 or 2 miles per hour, but the cost in lost time to drivers can total hundreds of millions of dollars annually.

Market Value in 2007 of Land Needed for the Reserve

To estimate the 2007 market value of land needed for the reserve, we developed a statistical model of land values based on sales records from the Riverside County assessor's office for January 2000 through October 2007. The model considers such factors as parcel size, current land use, purchase date, zoning, slope, proximity to roads and freeways, job accessibility, and average household income in the surrounding area. After estimating the model based on past sales data, we used it to project the 2007 market value of the 35,526 acres that RCA had acquired through October 2007 and of the 117,474 acres remaining to be assembled. To identify the land remaining to be acquired, we developed a number of reserve-assembly scenarios based on an outline that USFWS had developed for the reserve. This so-called conceptual reserve design (CRD) was based on the textual description in the MSHCP planning document of how the final reserve might be configured.

We estimate that the 35,526 acres already acquired through October 2007 were valued at approximately $9,000 per acre, on average, as of mid-2007. The average acquisition cost for this land was approximately $8,200 per acre in 2007 dollars, and the difference reflects the general rise in inflation-adjusted land values through mid-2007. As of mid-2007, the market value of land still needed for the reserve was approximately $36,000 per acre. The difference in the values of the land already acquired and yet to be acquired indicates that past acquisitions have focused on less expensive parcels.

Detailed examination of the parcels needed to complete the USFWS CRD revealed that the land needed for linkages between core habitat areas is disproportionately expensive because it runs through heavily developed areas. Modifying the linkages to avoid existing development could reduce the costs of assembling the reserve, and the cost reductions could be significant. If linkages are rerouted to avoid existing development, we estimate that the average value of land needed to complete the reserve could fall to as low as approximately $26,000 per acre (up to roughly a 25-percent decline). Whether the linkages could be rerouted without degrading the reserve's ecological integrity, however, would need to be investigated.

As of mid-2007, the market value of the land needed to complete the reserve was considerable. Assuming that linkages are not rerouted, the value of the land needed to complete the reserve is an estimated $4.2 billion, with a 95-percent statistical confidence interval running from approximately –10 percent to +20 percent of the total ($3.8 billion to $5.0 billion). Note that this total covers the land to be acquired by all levels of government and to be contributed through the development-authorization process, not just the land that is local government's responsibility to acquire. Our estimate of the overall value of the land in a 153,000-acre reserve is approximately double that in the initial MSHCP planning documents (which were completed in 2003), reflecting the rapid rise in land prices in western Riverside County between 2003 and 2007. Housing prices in Riverside County have fallen considerably since mid-2007. However, sales prices for open space and agricultural land in western Riverside County did not show a substantial downturn in price through October 2007, and more-recent data are not available as of this writing. Thus, it is not clear how the value of land held by RCA has changed since mid-2007.

Preferred Land-Acquisition Strategy

The substantial increase in the projected cost of assembling the reserve raises concern that current local revenue sources may be inadequate to fund local-government obligations under the plan. The overall cost of assembling the reserve, however, depends not on land prices in mid-2007 but on the trajectory of land values over time and the time frame in which RCA acquires the land needed for the reserve. The financial consequences of different price trajectories and purchase strategies can be enormous. For example, if the current downturn in housing prices causes land values to retreat substantially from the $36,000 average in mid-2007 and if RCA buys a substantial amount of land during the downturn, then reserve-assembly costs could be considerably less than estimates based on mid-2007 values. If, on the other hand, RCA spaces purchases over a long period and land prices continue to appreciate at historic rates, then the present value of the outlays needed to assemble the reserve could be far greater than estimates based on mid-2007 prices.

The optimal period over which to assemble the reserve depends on future land prices, but it is impossible to predict with certainty how land prices will evolve over time. To address this uncertainty, we constructed a wide range of price scenarios based on economic theory and historic trends in land prices. We then investigated the consequences of different land-acquisition strategies. While it is desirable to spread purchases over a long period in some land-price scenarios, we concluded that the preferred strategy overall is to acquire the land over approximately 10 years. Acquiring land in the next decade is desirable because the financial risks of spreading land purchases over a much longer period are substantial, while the potential excess costs of buying land too quickly are not nearly as large.

Assembling the remaining acreage needed for the reserve over 10 years would entail a considerable acceleration in land acquisition. Land acquisitions during the first three years of plan operation (2005 through 2007) averaged approximately 5,500 acres per year. Acquisitions would need to increase to nearly 12,000 acres per year to complete the reserve in 10 years.

Our findings also suggest that it would be preferable for RCA to set annual land-acquisition goals in terms of the dollar amount of land purchased rather than the number of acres purchased. In this way, more land will be purchased when land prices are low than when they are high. This strategy appears to be especially beneficial if RCA assembles the reserve over a period of several decades but has less effect if RCA can complete assembly within 10 years or less.

Costs of Implementing the Plan and Operating the Reserve

The cost of the MSHCP includes not only the cost of acquiring the land needed for the reserve but also the costs of implementing the plan and operating the reserve over time. These include the costs of routine habitat management, adaptive management, biological monitoring, and plan implementation and oversight. Routine habitat management consists primarily of controlling public access to conserved lands by installing and maintaining fences and gates and by regularly patrolling areas that frequently experience illegal dumping, off-highway vehicle (OHV) use, hunting, and other illegal trespass. Adaptive management uses the results of information gathered through the biological-monitoring program and from other sources to adjust habitat-management strategies and practices. Biological monitoring involves developing an initial baseline inventory of the 146 species that the MSHCP covers and ongoing annual monitoring to follow their status. Plan implementation and oversight costs arise from the day-to-day operational expenses that RCA incurs to implement the plan. These include managing reserve assembly, complying with reporting requirements, and overseeing management and monitoring programs.

We project the costs to operate the reserve from 2008 through the plan's expiration in 2079, using historical data on program expenditures as well as qualitative information elicited from subject-matter experts. Table S.2 shows the present value of projected management, monitoring, and plan implementation and oversight costs in 2007

Table S.2
Present Value of the Costs of Implementing the Plan and Operating the Reserve Through 2079 (millions of 2007 dollars)

Cost Category	Estimate		
	Low	Baseline	High
Habitat management	51	146	309
Adaptive management	27	41	58
Biological monitoring	47	55	65
Plan implementation and oversight	189	232	258
Total	314	474	690

dollars for the MSHCP's remaining 72-year life. The baseline estimate is the value we calculate using assumptions that we consider most reasonable and is typically a continuation of historical values. The high and low estimates are calculated using a reasonable set of optimistic and conservative assumptions.

Discounted back to 2007 using a 3-percent real discount rate, the present value of reserve-operation costs over the MSHCP's remaining life is projected to total $474 million. The range into which these costs can be reasonably expected to fall runs from $314 million to $690 million.

Our undiscounted operating-cost projection exceeds the original forecast in MSHCP planning documents by $345 million (increasing from $937 million to $1,282 million). The increase is due primarily to plan implementation and oversight costs that were not included in the original cost analysis.

Revenues for the Plan

RCA receives revenues from local, state, and federal sources. Forecasting RCA revenue is a difficult task, as the funding program is still relatively new and reaches far into the future. Therefore, projections are made for a range of assumptions about underlying economic and demographic conditions. Figure S.2 shows our baseline forecast for revenue from local sources through 2079, in 2007 dollars. Local revenues are projected to peak at approximately $40 million per year over the next few years before falling to between $25 million and $30 million through 2035 and then to between $15 million and $20 million for the remainder of the plan.

The baseline projections translate into $770 million in present value. In recognition of the uncertainty in underlying parameters, we constructed low-revenue and high-revenue scenarios. The present value of the revenue streams is $635 million in the low-revenue scenario and $962 million in the high-revenue scenario. Revenues from state and federal sources are projected to add $180 million in present value over

**Figure S.2
Baseline Forecast for Local Revenue Program in 2007 Dollars**

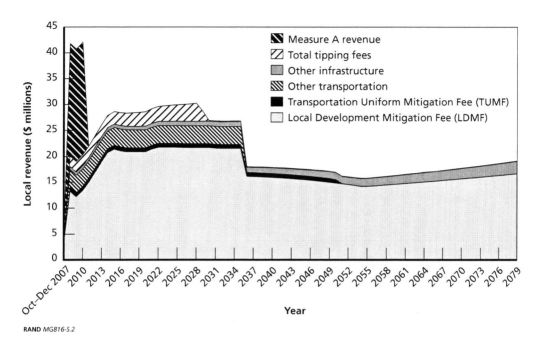

RAND *MG816-S.2*

the plan's life, with estimates for the low- and high-revenue scenarios ranging from $121 million to $237 million.

Gap Between Local Costs and Revenue

Comparing the plan's projected costs and revenues raises two main issues: the timing of revenues relative to expenditures and the overall adequacy of revenues. Regarding the first issue, the expected receipts from revenue sources that are already in place do not line up well with a strategy of acquiring land in a relatively compressed time frame. To finance acquisition of the reserve in a relatively short period, RCA will need to pursue financial strategies that allow it to decouple annual expenditures from annual revenues. Strategies that would enable this include bonding against a future revenue stream or borrowing funds with repayments made over time from ongoing revenues.

Regarding the overall adequacy of revenue, our analysis does not allow us to conclude with certainty whether existing local revenue streams will be sufficient to finance the local share of reserve assembly and operation costs. The gap between costs borne by local permittees and local revenue sources depends on a number of factors, including the trajectory of future land prices, RCA's adopted acquisition strategy, the amount of acreage obtained though the entitlement and authorization processes for private development projects, and the economic and demographic trends that influence revenue.

Given the wide range of potential outcomes, we provide estimates of the local funding gap under favorable and unfavorable realizations (from RCA's point of view) of the underlying uncertainties. In some scenarios that combine very optimistic assumptions about land prices (from RCA's point of view) and local developer contributions through the development-authorization process with optimistic assumptions about revenue, the present value of existing revenue streams will be adequate to cover the present value of expenditures. In less favorable scenarios in which land prices remain relatively high, land contributions through the development process remain low, and revenue ends up at the low end of the projected range, the present value of revenue could fall several billion dollars short of expenditures. We cannot assign probabilities to the various outcomes but note that the factors that could lead to low land values (e.g., a drop in the housing market) could also lead to low revenues (e.g., a decline in revenue from the LDMF), decreasing the likelihood of scenarios in which current revenue sources are adequate.

To determine whether additional local revenue instruments will be acquired, RCA should pay close attention to the changes in land prices over the next few years. If land prices fall substantially from the levels paid for comparable parcels in mid-2007 and RCA can purchase a substantial amount of acreage at the reduced prices, then it is conceivable that additional revenue from local sources will not be needed. If, on the other hand, land prices do not decline much over the next few years, it will become increasingly likely that revenue from existing instruments will be inadequate and that additional local revenue sources will be required.

Additional Revenue Options

A wide range of options exists for raising additional revenue from local sources. We examined 10 sources of additional revenue, including property-based revenue sources, development-based revenue sources, transportation-based revenue sources, and sales tax–based revenue sources. Table S.3 provides estimates of the amount by which each tax or fee would need to increase in order to raise $1 billion on a present-value basis. The projections assume that the tax is levied on all Riverside County property, development, transportation, or sales, respectively. If any of the revenue mechanisms is implemented only in western Riverside County or if revenue from a countywide tax is shared with eastern Riverside County, then the increases in Table S.3 would need to be somewhat larger to generate $1 billion in revenues for the MSHCP.

Each option considered has advantages and disadvantages in terms of equity, efficiency, and political feasibility. If additional revenue is necessary, policymakers will need to weigh the trade-offs in deciding what options to pursue.

Funding mechanisms that consider the construction of transportation facilities and habitat conservation as one integrated project offer the prospect of more flexible

Table S.3
Increases in Revenue Sources Needed to Raise $1 Billion in Present Value

Basis of Revenue Source	Tax or Fee Duration			
	10 Years	20 Years	30 Years	Life of MSHCP
Property				
Ad valorem property tax (percentage-point increase)	0.04	0.02	0.01	—
Parcel tax ($ increase per parcel)	133	69	49	27
Special property assessment ($ increase per dwelling unit)	140	73	51	28
Mello-Roos tax ($ increase per parcel)[a]		Similar to parcel tax		
Documentary transfer tax (% increase)	342	178	127	70
Development				
LDMF (% increase)	636	336	253	183
Transportation				
Highway tolls ($ per mile)	—	—	0.07–1.03[b]	—
Vehicle-license fee (VLF) (percentage-point increase)[c]	0.62	0.32	0.23	0.13
Vehicle-registration fee ($ increase)	63	33	23	13
Sales taxes				
Sales tax (percentage-point increase)	0.26	0.12	0.08	—

[a] The Mello-Roos Community Facilities Act of 1982 provides an alternative method of financing improvements and services. See California Government Code §§53311–53368.3.

[b] Depending on traffic volume and number of miles tolled.

[c] Current level is 0.65 percent.

funding that may reduce the overall project cost. For example, sources of funds that could be used both for infrastructure construction and habitat acquisition could allow RCA to accelerate reserve assembly and reduce overall land-acquisition costs. Currently, major funding sources on which RCA relies do not allow constructing transportation infrastructure and conserving habitat on a fully integrated basis. Federal or state legislation would be required to enable such mechanisms. Infrastructure banks could likewise offer loans that allow flexibility in allocating funds between construction and habitat conservation. Infrastructure banks do exist in California, but the two we were able to identify do not provide loans large enough to make much of a difference in western Riverside County. Developing programs that integrate transportation funding and habitat conservation warrants further attention.

Prospects for Achieving the Habitat-Conservation Goals of the Reserve

To ensure the viability of species that the MSHCP covers, the plan requires that RCA conserve a minimum number of acres of various habitat types spread across different regions of western Riverside County. This has been operationalized as a set of specific acreage requirements for seven distinct vegetation communities within nine subregions of the plan area, referred to as *rough-step accounting areas*.

We found that individual acreage goals cannot all be met using the USFWS CRD. That said, we found that, for all but one of the vegetation communities, the number of acres in the USFWS CRD across all rough-step areas exceeds the sum of acreage targets across all rough-step areas. In other words, while there are numerous shortfalls in specific rough-step areas, there appears to be sufficient acreage in total for most of the vegetation communities. The RCA-assembled reserve will not necessarily precisely follow the USFWS CRD. We have not examined the extent to which different reserve configurations that are consistent with the MSHCP's land-acquisition criteria would satisfy the rough-step requirements. However, our analysis shows that one configuration, the USFWS CRD, will not meet the rough-step requirements as currently written, and it is plausible that other configurations will face similar problems. It also shows that it may be worth revisiting rough-step requirements to determine whether it is appropriate to allow some fungibility of acreage requirements across rough-step areas.

Moving Forward

Our analysis has identified a number of MSHCP benefits and some areas in which improvements could be made to further the plan's goals. Based on our findings, we recommend that the RCA Board of Directors, staff, and stakeholders

- explore ways to increase the acreage obtained through the entitlement and authorization processes for private development projects
- examine how to route the linkages between the core habitat areas so as to minimize acquisition costs but meet the ecological goals for the reserve
- reexamine the rough-step requirements to determine whether they are overly prescriptive with regard to the spatial distribution of vegetative-community acreage, and explore how the rough-step accounting system could be modified to better reflect progress in achieving the plan's conservation goals
- determine the time frame in which the reserve should be completed, taking into consideration the potential financial savings of completing it within the next decade

- develop bonding or other financial strategies that allow decoupling of annual revenue and annual expenditures and enable reserve completion in the next decade
- regularly update land-acquisition cost and revenue projections to determine whether additional revenue will be necessary
- prepare a strategy for raising additional revenue that could be implemented should additional revenue become necessary
- work with federal and state authorities to determine whether transportation and habitat-conservation funding programs could be integrated to permit more-comprehensive resource planning and investment
- investigate how to increase the plan's benefits for commercial, industrial, and residential development projects
- explore how to limit the apparent plan-induced increase in permitting costs for transportation projects.

Being proactive with respect to these issues can help ensure the plan's success and the ongoing economic and ecological health of western Riverside County.

Acknowledgments

Many people made important contributions to this monograph. Thomas B. Mullen, former RCA executive director, provided a vision for how the study could contribute to the policy and practice of reconciling development and habitat conservation. Joe Richards, former deputy executive director at RCA, provided valuable insight and feedback on plan operation and interim drafts of the monograph. Charles Landry, current RCA executive director, brought extensive experience with the plan to provide very helpful comments during the latter part of the project. Pat Egetter, Sharon Baker-Stewart, Gary Poor, and Brian Beck, also at RCA, helped enormously in obtaining the large amount of data needed for the project.

John Husing of Economics & Politics, Inc., provided helpful guidance on economic issues related to Riverside County, and Joe Monaco and Stephanie Standerfer at Dudek Engineering + Environmental helped bring us up to speed on the MSHCP and provided useful comments on the stakeholder questionnaire.

Michael Allen, director of the Center for Conservation Biology (CCB), arranged for our team to tour the habitat areas in western Riverside County and shared his perspectives on implementing the MSHCP. CCB staff, especially Kristine L. Preston and Cameron W. Barrows, shared their knowledge of the habitat biology and habitat-conservation practices in the region. Yvonne Moore and Ronald J. Baxter graciously shared their intimate knowledge of the history, challenges, and operational details of the Western Riverside County MSHCP biological-monitoring and habitat-management programs.

We are indebted to John D. Landis, formerly of the University of California, Berkeley, and now at the University of Pennsylvania, for the advice he provided at the beginning of the project on specifying and estimating land-value models. We benefited tremendously from his past work and expertise in this area. John also provided insightful reviews on the interim and final drafts of the monograph. We would also like to thank Edward G. Keating, a senior economist at RAND, for his very thorough reviews under tight deadlines of the interim and final reports. The quality of this monograph improved substantially as a result.

Analysis of the effect of accelerating the completion of large freeway projects in western Riverside County was done under contract using the Southern California

Planning Model. Peter Gordon at the University of Southern California and Qisheng Pan, now at Texas Southern University, adapted and ran the model. We thank them for the timeliness and quality of their work.

At RAND, Alisher Akhmedjonov at the Frederick S. Pardee RAND Graduate School assembled data on the revenue sources of other habitat-conservation plans, Nancy Good and Lynn Polite provided administrative assistance, and Lisa Bernard skillfully edited the document.

Finally, the study would not have been possible without the participation of stakeholders familiar with the MSHCP who agreed to be interviewed or completed a questionnaire about the effects of the MSHCP on the placement of infrastructure. We cannot thank them by name because the interviews and questionnaires were completed on a confidential basis, but we thank them for generously giving their time.

Abbreviations

AADT	average annual daily trips
AASHTO	American Association of State Highway and Transportation Officials
AB	assembly bill
APN	assessor's parcel number
Caltrans	California Department of Transportation
CCB	Center for Conservation Biology
CDFG	California Department of Fish and Game
CEQ	Council on Environmental Quality
CEQA	California Environmental Quality Act
CESCF	Cooperative Endangered Species Conservation Fund
CETAP	Community and Environmental Transportation Acceptability Process
CFD	community-facility district
CNLM	Center for Natural Lands Management
CPI	consumer price index
CRD	conceptual reserve design
CREATE	National Center for Risk and Economic Analysis of Terrorism Events
CWA	Clean Water Act
DBESP	Determination of Biologically Equivalent or Superior Preservation
DBF	density bonus fee
DEIR	draft environmental-impact report

DEIS   draft environmental-impact statement

DMV   department of motor vehicles

DU   dwelling unit

EIR   environmental-impact report

EIS   environmental-impact statement

EMP   Environmental Mitigation Program

EO   executive order

EPA   U.S. Environmental Protection Agency

ESA   Endangered Species Act

FEIR   final environmental-impact report

FEIS   final environmental-impact statement

FHWA   Federal Highway Administration

FY   fiscal year

GFA   gross floor area

GIS   geographic information system

GO   general obligation

GPS   Global Positioning System

HANS   Habitat Evaluation and Acquisition Negotiation Strategy

HCP   habitat-conservation plan

HOV   high-occupancy vehicle

I-Bank   Infrastructure and Economic Development Bank

ILF   in-lieu fee

I/O   input-output

ISE   RAND Infrastructure, Safety, and Environment

ISRF   Infrastructure State Revolving Fund

ISTEA   Intermodal Surface Transportation Efficiency Act

JPR   joint project review

LDMF	Local Development Mitigation Fee
LFP	local funding program
MFH	multifamily housing
MIS	major investment study
MOU	memorandum of understanding
MSHCP	Multiple Species Habitat Conservation Plan
NCCP	Natural Community Conservation Planning Act
NEPA	National Environmental Policy Act
OCTA	Orange County Transportation Authority
OHV	off-highway vehicle
OLS	ordinary least squares
OSA	Open Space Authority (Santa Clara County)
PPP	public-private partnership
PQP	public or quasipublic
RCA	Western Riverside County Regional Conservation Authority
RCHCA	Riverside County Habitat Conservation Agency
RCIP	Riverside County Integrated Project
RCTC	Riverside County Transportation Commission
RCWMD	Riverside County Waste Management Department
RMOC	Reserve Management Oversight Committee
ROCA	Riverside Orange Corridor Authority
SAMP	special area management plan
SAWA	Santa Ana Watershed Association
SCAG	Southern California Association of Governments
SCPM	Southern California Planning Model
SFH	single-family housing
SIB	State Infrastructure Bank

SR	state route
SUV	sport-utility vehicle
TAZ	traffic-analysis zone
TCA	Transportation Corridor Agencies
TEA-21	Transportation Equity Act for the 21st Century
TFB	Transportation Finance Bank
TIFIA	Transportation Infrastructure Finance and Innovation Act
TIGER	Topically Integrated Geographic Encoding and Referencing system
TST	Transportation, Space, and Technology
TUMF	Transportation Uniform Mitigation Fee
USACE	U.S. Army Corps of Engineers
USFWS	U.S. Fish and Wildlife Service
USGS	U.S. Geological Survey
VLF	vehicle-license fee
VMT	vehicle-mile traveled
WRCOG	Western Riverside Council of Governments

CHAPTER ONE

Introduction

With increasing frequency across the country, population growth and development interests are colliding with environmental goals and regulations that protect threatened and endangered species' habitats. Perhaps nowhere is this clash more evident than in western Riverside County, California—one of the fastest-growing metropolitan areas in the United States and the home of a diverse array of increasingly rare species. In the 1990s, policymakers in Riverside County found the regulatory process for reconciling environmental and development interests both ineffective and inefficient. Regulatory and legal systems slowed development projects and increased their costs. The required project-by-project mitigation for endangered-species impacts resulted in a patchwork assembly of uncoordinated habitats. There was legitimate concern that these problems would only grow worse over time.

Responding to this challenge, in 1999, the Riverside County Board of Supervisors and the Riverside County Transportation Commission (RCTC) initiated a comprehensive regional-planning effort called the Riverside County Integrated Project (RCIP). A key element of the RCIP is the Multiple Species Habitat Conservation Plan (MSHCP), a plan to conserve half a million acres of species habitat in the western part of the county. In return for establishing the conservation reserve, the U.S. Fish and Wildlife Service (USFWS) and the California Department of Fish and Game (CDFG) issued the county and 14 cities in western Riverside County a 75-year "take" permit for endangered species. Finalized in June 2004, the take permit allows the cities and county to approve development projects outside the reserve that may negatively impact the plant and animal species covered by the plan, thus allowing for continued growth and development outside of the reserve area. Responsibility for acquiring and managing the reserve was vested with the Western Riverside County Regional Conservation Authority (RCA). RCA will not be able to use powers of eminent domain to assemble the reserve. Rather, the reserve will be assembled through willing property sales and transfers.

The MSHCP is an ambitious effort, mitigating development impact on 146 plant and animal species. While it is a potential model for other areas in the county, questions remain about the costs of assembling such a reserve, the adequacy of revenue sources, and how it will affect the length and cost of the approval processes for transportation and development projects. This monograph examines a series of issues that address these questions.

The Multiple Species Habitat Conservation Plan

The plan area for the MSHCP encompasses the unincorporated lands in Riverside County west of the crest of the San Jacinto Mountains as well as the cities of Banning, Beaumont, Calimesa, Corona, Hemet, Lake Elsinore, Moreno Valley, Murrieta, Norco, Perris, Riverside, San Jacinto, and Temecula. RCA, a joint-powers authority that includes each of these jurisdictions, is implementing the plan. Acting through RCA, the county and municipalities share responsibility for funding the assembly, management, and monitoring of the reserve area, and each in turn gains greater local control over land-use and development decisions consistent with the plan (TLMA, 2003).

Figure 1.1 provides an overview of the MSHCP plan area in western Riverside County, including existing public land and the additional area from which the

Figure 1.1
Location of the MSHCP and Targeted Areas for Conservation

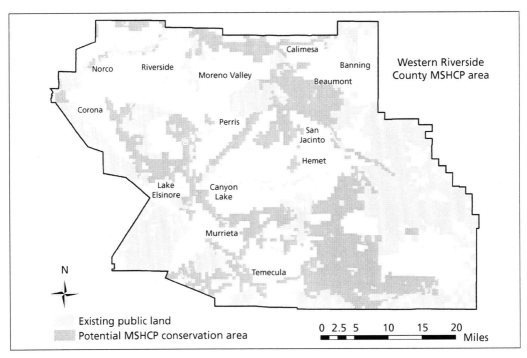

SOURCE: Data provided by Western Riverside County Regional Conservation Authority in 2007.
RAND MG816-1.1

reserve will be drawn. The region of western Riverside County included in the MSHCP scope spans 1.26 million acres; of these, approximately 500,000 (40 percent) will be preserved, making this one of the largest habitat-conservation plans (HCPs) ever attempted. The 500,000 acres includes about 350,000 acres already held in public trust along with 153,000 additional acres that will be conserved under the MSHCP agreement. The 153,000 acres will be drawn from approximately 300,000 acres that constitute the potential MSCHP conservation area shown in Figure 1.1.

The MSHCP encompasses a wide variety of bioregions—including the Santa Ana, San Jacinto, and San Bernardino Mountains; the Riverside Lowlands; the San Jacinto Foothills; Agua Tibia Mountain; and the desert transition—preserving habitat for 146 distinct endangered species. While there is some flexibility in the exact set of land parcels that will ultimately be included in the habitat reserve, the land-assembly process will be guided by tenets described in California's Natural Community Conservation Planning Act of 1991 (NCCP) (California Fish and Game Code §§2800–2835). Specifically, the reserve's design should (1) focus on critical species and their habitats throughout the plan area, (2) conserve large habitat blocks, (3) conserve contiguous and connected blocks of land, and (4) protect against encroachment and invasion by nonnative species (TLMA, 2003).

A key issue in developing the MSHCP was distributing the costs associated with assembling and managing the conservation area. Without the MSHCP, responsibility for conserving endangered species would rest solely with public and private entities whose construction projects and other activities directly affected declining species and their habitats. Stakeholders on the MSHCP Advisory Committee determined, however, that the conservation plan's benefits would accrue broadly—not only to existing and future communities in western Riverside County but also to the citizens of California and the United States as a whole. For this reason, responsibility for funding the MSHCP has been divided among federal, state, and local jurisdictions along with private development interests.

Of the 500,000 acres to be assembled, a large portion was already in public ownership when the take permit was issued. This includes approximately 248,000 acres of federal land, 34,000 acres of state land, and 65,000 acres of locally owned public or quasipublic (PQP) land (see Table 1.1). This left a total of 153,000 acres that still needed to be acquired to complete the MSHCP reserve. While RCA manages the assembly process, federal, state, and local governments as well as private developers are all expected to contribute either funding or land.

Of the 153,000 acres still required when the plan was adopted, federal and state agencies are obligated to fund the acquisition of about 56,000 acres. Anticipated methods of acquisition include direct purchase from willing sellers,[1] cooperative federal and state programs for conserving threatened or endangered species, land exchanges,

---

[1]   Eminent domain will not be used.

Table 1.1
Responsibility for Assembling the Reserve (acres)

Resource	Target Acreage	Acreage Acquired as of October 2007
Existing PQP open space		
Federal	248,000	248,000
State	34,000	34,000
Local	65,000	65,000
Subtotal	347,000	347,000
Land for RCA to assemble		
Federal and state acquisition	56,000	14,677
Purchases by local government	56,000	20,192
Contributions by private developers through development-authorization process	41,000	657
Subtotal	153,000	35,526
Total	500,000	382,526

SOURCE: Data on target acreage from TLMA (2003, pp. 4-3–4-13. Data on acquired acreage provided by RCA in 2007.

NOTE: There are 1.26 million acres in western Riverside County.

tax credits, purchases to mitigate state or federally funded projects (such as state and federal highways), and other government programs, such as the U.S. Department of Defense's Base Realignment and Closure program and the Federal Deposit Insurance Corporation. Potential funding sources include Land and Water Conservation Fund appropriations, grant funds from such entities as the Wildlife Conservation Board and the National Fish and Wildlife Foundation, federal funds provided pursuant to Section 6 of the federal Endangered Species Act (ESA) (Pub. L. Nos. 93-205, 107-136), Transportation Equity Act for the 21st Century (TEA-21) (Pub. L. No. 105-178) funds, state bond acts, funds generated from the sale of public-agency lands, and federal aid programs (TLMA, 2003).

Local governments, in turn, are expected to purchase an additional 56,000 acres from willing sellers through the Habitat Evaluation and Acquisition Negotiation Strategy (HANS) process (for more details, see TLMA, 2003) or other suitable mechanisms. These holdings may be acquired in fee or through conservation easements, deed restrictions, land exchanges, flood-control easements, or other types of interest acceptable under the MSHCP. Eminent domain will not be used. Funding sources to finance these purchases include local development fees, density bonus fees (DBFs), regional infrastructure contributions (as mitigation for transportation projects, regional utility projects, local public capital construction, or regional flood control), landfill tipping fees, and other potential new revenue sources, such as special assessments (TLMA, 2003).

It is anticipated that an additional 41,000 acres will be conserved though the entitlement and authorization processes for private development, relying on incentive structures as well as existing local, state, and federal development regulations. Relevant incentives include land exchanges, waiver or reduction of fees, fast-track entitlement processing, density bonuses, clustering, density transfers, and property reassessment. Private landholders may also donate land to federal or state wildlife agencies, local governments, or qualified nonprofit conservation organizations in order to assist with the habitat-conservation effort. Alternative forms of donation include gift of fee title, donation with retention of a term or life estate, sale at fair market value with donation of a portion of the proceeds, use of tax credits, or use of state and federal programs to conserve agricultural lands (TLMA, 2003). If local governments cannot acquire 41,000 acres through the development process, they will need to purchase the balance themselves.

According to RCA staff, 35,526 acres were acquired as of October 2007 (see rightmost column of Table 1.1). While considerable shares of the targets for federal and state acquisition and local purchases have been acquired (26 percent and 35 percent, respectively), only 2 percent (657 acres) of the target for developer contributions has been conserved. The low level of contributions indicates that developers have been able to avoid situations in which they are required or expected to make contributions to the reserve. Parties familiar with the development process provided the following explanation for how developers have been able to avoid land contributions. If the land proposed for development is all needed for the reserve, then RCA will make an offer to purchase the entire property. If the land proposed for development is not needed for the reserve, then there will be no requirement to contribute land. It is only when part of the land proposed for development is needed for the reserve that property owners will potentially contribute to the reserve. The low level of contributions to date suggests that landowners have been able to avoid developing properties that are partially needed for the reserve. Over time, as the amount of land available for development declines, it may become more common for properties that are partially needed for the reserve to be developed. However, the low rate of contribution to date raises concern that local government will need to find funding to purchase a substantial fraction of the acreage included in this category.

Contribution of This Monograph

This monograph begins by examining the value of the land needed for the reserve. Chapters Two and Three estimate the value of land already acquired by RCA, the value of land in a completed reserve, and the value of land yet to be acquired. This analysis allows us to compare the average value per acre of land already acquired and the average value of land yet to be acquired and thus to assess how good a guide past acquisitions are to the ultimate cost of the reserve. This detailed examination of the land that remains to be acquired allows a better understanding of what drives the overall acquisition cost and what types of adjustments in the acreage targeted for conservation might yield substantial cost savings. The details of the statistical models used to estimate land values and the regression results are reported in Appendix A.

The plan sets targets for the number of acres for different vegetation communities in different subregions of western Riverside County. Chapter Three also examines whether these targets can be met given the current planned configuration of the reserve.

The analyses in Chapters Two and Three develop estimates of the cost of completing the reserve given land values in mid-2007. The remaining land will not be purchased all at once, however, and both the time frame in which the land is purchased and the future trajectory of land prices will determine the ultimate cost of assembling the reserve. In Chapter Four, we examine the advantages and disadvantages of buying land for the reserve in different time frames and evaluate temporal acquisition strategies that will tend to reduce reserve-assembly costs. Appendix B contains examples of the range of future land-price trajectories that are considered.

The cost of the land needed for the reserve is the largest component of the overall cost of the plan, but costs of administering the plan and operating the reserve are also considerable. In Chapter Five, we forecast RCA's future expenditures on habitat management, biological monitoring, and MSHCP implementation and oversight. These implementation and administrative costs are combined with projected land-acquisition costs to give an estimate of the overall cost of plan.

Chapters Two through Five address the plan's costs. The subsequent two chapters examine its revenues. Chapter Six describes existing revenue sources and forecasts revenue through the end of the plan in 2079. The present value of the revenue projections are then compared with cost estimates from the preceding chapters to determine whether additional revenues will be necessary to fund the plan. Potential sources of additional revenue are explored in Chapter Seven. The chapter begins with a review of the revenue for other HCPs that have been established and then investigates a wide range of local (as opposed to state and federal) measures for raising additional revenue. Estimates of the amount that each tax or fee would need to be increased to raise $1 billion in present value are provided. Appendix C details the revenue sources for 20 HCPs that are at least 1,000 acres in size, and Appendix D examines the extent to which existing funding mechanisms allow integration of transportation and habitat-conservation projects and what types of changes are required to increase funding flexibility in the future.

An important expectation of the MSHCP is that it streamline the permitting processes for transportation and commercial, industrial, and residential development projects in western Riverside County. Chapter Eight explores this aspect of MSHCP benefits. Based on interviews and a detailed questionnaire filled out by knowledgeable stakeholders, Chapter Eight provides an initial assessment of the extent to which the MSHCP has accelerated the permitting processes for transportation and development projects. It reports perceptions of the effects to date and those expected in the next 10 years. It also reports stakeholder perceptions of the MSHCP's impact on the frequency and scope of lawsuits that attempt to stop or modify projects.

Faster placement of major roads and freeways in western Riverside County will presumably improve mobility in the county. Appendix E quantifies some of the MSHCP's mobility benefits. It uses a detailed computer model to examine the effects of the faster completion of four major transportation corridors in western Riverside County on average travel speeds and travel times and then translates these impacts into dollar values.

The permitting process under the MSHCP will change at least to some extent once the reserve has been established and the objectives concerning the species covered by the plan have been met. In Appendix F, we examine how the roles of the wildlife agencies and the permitting process may change. This analysis provides insight into how MSHCP benefits may change over time.

The final chapter of the monograph, Chapter Nine, provides overall observations on the findings and identifies issues raised by our analysis that the RCA Board of Directors, RCA staff, and stakeholders should address moving forward.

CHAPTER TWO

Value of Parcels Already Acquired by RCA

Estimating the current fair market value of parcels already acquired by RCA for conservation serves several ends. First, against the backdrop of an extremely volatile housing market, it provides RCA with a sense of how land values have changed during the period over which RCA has been assembling the reserve. Such information is helpful as RCA negotiates to purchase additional parcels. Second, once estimates of the land needed for the entire reserve are developed (as will be done in the following chapter), it allows projection of the funds needed to complete the reserve.

To estimate the current value of RCA's portfolio, we developed a statistical model of land values based on sales records from the Riverside County assessor's office from January 2000 through October 2007. The model considers such factors as parcel size, current land use, purchase date, zoning, slope, proximity to roads and freeways, job accessibility, and average household income in the surrounding area. After estimating the model based on past sales data, we then used it to project the 2007 market value of those parcels assembled by RCA through October 2007.

In the remainder of this chapter, we first review the number and total cost of parcels that RCA has already acquired. Then, we describe the land-use model developed for this analysis and the data used to estimate it. Finally, we report our projections of the value of RCA's land portfolio as of mid-2007.

Land Purchased by RCA as of 2007

Table 2.1 shows a summary of the conservation land acquired by RCA between February 2000 and October 2007.[1] During this period, RCA assembled just over 35,500 acres, of which a little less than 1,000 were contributed[2] (the rest were

---

[1] The take permit resulting from the MSHCP was issued in June 2004, but RCA was given credit for some land that had been purchased previously.

[2] The Riverside Land Conservancy gave the state about a third (close to 330 acres) of the contributed acres. The remaining two-thirds (just under 660 acres) were granted to local permittees. The majority of local contributions were received from real-estate developers through the project-approval process.

Table 2.1
Acres Assembled by RCA as of October 2007

Year	Assembled Acres			Cost ($)		Cost in 2007 Dollars	
	Contributed	Purchased	Total	Total (millions)	Per Acre (thousands)	Total (millions)	Per Acre (thousands)
2000	0	1,658	1,658	27.6	16.6	34.8	21.1
2001	0	0	0	0	—	0	—
2002	38	1,919	1,958	14.3	7.5	17.0	8.8
2003	328	13,965	14,292	84.2	6.0	97.4	7.0
2004	0	1,370	1,370	10.1	7.4	11.3	8.3
2005	31	2,964	2,995	15.4	5.2	16.5	5.6
2006	574	9,252	9,826	61.9	6.7	63.6	6.9
2007	14	3,413	3,427	41.8	12.2	41.8	12.2
2000–2007	985	34,541	35,526	255.3	7.4	282.4	8.2

SOURCES: Land-assembly and cost data provided by RCA staff; purchase cost adjusted to 2007 dollars using the Los Angeles–Anaheim–Riverside consumer price index (CPI) (see California Department of Industrial Relations, 2007).

purchased). The total acquisition cost was just over $255 million, implying an average per-acre price of about $7,400 (this calculation does not include the acres that were contributed). Adjusted to 2007 dollars, the total acquisition cost is closer to $282 million, or about $8,200 per acre. For reference, Figure 2.1 shows the location of the acreage that RCA has assembled to date.

Later in this chapter, we examine the characteristics of the existing assembly in greater detail. A key point to note here, however, is that almost 34,000 of the acres assembled to date—about 95 percent—were open-space land when purchased, and many of the parcels were located far from existing urban areas. Both of these factors contributed to the relatively low per-acre price. Parcels with existing development or proximal to urban areas, as we will see, are, on average, much more expensive.

Data and Methods Used to Project the Value of the Current Portfolio

To forecast the value of parcels in the reserve, we developed a *hedonic land-value model* based on prior parcel-sales records in western Riverside County. Hedonic models relate the purchase price to a number of different characteristics of the land, such as size, slope, and proximity to major roads. Numerous studies have examined the variables that influence the price of land and housing (see, for instance, Case and Mayer, 1995,

Figure 2.1
Location of Land Acquired by RCA as of October 2007

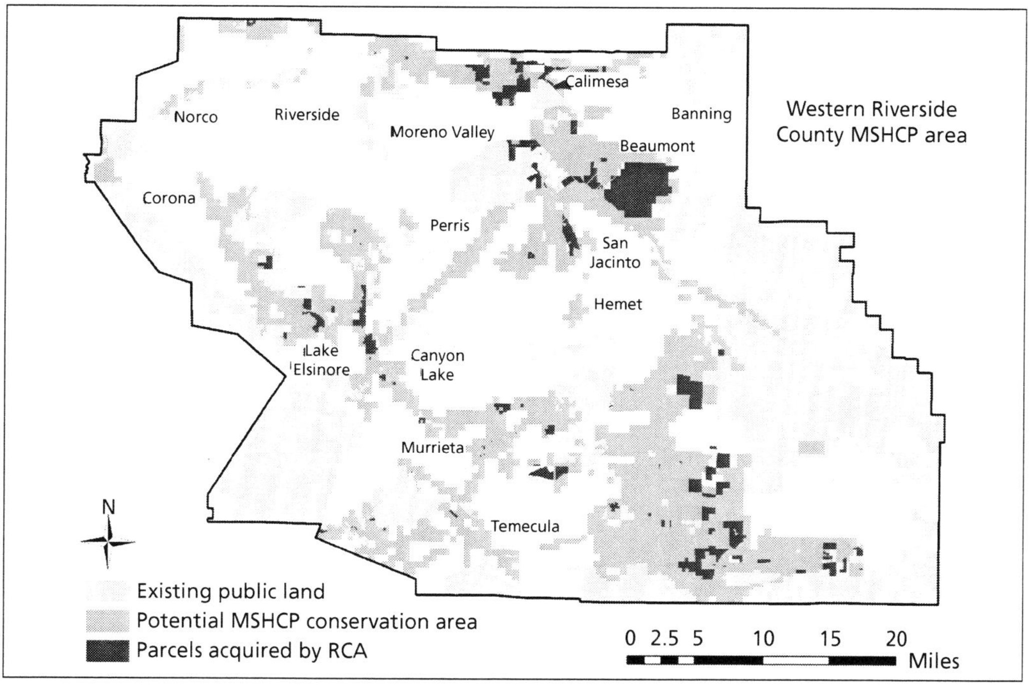

SOURCE: Data provided by RCA in 2007.
RAND *MG816-2.1*

and Clapp, Rodriguez, and Pace, 2001), and we draw heavily on such studies to specify the variables included in our model.

RCA will, in most cases, be acquiring open-space or agricultural parcels in the process of assembling the reserve. In certain limited cases, though, RCA may find it necessary to acquire properties with some existing development in order to complete the reserve. Because the relationship between parcel characteristics and property values may differ depending on current land use, we found it helpful to estimate separate statistical models for five major land-use categories: open space (undeveloped), agricultural, single-family housing (SFH), multifamily housing (MFH), and other developed properties (including commercial and industrial land uses).[3]

The statistical models are used to estimate both the value of land already assembled by RCA (the subject of this chapter) and the cost of acquiring the remaining land needed to complete the reserve (the subject of the next chapter). Because the majority of parcels that RCA has acquired so far and is expected to ultimately purchase fall in

---

[3] Single-family homes on individual lots (including manufactured homes on individual lots) have been categorized as SFH. MFH includes condominiums, apartment buildings, duplexes, triplexes, and mobile-home parks.

the categories of open space and agricultural use, we pay particular attention to parcel characteristics that influence the value of land absent additional improvements.

Next, we describe the parcel characteristics used in our analysis and discuss how they might be expected to affect land value. We then provide an overview of the statistical methods used to estimate the hedonic land-value model.

Parcel Characteristics

To estimate the hedonic land-value models, we began by collecting data on the purchase price for all parcel sales completed in western Riverside County between January 2000 and October 2007 (including RCA purchases, although these represented a very small share of the total transaction volume).[4] We then assembled a broad range of independent variables that should have some relationship to purchase price, including parcel size; zoning; slope; proximity to amenities, such as parks or water bodies; proximity to the existing transportation network; accessibility to jobs; income in the surrounding area; presence in an incorporated municipality; and characteristics of built improvements (such as the number of bedrooms in a single-family dwelling unit), where available.

Some of the variables included in our models—such as sales price, year of sale, and current land use—were obtained from the Riverside County assessor's office. The majority, however, were constructed through geographic information system (GIS) analysis. For example, using standard GIS capabilities, we calculated the distance to the nearest highway and the distance to the nearest major road for each parcel. Appendix A provides additional details on the source and derivation of all variables included in our hedonic models.

The full set of variables included in our models can be organized into several categories, including price, year of sale, physical features, legal and jurisdictional features, built improvement features, distance and accessibility features, and neighborhood features. Table 2.2 lists the variables included in each of these categories. It also provides summary statistics—including the number of observations, the mean, and the standard deviation—for each of the variables that are not indicator (binary) variables.

Purchase Price. Our data include information about the sales prices of all property transactions in western Riverside County between January 2000 and October 2007 that were available from the assessor's office (not just sales of parcels already acquired by RCA).[5] We also divide the sales data into five land-use categories, as already discussed: open space, agricultural, SFH, MFH, and other development. This segregation

---

[4]   For 2000 and 2001, the Riverside County assessor's office could provide only a small number of sales records in electronic format. For 2002 through 2006, we have much more complete data; for 2007, we have records for transactions completed between January and October.

[5]   Given that the county uses the sales data records we received from the assessor's office as a basis for collecting property taxes, we suspect that the data are likely to be relatively free of errors.

enables us to examine how sales values vary depending on the *current* land use. The vast majority of sales records—about 127,000 out of a total of about 144,000—are for single-family homes. There are also significant numbers of sales for MFH units and open-space parcels but relatively few sales for other land uses (including commercial and residential) and agricultural parcels. The price statistics listed in the table have been shown on a per-acre basis and have been converted into 2007 dollars.[6] SFH, MFH, and other development are by far the most expensive—averaging more than $2 million per acre, reflecting, in part, the value of the built improvements—while open-space and agricultural parcels are comparatively cheap on a per-acre basis.

Year of Sale. With several years of rapid appreciation in the Riverside real-estate market since 2000, followed by several more of rapid decline, the year of sale will likely have a strong influence on a parcel's predicted value. We thus include a set of variables for year of sale in the model.[7] Including year of sale also allows us to predict the prices of all sales as if they had occurred in 2007. This is necessary in order to estimate the current value of the parcels assembled by RCA to date. As shown in Table 2.2, the number of sales rose between 2002 and 2005 and then began to decline in 2006 and 2007.[8] This correlates roughly with the rise and subsequent fall in home prices in Riverside County.

Physical Parcel Features. Many physical characteristics of a parcel will affect its value. Of these, size is perhaps the most obvious. Slope is another important factor, one that will influence how easy or difficult it is to develop the property. Also potentially relevant are water-related features, such as location in a designated flood zone, presence of a water body, and presence of wetlands.

Legal and Jurisdictional Parcel Features. Other factors that may affect a parcel's value stem from legal or jurisdictional considerations. Perhaps foremost among these is zoning, which governs, according to municipal and county general plans, the type and density of allowable development on a parcel, which, in turn, influences the potential profitability of development activities and, ultimately, the amount that a developer would be willing to pay for the parcel. Note that, whereas the land-use variable describes how a parcel is currently being used, the zoning variable specifies potential uses for the land under current municipal and county zoning regulations. Additional features that may have bearing include whether the parcel falls within incorporated city limits or an area soon to be annexed by a city, whether some portion of the parcel has already been protected with a conservation easement, and whether it lies within the

---

[6] Sales prices were converted to 2007 dollars using the Southern California CPI (see California Department of Industrial Relations, 2007).

[7] These are coded as indicator variables: 1 if the sale occurred in that year and 0 if it did not.

[8] It is difficult to judge trends in the number of sales prior to 2002, given that the assessor's sales data that we received for 2000 and 2001 appear to be incomplete. Note that the sales-record count for 2007 includes transactions recorded only between January and October. The total for the year is therefore likely to be higher but still well below the peak in 2005.

Table 2.2
Land Parcels Sold in Western Riverside County, January 2001–October 2007

Characteristic	Sales with Characteristic	Mean	Standard Deviation
Purchase price by current land use in 2007 dollars ($ thousands per acre)			
Open space	7,272	343	6,597
Agricultural	342	83	80
SFH	127,120	2,210	1,245
MFH	6,698	2,683	2,010
Other	1,606	1,804	2,100
Year of sale			
2000	51	—	—
2001	178	—	—
2002	11,593	—	—
2003	23,697	—	—
2004	28,452	—	—
2005	35,808	—	—
2006	30,867	—	—
2007	12,392	—	—
Physical features			
Acreage (acres)	143,038	0.68	4.96
Slope (percentage)	143,038	12.54	14.49
In a flood zone	19,712	—	—
Body of water present	755	—	—
Wetlands present	215	—	—
Legal and jurisdictional features			
Zoning			
Open space	6,874	—	—
Agricultural	9,311	—	—
SFH	87,943	—	—
MFH	30,914	—	—
Other	7,996	—	—
In a city	91,254	—	—

Table 2.2—Continued

Characteristic	Sales with Characteristic	Mean	Standard Deviation
In area intended to be annexed to a city	19,476	—	—
Conservation easement on parcel	1,957	—	—
In USFWS CRD	16,263	—	—
Built improvement features			
Bedrooms (SFH only)	127,120	3.46	1.02
Manufactured housing (SFH and MFH) (0/1)	6,691	—	—
Owner occupied (MFH only) (0/1)	1,388	—	—
Distance and accessibility features			
Distance to nearest highway (miles)	143,038	1.3	1.1
Distance to nearest road (miles)	143,038	0.3	0.3
Jobs within 30 minutes (thousands)	143,038	372	398
Distance to nearest park (miles)	143,038	1.1	1.2
Distance to existing sewer line (miles)	143,038	0.2	0.9
Neighborhood features			
Land within 1 mi. developed (%)	143,038	52	20
Land within 1 mi. developable (%)	143,038	35	20
Difference in percentage of land developed within 1 mi. and 2.5 mi.	143,038	42	16
Difference in percentage of land developable within 1 mi. and 2.5 mi.	143,038	38	16
Median income of surrounding census tract ($ thousands)	143,038	49.7	16.7

area of intended conservation under the MSHCP. Note that this latter element should not, in theory, influence a parcel's value, in the sense that the specified appraisal process for determining the purchase price for parcels to be acquired by RCA is not intended to consider a parcel's potential value with respect to RCA's conservation activities (TLMA, 2003). In practice, however, many land owners and speculators are aware of the areas that RCA is working to conserve, so this may affect the price that a parcel commands.

Built Improvement Features. We included only a few characteristics in our land-value models related to built improvements on a parcel. There were two main reasons for this. First, the vast majority of land to be purchased by RCA is open space and thus has no improvements. Second, the property data provided by the county assessor's office included just a few such variables for residential land uses and none for commercial or industrial properties. For the SFH category, we included information about the number of bedrooms (as a general proxy for other size-related variables) along with whether the home would be classified as manufactured (including, for instance, trailers and modular homes), which should tend to reduce the value. For MFH, we captured information about whether the home might be owner-occupied (such as a condominium) or would instead be rented (such as an apartment).

Distance and Accessibility Features. The value of parcels derives not just from site-specific features but also from proximity to roads, amenities, and jobs. For instance, being closer to major roads and highways improves accessibility, which should tend to enhance a parcel's value. For residential (or potential residential) land uses, proximity to job centers is also desirable. Proximity to amenities, such as parks, should likewise augment a property's value. Proximity to existing sewer lines may reduce the cost of development and thus increase land value.

Neighborhood Features. The final set of variables considered relates to characteristics of the neighborhood surrounding each parcel. A potential factor here is the relative percentage of developed and developable land within a given radius of a parcel. We chose to include measures of both (note that, because permanently conserved land counts as neither developed nor developable, the two retain some degree of independence), and they may interact in subtle ways. On one hand, a lower level of development in the surrounding area corresponds to a higher level of open space, and many potential buyers may view this as an amenity. On the other hand, higher levels of development likely correspond to increased accessibility to desirable amenities, such as restaurants and shops, and may also confer a scarcity-related premium on any remaining open-space parcels. In addition to tracking the amount of developed and developable land in a neighborhood, we also considered the median household income in each census tract. This serves as a proxy for the desirability of the neighborhood surrounding each parcel.

Statistical Methods

We used statistical regression techniques to estimate the relationship between sales price and parcel characteristics for 143,038 recorded sales[9] that took place in western Riverside County between January 2000 and October 2007. The details of the specification and the results of the regression are reported in Appendix A. As noted, we estimated separate models for each of the five land-use categories. Overall, the models did a good job of explaining the variation in parcel purchase price (the R-squared for the regression was reasonably high for cross-sectional data). Encouragingly, the model with the highest explanatory power was the model for open-space parcels; the vast majority

---

[9]   Some of the sales records we received from the assessor's office were described as including multiple parcels for a single transaction price; these records were not included in the data used to estimate the models.

of parcels that RCA has already bought and will need to buy in the future fall into this category.

We then used the model to estimate the current market value (as of mid-2007) of the parcels already acquired by RCA. The procedures used to make the projections and to generate statistical confidence intervals for the estimates are detailed in Appendix A.

Current Value of Parcels Already Acquired by RCA

Estimates of the mid-2007 market value of parcels assembled by RCA as of October 2007 are presented in Table 2.3. In the table, the first column lists the five land-use categories, the second column shows the number of parcels already acquired by RCA for each category, and the third column presents our point estimate for the total current value of those parcels. The fourth column provides the 95-percent statistical confidence interval for the estimate; that is, there is a 95-percent probability that the actual value falls between the lower and upper bounds of this interval. The fifth column lists the total acres for parcels in each land-use category, while the last column provides an estimate for the average price per acre in each land-use category. The last row in the table aggregates the results across all land uses.

We estimate that the 35,526 acres so far acquired by RCA were worth approximately $321 million as of mid-2007. Open-space parcels are, by far, the least valuable on a per-acre basis, followed by agricultural parcels. Single-family and multifamily residential parcels, on the other hand, are much more valuable on a per-acre basis. From the perspective of the overall cost of assembling the reserve, the much lower cost of open space is good, as the vast majority of RCA's acquisitions to date fall into this category.

Table 2.3
Estimated Mid-2007 Market Value of Parcels Acquired by RCA as of October 2007

Land Use	Total Parcels	Value ($ millions)	95% Confidence Interval ($ millions)	Total Acres	Price per Acre ($ thousands)
Open space	513	289.9	[255.5, 328.6]	33,914	8.5
Agricultural	20	26.5	[18.2, 45.2]	1,558	17.0
SFH	3	1.4	[1.4, 1.5]	11	133.2
MFH	3	3.0	[2.3, 3.7]	43	69.8
Other	0	0	—	0	—
All land uses	539	320.8	[287.5, 368.9]	35,526	9.0

As shown in the confidence-interval column, we have estimated that the total value of all parcels as of mid-2007 likely falls between $288 million to $369 million (with a confidence level of 95 percent). This range corresponds to a difference of as much as 10 percent below or 15 percent above our point estimate of $321 million. We have also calculated confidence intervals for the value of parcels in the different land-use categories.

A close examination of the numbers indicates that spread of the confidence interval is smaller for some land uses and larger for others. For example, the bounds are quite tight for SFH, while the percentage spread for agricultural parcel values is much greater. Generally speaking, the land-use categories with more transaction records have tighter confidence intervals (in the case of SFH, we were also able to employ helpful explanatory variables, such as number of bedrooms), while land-use categories with fewer transaction records have looser confidence intervals. For open space, the bounds are relatively tight, ranging from about 12 percent below to about 13 percent above our point estimate. This relatively narrow confidence interval is helpful when predicting the current value of RCA purchases because the vast majority of parcels already acquired by RCA, as well as those yet to be acquired, fall into this category.

Earlier in Table 2.1, we provided data about the purchase price for parcels that RCA had assembled as of October 2007. The sum, in inflation-adjusted dollars, was about $282 million. This falls well below our point estimate of $321 million for the current market value of these parcels and slightly below the lower bound of $288 million in our 95-percent confidence interval. In short, it appears likely that the market value of land has appreciated significantly during the past few years as RCA has been assembling the reserve.[10]

As a side note, the inclusion of the year-of-sale variable in the hedonic land-value model allows us to estimate the annual percentage change in land values for various land uses. Table 2.4 provides several of these estimates, along with the change in median single-family-home prices in Riverside County during this period for comparison.[11] There are two key observations to note in this table. First, the estimated annual percentage change in SFH lots based on the hedonic model is very close to the observed annual change in median home price. This provides some confidence that the model is effective in accurately capturing the appreciation in property values. Second, it appears that the rate of appreciation for open-space and agricultural parcels has been much greater than for SFH parcels(and may also lag changes in home prices by a year or two). There are theoretical reasons for this, which we discuss further in Chapter Four.

---

[10] The $282 million figure represents the price for the 34,541 acres that were purchased and does not include an estimate of the market value for the remaining 985 acres that were donated. Accounting for the value of these acres on a pro rata basis would increase the $282 million to $290 million. This is slightly higher than the lower bound of the 95-percent confidence interval but still well below the point estimate of $321 million.

[11] Because the sales data we received from the assessor's office for 2000 and 2001 appear to be incomplete, the table does not include appreciation estimates for 2001 or 2002.

Table 2.4
Estimates of Annual Appreciation in Property Values in Constant Dollars

| Year | Estimated Annual Percentage Change in Sales Price from Land-Value Models, by Parcel Type | | | Single-Family Home Sales in Riverside County | |
	Open Space	Agricultural	SFH	Median Price ($ thousands)	Annual Percentage Change
2003	24	86	17	311	15
2004	68	18	26	389	25
2005	45	59	17	448	15
2006	3	2	4	470	5
2007	4	−4	−9	437	−7

SOURCE: Sales data for single-family homes from Riverside County EDA (2008), converted to 2007 dollars using the Southern California CPI (see California Department of Industrial Relations, 2007).

The annual appreciation in values for different land uses as estimated in our modeling results shows a similar pattern to the trajectory of the median home price in Riverside County observed for the same period. Prices increased dramatically between 2003 and 2005 and then began to slow or even decline in 2006 and 2007.

Conclusion

RCA holdings appear to have appreciated in the past several years, reaching a value of approximately $320 million as of mid-2007 (compared to nominal acquisition costs of about $255 million). Housing prices have declined substantially during the past year, and the value of RCA's portfolio may have fallen since mid-2007. Median home prices in Riverside County fell 31 percent between June 2007 and June 2008 ("Southland Home Sales Drag Along Bottom," 2008). As will be discussed in Chapter Four, sales prices for open space and agricultural land in western Riverside County did not show a substantial downturn in price through October 2007, but more-recent data are not available as of this writing. Thus, it is not clear how the value of land held by RCA has changed since mid-2007.

The approximately 35,500 acres that RCA had acquired as of October 2007 amounts to 23 percent of the 153,000 acres needed to complete the MSHCP reserve.[12] If one assumed that the per-acre value of land already acquired were comparable to the per-acre value of land that RCA must still buy, then a first-cut estimate of the total value of the land in a 153,000-acre reserve would be about $1.37 billion ($9,000 per

---

[12] A small number of acres acquired so far fall outside of the area targeted for acquisition and thus would not be counted.

acre times 153,000 acres). As we shall see in the next chapter, though, the estimated per-acre value of the land acquired to date is much lower than the estimated per-acre cost of land yet to be acquired. In other words, it appears that RCA's acquisition efforts to date have focused, for the most part, on relatively cheap parcels on a cost-per-acre basis and that the majority of more-expensive parcels have yet to be acquired.

CHAPTER THREE

Value of Land Required for the MSHCP Reserve

In this chapter, we develop estimates for the market value (as of mid-2007) of the land that will be needed for the entire reserve. In the context of this chapter, the term *reserve* (or *reserve assembly*) refers to the additional 153,000 acres that RCA must assemble (including parcels that RCA has already acquired and parcels yet to be assembled—either through direct purchases or through developer transfers as part of the real estate–approval process), which, in turn, will complement the existing 350,000 acres of public land in western Riverside County to provide an overall conservation area of approximately 500,000 acres.

The MSHCP agreement allows flexibility in the reserve's design, and, accordingly, we examine several scenarios for the types and locations of parcels that will be assembled to complete the reserve. Our scenarios are based on an existing map of what the reserve might look like, the so-called *conceptual reserve design* (CRD) developed by the USFWS (2004). It is important to note that the reserve assembled by RCA need not follow the USFWS CRD. Rather, the reserve must ultimately support the biological goals that underlie the plan's conservation criteria, and numerous reserve-assembly configurations could fulfill this aim. Our primary motivation for examining scenarios based on the USFWS CRD is one of analytic convenience. By using the USFWS CRD as a starting point, it is possible to identify a representative sampling of the types and locations of parcels that RCA might seek to acquire, and this, in turn, makes it possible to develop more-reasonable estimates of what it could cost to assemble the reserve.

We also examine the performance of the USFWS CRD–based assembly scenarios with respect to the conservation goals outlined in the plan. These include goals for the total number of acres in the reserve as well as for the number of acres for different vegetation communities in different subregions in the plan.

Analytic Approach

This section begins by outlining the broad guidelines for assembling the reserve as specified in the MSHCP. We then describe the USFWS CRD and our process for developing alternative assembly scenarios based on this map. We move on to discuss the criteria according to which each scenario is evaluated, including the estimated market value and performance against the conservation guidelines outlined in the MSHCP agreement. The section concludes with a brief overview of the computational methods employed in the analysis.

Broad Guidelines for Reserve Assembly

The MSHCP agreement specifies several important guidelines related to reserve size and configuration. Here, we discuss the most salient concerns with respect to assembling the reserve.

Total Acres. As discussed in Chapter One, the MSHCP planning documents envision acquisition of 153,000 acres. Note that, while RCA will manage the assembly of these additional 153,000 acres, it is expected that the state and federal governments will fund about a third of the acquisition costs. RCA is responsible for funding the acquisition of the remainder. RCA will need to acquire some of these acres through direct purchase, while others may be granted to RCA, either by developers as part of the entitlement process for private real-estate projects or by other donors.

Criteria Area. The MSHCP documentation outlines a set of criteria cells that specify the areas in western Riverside County in which the reserve is to be assembled.[1] Collectively, the criteria cells are referred to as the *criteria area*, which covers about 300,000 acres.[2] With a total reserve goal of 153,000 acres, roughly one half of the criteria area will need to be included in the final reserve.

Core Habitat. To ensure the viability of species covered by the MSHCP, the plan requires that RCA conserve a minimum number acres of different habitat types spread across different subregions (referred to as *rough-step areas*) in the overall plan area. This mandate has been operationalized as a set of specific acreage requirements for seven distinct vegetation communities in nine rough-step accounting areas.[3] For instance, the plan specifies that RCA must conserve at least 800 acres of coastal sage scrub within rough-step area 1. The current acreage targets for different vegetation communities in eight rough-step areas are listed in Table 3.1.[4] No specific acreage targets for different vegetation communities have been enumerated for the ninth rough-step area.

---

[1]   Most of the criteria cells are square and cover 160 acres. Not all, however, are exactly square, and some are smaller than 160 acres, while others are larger.

[2]   The criteria area is divided into criteria cells. For each cell, the MSHCP provides a rough description of the land needed for the reserve. The following is an example of such a description: "Conservation within this Cell will range from 25%–35% of the Cell focusing in the central portion of the cell" (TLMA, 2003, p. 3-162).

[3]   Loosely defined, a *vegetation community* represents suitable habitat for one or more species. Note that the calculation of the number of acres available for conservation for each vegetation community in each rough-step area was based on a vegetation map developed in the 1990s for western Riverside County (TLMA, 2003).

[4]   These acreage targets reflect a slight amendment to the plan adopted in 2007 (RCA, 2007b).

Table 3.1
Acreage Requirements for Vegetation Communities, by Rough-Step Area

Vegetation Type	Rough-Step Area								Total
	1	2	3	4	5	6	7	8	
Coastal sage scrub	765	10,340	2,050	17,590	370	3,827	7,090	4,940	46,972
Desert scrub	0	0	0	3,680	0	0	0	0	3,680
Grassland	180	4,780	900	5,930	1,010	3,638	1,550	1,840	19,828
Playas and vernal pools	0	0	3,830	0	0	0	0	0	3,830
Riparian scrub, woodland, and forest	550	460	110	1,320	460	208	460	250	3,818
Riversidean alluvial-fan sage	0	1,110	100	1,099	260	0	350	130	3,049
Woodlands and forest	0	170	0	870	1,000	98	330	0	2,468
Total	1,495	16,860	6,990	30,489	3,100	7,771	9,780	7,160	83,645

SOURCE: RCA (2007b).

NOTE: There are no acreage requirements for the ninth rough-step area.

Figure 3.1 shows a map of vegetation communities, rough-step area divisions, and the criteria area in which the conservation activities must occur.[5] A key observation from this map is that the distribution of vegetation communities is quite granular, suggesting that the task of keeping track of and achieving the rough-step goals during the process of assembling the reserve will be quite complex.

Note that the underlying purpose of the rough-step areas is to provide a mechanism for state and federal wildlife agencies (CDFG and USFWS) to verify that local permittees are not allowing land in the criteria area to be developed, which would preclude RCA from assembling a reserve that provides the necessary habitat to support species covered by the plan. In each rough-step area and for each vegetation community, RCA must keep track of (1) the number of open-space acres initially available when the plan was approved, (2) the number of acres that have since been developed (or approved for development), and (3) the number of acres that RCA has conserved

Figure 3.1
Vegetation Communities, Rough-Step Areas, and Criteria Cells

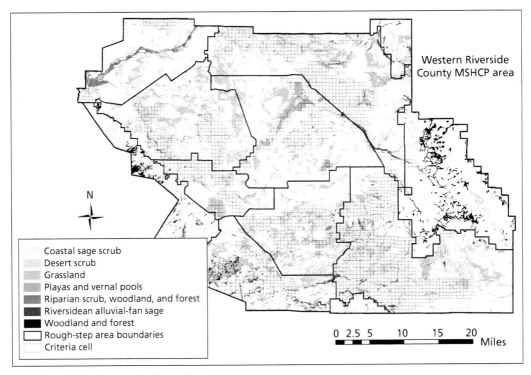

SOURCE: Data provided by RCA in 2007.
RAND MG816-3.1

---

[5] Note that we have shown only the seven vegetation-community categories that are tracked in the rough-step requirements. There are other vegetation communities as well, but we have not added these, as the map is already quite complex.

thus far. A formula is then applied to these parameters to verify that RCA's assembly activities have been keeping pace—that is, keeping in rough step—with allowed development. RCA must update the rough-step calculations each year and publish the results in its annual reports. In cases in which RCA falls out of compliance with the rough-step accounting formula, the wildlife agencies may suspend development authorizations until RCA has assembled enough additional acreage to comply with the formula.

Habitat Linkages. To complement the core habitat areas, parcels must be acquired that provide "linkages" that enable certain endangered species to travel from one core area to another. If linkage parcels include acres for vegetation communities specified in the core habitat requirements, then those acres will count toward meeting the requirements for the relevant rough-step area. That said, the linkages must be assembled whether or not they provide acreage that counts against the core habitat goals. Dudek Engineering + Environmental Consulting (Dudek), a consultant to RCA, has identified parcels that could be acquired to provide the necessary linkages; these potential linkage parcels are included in all of the assembly scenarios considered in this analysis.

The U.S. Fish and Wildlife Service Conceptual Reserve Design

As discussed in the MSHCP documentation, developing a reserve plan that includes compact and contiguous core areas connected by suitable linkages enhances the biological integrity of habitat conservation. Given that the criteria area covers approximately 300,000 acres and that only 153,000 acres must be conserved, there is a significant degree of flexibility in the assembly process. It would certainly be possible to conserve a set of parcels that meets total acreage requirements as well as individual vegetation-community requirements in different rough-step areas but nonetheless results in a highly fragmented, and therefore less effective, reserve. To avoid such an outcome, the MSHCP provides guidelines for what an effective reserve pattern—that is, one with a sufficient level of compactness and contiguity—might look like.

The suggested guidelines in the MSHCP documentation are presented not as a map but rather as a set of textual descriptions of the areas in different criteria cells that might be included in the reserve. For instance, that plan might state that, in a given subset of the criteria cells, the goal would be to acquire between 25 and 35 percent of the available acres, focusing on acquisitions in the northwest quadrant. Based on these textual descriptions, USFWS has developed a map representing what a biologically suitable reserve assembly could look like (USFWS, 2004). This map, the USFWS CRD, is illustrated in Figure 3.2.

Figure 3.2 maps existing public lands (such as national forests and state wildlife reserves), the criteria cells in which the conservation must occur, and the areas included in the USFWS CRD. Note that, in the CRD, the larger contiguous blocks,

Figure 3.2
The USFWS Conceptual Reserve Design

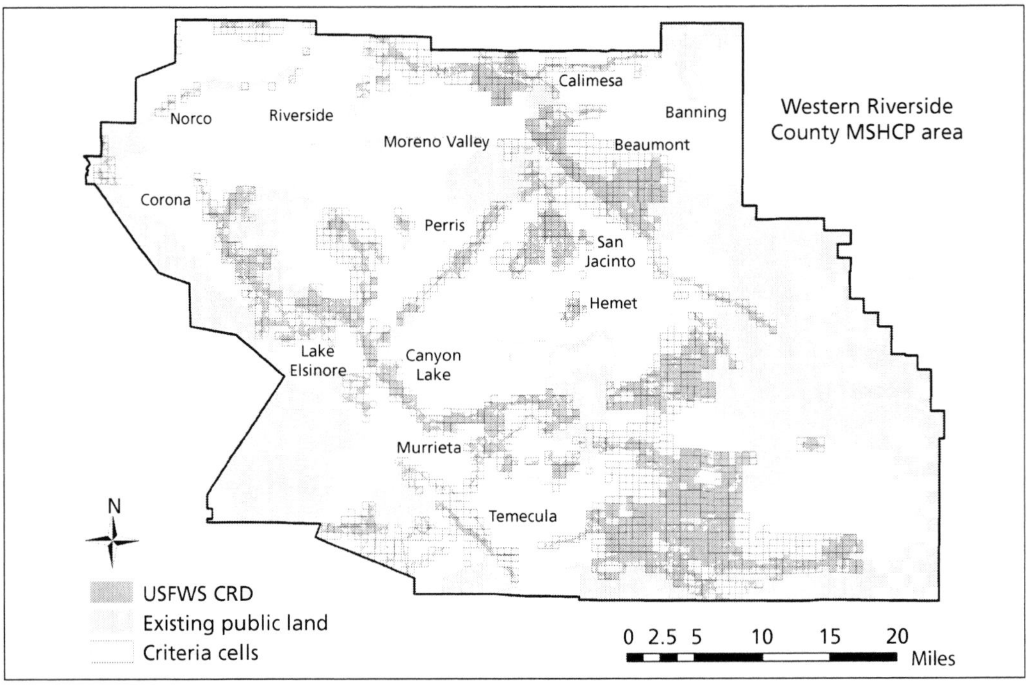

SOURCE: Data provided by RCA and USFWS in 2008.
RAND *MG816-3.2*

which often complement existing public lands, represent the significant areas of core habitat conservation. The linear features, in turn, represent the linkages that connect these core areas.

For the purposes of our analysis, we relied on the USFWS CRD as a starting point for what the reserve might look like. The CRD spans an area of almost 165,000 acres, of which a little more than 1,000 are PQP lands. The USFWS CRD is larger than the 153,000 acres ultimately required because it contains some areas, such as road rights-of-way or scattered development, that are unlikely to be conserved.

While we recognize that the USFWS CRD is but one example of a suitable reserve design, using this map makes it easier to identify a set of parcels—that is, an assembly scenario—that should be able to meet the size and spatial-configuration goals for the reserve.[6] It should be stressed that, while the USFWS CRD is a helpful analytic tool for building reserve-assembly scenarios, it is not prescriptive. The plan, as noted earlier, was crafted to ensure sufficient flexibility such that RCA would not need to exercise eminent domain to wrest specific parcels from unwilling sellers (TLMA, 2003).

---

[6]   Specifically, by using GIS, one can simply identify those parcels that fall within or partially overlap the CRD to consider for potential acquisition.

Parcel-Level Issues That Affect Reserve-Assembly Scenarios

Even with the USFWS CRD as a starting point for the assembly scenarios analyzed in this chapter, there are still many decisions to make about parcel-specific acquisitions, including whether to include a specific parcel based on its current land use and whether to include a parcel in its entirety or instead assume that RCA would seek to acquire just a portion of the parcel. Such decisions could affect the estimated value of the reserve, the total number of acres assembled, and the number of acres in different vegetation communities and rough-step areas. Here, we outline assumptions about the selection of specific parcels that we have used to create several reserve-assembly scenarios based on the USFWS CRD.

Land Use. Our parcel-assembly scenarios include three distinct groups of parcels: those that RCA has already acquired, those that will be used to create linkages among core areas, and those that will make up the core areas of habitat.

Given that the first group of parcels has already been acquired, we include such parcels in all the scenarios examined regardless of land use. The same is true for linkage parcels, though for a different reason. For linkages to be functional, they must be uninterrupted. In other words, if a linkage consists of a string of 10 adjacent parcels, then RCA will need to acquire all 10 of these parcels—regardless of land use—to make sure that the linkage corridor allows species mobility from one core area to another. If any of the 10 parcels were omitted, the corridor would be incomplete and therefore ineffective. For this reason, our base scenarios assume that the potential linkage parcels that Dudek identified would all be included in the assembly. Note that, in practice, it may be possible for RCA to alter the alignment of certain linkages so as to avoid the purchase of more-expensive, already developed parcels, so we also consider that possibility when developing value estimates for the different assembly scenarios.

For the core-area parcels, there is a much greater degree of latitude. In the core areas, RCA would undoubtedly seek to acquire the majority of open-space and agricultural parcels in the USFWS CRD. However, if needed—either to achieve the total acreage goal or to achieve individual goals for different vegetation communities and rough-step areas—RCA could also seek to acquire properties with some level of development, such as larger residential lots or even commercial or industrial properties. In constructing the assembly scenarios examined in this chapter, we therefore incorporate three possible assumptions regarding the types of parcels that would be included in the core areas of the USFWS CRD:

- all open-space and agricultural parcels
- all open-space and agricultural parcels along with residential lots greater than 10 acres in size
- all parcels, including open-space, agricultural, residential, commercial, and industrial lots.

Even though we consider a scenario in which the reserve assembly encompasses all parcels in the USFWS CRD, including heavily developed parcels, we do not envision that such a scenario would occur in practice. To begin with, the purchase price of developed parcels will certainly be much higher than for open-space land. In addition, it would be necessary to spend even more money on demolition and restoration to return these parcels to a suitable state for species habitat. Flexibility in the final form of the reserve will presumably allow RCA to construct a reserve that does not include such parcels. Even so, evaluating such a scenario is helpful in determining a reasonable upper bound on the current market value of the full reserve.

Approved Development. A small but nontrivial number of parcels in the criteria area have received the necessary approvals for real-estate projects but have not yet been developed. To meet certain habitat-conservation goals, RCA could consider trying to purchase these parcels as well. Since they have not yet been developed, they should be cheaper than existing residential, commercial, or industrial properties. Our assembly scenarios therefore consider the possibilities that (1) parcels with approved development will not be included in the reserve or (2) such parcels can be acquired as part of the reserve.

Excess Road Right-of-Way. The criteria area is crisscrossed with road right-of-way that has been reserved for future road development. With the MSHCP reserve in place, however, at least some of these once-planned roads may no longer be needed. That is, they can now be thought of as excess road right-of-way. The scenarios examined in this chapter include the possibilities that (1) future road right-of-way would not be acquired in assembling the reserve[7] or (2) future road right-of-way in the USFWS CRD would be acquired for conservation.[8]

Parcel Subdivision. RCA will, in many cases, purchase parcels in their entirety. In certain circumstances, however, such as when only a portion of a parcel provides valuable habitat, RCA may seek to subdivide the parcel and purchase only the amount needed for conservation. Such subdivisions, where possible, should help to reduce the overall cost of assembling the reserve.

In practice, whether or not RCA will be able to convince a landowner to sell a portion of his or her parcel to RCA likely depends on the size of the parcel as well as the amount that RCA wishes to purchase. Imagine, for instance, that a developer holds a 50-acre parcel and RCA would like to acquire 45 of those acres for the reserve. It is

---

[7] That is, when the right-of-way crosses a parcel to be conserved by RCA, we subtract the acres covered by the right-of-way and then prorate the parcel's estimated value accordingly.

[8] In practice, it is unlikely that RCA would purchase all future road right-of-way, as some of the roads may still be needed. It is beyond the scope of our analysis, however, to distinguish between right-of-way that is no longer needed and right-of-way that must be kept in place for future roads. For this reason, our scenarios assume that the reserve will include either none of the future road right-of-way or all of it. This helps to provide upper and lower bounds—with respect to both the reserve's value and its conservation attributes—based on decisions to acquire some portion of the corridors currently designated as future road right-of-way.

unlikely that a developer could do much with the remaining five acres, so the developer would likely insist that RCA purchase the parcel in its entirety or not at all. On the other hand, if RCA wanted to buy only 10 of the acres, the developer would still be able to make productive use of the remaining 40 acres and might therefore be more willing to sell a portion to RCA.

In developing the hypothetical assembly scenarios based on the shape of the USFWS CRD, we begin with the assumption that RCA would attempt to exactly subdivide parcels that partially overlap the CRD—that is, it would attempt to purchase just those components of parcels that fall entirely within the CRD. If successful, the current owner would retain any portion of the parcel lying outside the CRD, and the purchase price for the parcel would be prorated accordingly. We then consider two potential assumptions about how landowners would respond. Under the first of these, we assume that landowners would always allow RCA to subdivide parcels that overlap the CRD boundary, regardless of the size of the portion that falls outside the CRD. This assumption is likely unrealistic, but it suggests a reasonable upper bound on the amount that RCA could save through parcel subdivision. Under the second, more realistic assumption, a landowner would allow RCA to acquire a subdivided portion of a parcel only if the remainder would be large enough to pursue reasonable development activities.

In determining whether the remainder of a parcel could support development activities, we used slightly different rules for linkage and core-area parcels. For linkages, we first calculated the average size of other parcels in that same linkage. If the part of a parcel falling outside the USFWS CRD boundary was at least as large as the average size of other parcels in the linkage corridor, we assumed that subdivision could take place. For core-area parcels, in turn, we assumed that subdivision could take place only in cases in which the portion of a parcel lying outside the USFWS CRD was at least 25 acres. Both of these rules were determined through consultation with RCA staff based on their experience in acquiring and subdividing parcels to date.

Reserve-Assembly Scenarios

Drawing on these considerations, we developed three scenarios of the parcels that would be included in the reserve, taking for granted the parcels that RCA already holds. We refer to these as the *base-case scenario*, the *lightly developed scenario*, and the *heavily developed scenario*. The three scenarios vary in terms of the numbers and types of parcels included in the reserve, gradually increasing in both total acres and total value. Examining this range of scenarios makes it possible to illustrate how the reserve's value along with its conservation attributes may be influenced by the alternative parcel-assembly decisions that RCA could make.

In constructing the scenarios, we began with parcels that RCA has already assembled as well as the potential linkage parcels identified by Dudek. Both of these sets of parcels were included in all three of the scenarios. Our next step was to incorporate additional core-area parcels that fall within or overlap the USFWS CRD boundary. For the base-case scenario, we included only open-space and agricultural parcels in the core areas. For the lightly developed scenario, we augmented the core area–parcel selections to include parcels with approved development, future road right-of-way, and residential lots greater than 10 acres in size. Finally, for the heavily developed scenario, we augmented the core area–parcel selections to include smaller residential lots as well as commercial and industrial properties. Table 3.2 summarizes the selection of parcels included in each of the scenarios.

For each of the three parcel-assembly scenarios, we also explored the two assumptions about parcel subdivisions discussed earlier. In the *exact-subdivision scenario*, we assumed that it would always be possible to subdivide parcels overlapping the USFWS CRD to acquire just those portions that fall within the CRD. In the *partial-subdivision scenario*, we assumed that subdivisions could occur only if the size of the portion of the parcel outside the CRD met the specific subdivision rules described earlier (the *partial-subdivision scenarios*). By considering each of these two subdivision assumptions for the three parcel-selection scenarios, we arrived at a total of six cases to consider.

Evaluation Criteria

To compare the scenarios against one another, we developed several high-level statistics describing their land value as well as their performance with respect to the conservation goals of the MSHCP.

Total Value. This represents our estimate of the 2007 market value of each reserve scenario, using the hedonic land-value models described in the previous chapter. It includes parcels already held by RCA as well as linkage and core-area parcels still to be assembled.

Table 3.2
Parcels Included in Reserve-Assembly Scenarios

Type of Parcel	Scenario		
	Base Case	Lightly Developed	Heavily Developed
Parcels already assembled by RCA	X	X	X
All potential linkage parcels	X	X	X
Open-space and agricultural parcels	X	X	X
Approved development projects		X	X
Future road right-of-way		X	X
Residential lots > 10 acres		X	X
All other developed parcels			X

Total Acres. This is the total number of acres across all parcels in each scenario. The number includes acres in the USFWS CRD, other acres in the criteria cells but not in the USFWS CRD, and acres outside the criteria cells.

Value per Acre. This is simply the total value divided by the total acres. In other words, it represents the average per-acre value of the land in the reserve-assembly scenario.

Assembly Value of 153,000 Acres. This number is calculated by multiplying the per-acre value for each assembly scenario by 153,000 total acres. The basic idea here is that the reserve would include the same mix of parcel types used to construct the scenario but that only a total of 153,000 acres would be assembled. This is reasonable in the sense that RCA, to reduce acquisition costs, will strive to construct an assembly that meets conservation goals while not exceeding the required 153,000 acres by a significant amount. Accordingly, this number is likely to approximate the reserve's value more closely than the total value number discussed earlier.

Acres in Criteria Cells. This represents the total number of acres for the parcels that fall within the criteria cells and thus can be counted against the total acreage goal of 153,000. (Acres falling outside of the criteria cells, in contrast, would not be counted toward this goal, according to the MSHCP guidelines.)

Total Acre Shortfall. This number indicates whether there is a shortfall between the number of acres acquired in criteria cells and the total acreage goal of 153,000. If the number of targeted acres exceeds 153,000, the value for this statistic is set to zero.

Vegetation Community and Rough-Step Area Shortfall. In addition to examining the total number of acres acquired, we also determine the number of acres for each vegetation community and rough-step area that a specific assembly scenario would provide. These numbers are then compared against individual acreage goals for each vegetation community and rough-step area to see whether any shortfalls exist. This statistic represents the sum, across all vegetation communities and rough-step areas, of any such shortfalls that we identify for a given acquisition scenario. Because we set any acreage surplus for a vegetation community–rough-step area combination to zero, a shortfall for a particular vegetation community in one rough-step area is not offset in this accounting by a surplus for that vegetative community in another rough-step area. In evaluating the number of acres for a given vegetation community and rough-step area, we include only acres that fall within the criteria cells because acres falling outside this area are not considered eligible for meeting reserve requirements.

Computational Methods

As may be inferred from the preceding discussions, our analysis required the ability to examine a range of detailed spatial characteristics of individual parcels to make certain decisions or track certain statistics. For example, we needed to be able to answer such questions as the following:

- How many acres of a parcel fall outside of the criteria cells?
- What portion of a parcel does future road right-of-way or approved development cover?
- How many acres in a parcel correspond to a specific rough-step area and vegetation community?

To answer such questions, we used GIS to perform a spatial intersection of maps containing the different data layers of interest. Specifically, we analyzed the intersection of the following layers:

- parcel boundaries
- criteria cells
- USFWS CRD outline
- rough-step accounting area boundaries
- vegetation communities
- areas designated for future road right-of-way
- areas approved for future development.

The net effect of the intersection operation involving these layers was to divide each parcel into different component polygons according to the criteria just enumerated. For instance, we could identify the component polygons (and their size) for a parcel that fell outside the USFWS CRD, that contained a particular vegetation community, that fell within a given rough-step area, or any combination thereof. This enabled the types of calculations described earlier.

Value of Land in Reserve-Assembly Scenarios

We begin this section by presenting findings on the current land value (as of mid-2007) for the reserve-assembly scenarios just outlined. We also develop confidence intervals around the estimated total market value to provide a sense of how much the actual value might vary given the statistical uncertainty of our land-value models. Finally, we examine the potential savings that could be achieved by modifying certain linkage corridors so as to avoid purchasing heavily developed parcels. In subsequent sections, we consider the cost implications for local permittees as well as the performance of the assembly scenarios with respect to the conservation goals outlined in the plan.

Total and Average Land-Value Estimates for the Reserve-Assembly Scenarios

Table 3.3 presents land-value estimates for the three reserve-assembly parcel-selection scenarios discussed earlier: the base-case, lightly developed, and heavily developed scenarios. For each of these, we also examine both the exact parcel–subdivision assumption and the partial parcel–subdivision assumption, resulting in a total of six cases

Table 3.3
Estimated Reserve Value for the Six Reserve-Assembly Scenarios

Assembly Scenario	Total Parcels	Estimated Value ($ billions)	Total Acres	Value per Acre ($)	153,000-Acre Value ($ billions)
Base case					
Exact subdivision	11,387	3.90	151,587	25,700	3.93
Partial subdivision	11,387	4.77	162,224	29,400	4.50
Lightly developed					
Exact subdivision	12,164	4.14	161,332	25,700	3.93
Partial subdivision	12,164	5.06	173,371	29,200	4.47
Heavily developed					
Exact subdivision	15,490	5.91	168,570	35,100	5.37
Partial subdivision	15,490	7.24	182,240	39,700	6.07

included in the analysis. Recall that the partial parcel–subdivision rule allows for fewer subdivisions than the exact parcel–subdivision rule; as a result, the cases involving partial-parcel subdivision always include a larger total number of acres than the corresponding cases involving the exact parcel–subdivision rule.

In Table 3.3, the two left columns describe the parcel selection and subdivision scenarios and list the total number of parcels included in each scenario. The next three columns show the total estimated value in 2007 of the reserve scenario (including parcels already assembled by RCA as well as those not yet acquired), the total number of acres in the reserve, and the average value on a per-acre basis. The final column prorates the total value for a reserve of 153,000 acres; that is, it represents the value of the reserve under the assumption that RCA would assemble a comparable set of parcels but would constrain total acquisitions to 153,000 acres.

In evaluating these results, we start with the partial-subdivision scenarios because the exact-subdivision scenarios are not likely to be realistic, in the sense that it is improbable that RCA could convince all property owners to subdivide their parcels right at the reserve boundary. (Rather, these exact-subdivision scenarios might more properly be viewed as providing a bound on the most that RCA could save in purchasing a specific set of parcels through aggressive efforts to subdivide wherever possible.)

The 153,000-acre value estimates for the base-case and lightly developed parcel–selection scenarios under the partial parcel–subdivision assumption are both around $4.5 billion. For the heavily developed scenario, in contrast, the value is just above $6 billion. The implication is that, if RCA finds it helpful to purchase lightly developed properties, such as large residential lots, in order to acquire needed habitat, there will be little effect on the reserve's total value. On the other hand, if RCA finds it necessary to purchase and convert more–heavily developed properties, such as smaller residential lots or commercial and industrial developments, the cost of the reserve will escalate rapidly. Fortunately, given the inherent flexibility in the plan, it appears unlikely that RCA would need to acquire many heavily developed parcels.

Another observation from Table 3.3 is that there tends to be a considerable difference in the per-acre values between the exact- and partial-subdivision scenarios. Recall, again, that the distinction between these two sets of scenarios is whether all parcels at the reserve boundary will be subdivided. Our data suggest that, because such parcels lie closer to existing roads and development than parcels in the middle of the largely open-space criteria area, they will tend to have a higher per-acre value on average. In the partial-subdivision scenarios, fewer parcels at the edge of the reserve are subdivided, and, as a result, a greater percentage of the acreage in these parcels is included in the assembly. This raises the average per-acre value for the partial-subdivision cases.

Confidence Intervals for the Land-Value Estimates

As in the previous chapter, we developed confidence intervals for our estimates of the total market value for assembly scenarios (see Appendix A for details on the statistical bootstrap method used to develop the confidence intervals). Table 3.4 presents the results of this analysis for the three parcel-selection scenarios under the partial parcel–subdivision assumption. In each scenario, the results are broken down by land use and also presented in aggregate.

The data in Table 3.4 merit several observations. First, the confidence bounds on the overall assembly value are relatively tight, ranging from about –10 percent on the low side to about +20 percent on the high side for the base-case and lightly developed scenarios and growing slightly larger for the heavily developed scenario. We consider the former scenarios to be more realistic than the latter, as it is unlikely that RCA would choose to acquire such a large number of developed parcels, so the tighter bounds on the base-case and lightly developed scenarios are encouraging. That is, they enable RCA to view the total assembly-value estimates as being fairly reliable.

One of the reasons that the confidence interval widens for the heavily developed scenario is that it includes many more parcels falling into the "other" category. Looking at the confidence intervals for the individual land uses in Table 3.4, there is much greater uncertainty for land values in the "other" category than in the remaining four land-use groups. One reason for this is that there were relatively few sales observations available for use in estimating the "other" land-use model, as shown in Table 2.2 in Chapter Two, making it more difficult to estimate an extremely accurate model.[9]

---

[9]   In addition, we found that the values for some of the land-use characteristics (e.g., size and distance to nearest highway) for the "other" parcels in the reserve scenarios fell beyond the range of values found in the sales data for "other" parcels that were used to estimate the land-value model. That is, we faced out-of-sample values in the parcel predictions. This was likely an artifact of our choice to group miscellaneous land uses (e.g., airfields, mines,

Table 3.4
Confidence Intervals for Assembly-Scenario Land-Value Estimates

Scenario	Land Use	Total Estimated Value ($ billion)	95% Confidence Interval ($ billions)	Percentage Spread (%)
Base-case scenario with partial-parcel subdivision	Open space	2.42	[2.17, 2.64]	[−11, +9]
	Agricultural	0.40	[0.29, 0.64]	[−29, +58]
	SFH	1.20	[1.17, 1.23]	[−3, +3]
	MFH	0.10	[0.08, 0.12]	[−16, +18]
	Other	0.64	[0.24, 1.44]	[−62, +126]
	Total	4.77	[4.28, 5.72]	[−10, +20]
Lightly developed scenario with partial-parcel subdivision	Open space	2.55	[2.28, 2.77]	[−11, +9]
	Agricultural	0.45	[0.31, 0.71]	[−30, +58]
	SFH	1.32	[1.29, 1.36]	[−3, +3]
	MFH	0.10	[0.08, 0.12]	[−16, +18]
	Other	0.64	[0.24, 1.44]	[−62, +126]
	Total	5.06	[4.56, 6.03]	[−10, +19]
Heavily developed scenario with partial-parcel subdivision	Open space	2.55	[2.28, 2.77]	[−11, +9]
	Agricultural	0.45	[0.31, 0.71]	[−30, +58]
	SFH	2.57	[2.51, 2.64]	[−2, +2]
	MFH	0.26	[0.22, 0.31]	[−16, +17]
	Other	1.41	[0.53, 3.29]	[−63, +133]
	Total	7.24	[6.31, 9.25]	[−13, +28]

Confidence intervals for the remaining land-use categories are more reasonable. The spread for agricultural parcels is still wide—about 30 percent on the low end and 60 percent on the high end—but not nearly to the same degree as the "other" land use (note that agriculture is another land use for which we had relatively few sales records available to estimate the model). The bounds for MFH are less than 20 percent in the negative and positive directions, while the bounds for open space are around 10 percent in either direction. SFH, which had, by far, the most available sales records as well as a broader selection of explanatory variables (e.g., number of bedrooms) to estimate the model, exhibits very tight bounds of just 2 or 3 percent in either direction.

---

and water-transfer facilities) into the "other" category. The majority of sales records used to estimate the model represented traditional commercial and industrial properties rather than these less common land-use types.

In all three scenarios, open-space and SFH parcels represent the largest shares of the overall purchase price (open space actually dominates in terms of the number of acres, but SFH parcels cost more per acre). Because open space and SFH have the tightest bounds for individual land uses, this helps to maintain a relatively narrow confidence interval on the total assembly value (especially for the base-case and lightly developed scenarios, which have fewer parcels in the difficult-to-predict "other" category).

Again, as described in the previous chapter, note that our confidence intervals reflect uncertainty in the statistics of our land-value models. They do not, in contrast, take into consideration uncertainty relative to recent declines in the real-estate market. The sales records used to calibrate our models included transactions through October 2007. Thus, our "current" land-value estimates for 2007 likely reflect prices as of about May 2007 (the midpoint of our 2007 data between January and October). As noted in Chapter Two, median home prices in Riverside County fell 31 percent between June 2007 and June 2008. However, as discussed in Chapter Four, insufficient data were available at the time of this writing to determine whether open space and agricultural land prices have declined between mid-2007 and mid-2008.

Disaggregation of Land-Value Estimates by Land Use and Location

The aggregate nature of the results in Table 3.3 masks considerable variation in the per-acre value of parcels in different areas and for different land uses. To explore this issue, Table 3.5 provides a more detailed breakdown of the value estimates for the lightly developed–parcel selection scenario under the partial parcel–subdivision assumption. We have selected this scenario because it falls in the midrange—in terms of total value, number of acres, and types of properties included—of the other two reserve scenarios considered in our analysis and thus may offer insights that would hold across other scenarios as well.

In Table 3.5, we begin by dividing the parcels to be assembled into three broad groups: those already held by RCA, those required for the linkages, and those that will complete the core areas. In each of these parcel groups, we also categorize parcels by the five land uses recognized in our regression models: open space, agricultural, SFH, MFH, and other development (including commercial and industrial uses). For each parcel group and land-use category, we list the number of parcels, their total estimated value, their total acreage, and the corresponding average cost per acre. We also provide subtotals for each parcel group and aggregate the results across all groups.

Table 3.6 complements Table 3.5, presenting the percentage of total cost as well as the percentage of total acreage represented by each parcel group (that is, each subtotal line from Table 3.5).

As can be seen in Table 3.6, the linkages are disproportionately expensive, representing about 60 percent of the total estimated value (roughly $3.0 billion of about $5.1 billion) of the assembly for just 28 percent of the total acreage (just under 48,000 of the total of approximately 173,000). One reason for this, as can be discerned in

Table 3.5
Disaggregation of Land Values for the Lightly Developed Parcel–Selection Scenario Under
the Partial Parcel–Subdivision Assumption

Parcel Group	Land-Use Category	Parcels	Estimated Value ($ millions)	Acres	Per-Acre Value ($ thousands)
Parcels already owned by RCA	Open space	513	290	33,914	8.5
	Agricultural	20	27	1,558	17.0
	SFH	3	1	11	133.2
	MFH	3	3	43	69.8
	Other developed	0	—	—	—
	Subtotal	539	321	35,526	9.0
Additional linkage parcels	Open space	3,103	931	30,209	30.8
	Agricultural	243	169	3,480	48.6
	SFH	2,177	1,201	12,615	95.2
	MFH	127	96	346	278.9
	Other developed	214	638	1,260	506.3
	Subtotal	5,864	3,035	47,910	63.3
Additional core-area parcels	Open space	5,194	1,328	74,149	17.9
	Agricultural	300	252	10,518	23.9
	SFH	267	120	5,268	22.7
	MFH	0	—	—	—
	Other developed	0	—	—	—
	Subtotal	5,761	1,699	89,935	18.9
All parcels in scenario	Open space	8,810	2,549	138,273	18.4
	Agricultural	563	447	15,557	28.8
	SFH	2,447	1,322	17,893	73.9
	MFH	130	99	389	255.8
	Other developed	214	638	1,260	506.3
	Total	12,164	5,055	173,371	29.2

Table 3.5, is that most of the heavily developed parcels included in this reserve scenario, such as MFH, commercial, or industrial properties, lie within the linkages. Such properties have, on average, a much higher per-acre value than less-developed or open-space properties.

Table 3.6
Percentage of Acres and Price for Different Parcel Groups in the Lightly Developed Parcel–Selection Assembly Scenario

Parcel Group	Total Estimated Value ($ millions)	Share of Total Estimated Value (%)	Total Acres	Share of Total Acreage (%)
RCA-owned	321	6	35,526	21
Linkage	3,035	60	47,910	28
Core	1,699	34	89,935	52
All	5,055	100	173,371	100

A second reason that the linkages are disproportionately expensive is that average per-acre values for each of the land-use categories tend to be higher than they are for the parcels already acquired by RCA or for the additional parcels to be acquired in the core areas. As Table 3.5 shows, for instance, the estimated per-acre value for open-space land is about $8,500 for parcels already acquired, about $17,900 for parcels still to be acquired in the core areas, and about $30,800 for parcels still to be acquired in the linkage areas. Our interpretation of this observation is that the linkages typically run through areas that are already heavily developed, which, in turn, drives up the value of available land. Such factors as proximity to roads and surrounding development patterns tend to increase the per-acre land values in the linkages.

Cost Implications of Rerouting Linkage Corridors to Avoid Heavily Developed Parcels

Our analysis so far has focused on the total value of land for reserve-assembly scenarios based on the USFWS CRD. Each of the examined scenarios also included the potential linkage parcels identified by Dudek. As noted, these linkage parcels include numerous SFH, MFH, commercial, and industrial properties, and, as a result, they are very expensive. If the linkages could be shifted to avoid developed parcels, therefore, the overall market value of the modeled reserve scenarios could be reduced substantially. We should stress that we have not evaluated the ecological implications of shifting certain corridors in order to determine whether such shifts would be consistent with the conservation guidelines outlined in the plan.[10] We did, however, examine the potential savings that could be achieved by avoiding developed parcels in constructing the linkages.

To do so, we began by identifying the total number of acres and total value of the linkage parcels in our scenarios. Next, we looked at the total acres and total value of open-space and agricultural parcels in the linkages, calculating the average price per acre for such parcels. We then multiplied the average price per acre for open-space and

---

[10] RCA can move linkages in criteria cells without amending the plan. Moving linkages outside criteria cells, in contrast, would require a plan amendment (Landry, 2008).

agricultural parcels by the total number of acres for all parcels in the linkage corridors. The resulting figure represents an estimate of the total value of assembling the linkages, assuming that

- the linkages could be shifted to avoid all developed parcels
- the same total number of acres would be acquired in constructing the linkages
- the value of the new open-space and agricultural parcels replacing the more heavily developed parcels would be comparable, in terms of price per acre, to the open-space and agricultural parcels in the linkage alignments used in our scenarios.

It is not clear that all of these assumptions would hold in practice, but it is still useful to perform the exercise in order to get a sense of the potential magnitude of the financial benefits that would result if such shifts proved possible.

Note that the set of included linkage parcels was the same for each of the three parcel-selection scenarios (base case, lightly developed, and heavily developed). On the other hand, the total number of acres acquired with the linkage parcels varied between the exact parcel–subdivision and the partial parcel–subdivision assumptions. We therefore developed two estimates of the potential savings that might be achieved by aligning the linkage corridors so as to avoid developed parcels: one for each of the subdivision assumptions.

For the exact parcel–subdivision case, we estimated that the total savings that could be achieved by avoiding developed linkage parcels was about $0.81 billion. For the partial-subdivision scenarios, for which the total number of acres purchased was higher, our estimate of the potential savings was $1.12 billion. Table 3.7 shows the corresponding percentage savings, based on the prorated 153,000-acre values, for each of the six scenario and subdivision cases examined.

As the data in Table 3.7 suggest, the reserve's overall market value can be reduced considerably if RCA can align the linkage corridors in a manner that sidesteps heavily developed parcels, with potential savings falling between 15 and 25 percent. The question of whether this would be possible within the plan's ecological constraints was beyond the scope of this study, but it certainly merits further evaluation.

Remaining Costs for Local Permittees

The preceding analysis provided estimates of the total market value for a 153,000-acre reserve, including the land that RCA has already assembled. In this section, we consider the share of the remaining assembly costs for which local MSHCP permittees—Riverside County and the 14 cities in western Riverside County—may be responsible.

To address this question, it is first necessary to estimate the number of acres that local permittees will ultimately need to purchase. In crafting the MSHCP

Table 3.7
Estimated Percentage Savings from Aligning Linkage Corridors to Avoid Developed Parcels

Assembly Scenario	153,000-Acre Value ($ billions)	Estimated Linkage Savings ($ billions)	Adjusted Reserve Value ($ billions)	Value per Acre ($ thousands)	Savings (%)
Base case					
Exact subdivision	3.93	0.81	3.12	20.4	20.6
Partial subdivision	4.50	1.12	3.38	22.1	24.9
Lightly developed					
Exact subdivision	3.93	0.81	3.12	20.4	20.6
Partial subdivision	4.47	1.12	3.35	21.9	25.1
Heavily developed					
Exact subdivision	5.37	0.81	4.56	29.8	15.1
Partial subdivision	6.07	1.12	4.95	32.4	18.5

agreement, policymakers deemed it appropriate that all parties benefiting from the plan—including the federal and state governments, local permittees, and local development interests—contribute to the reserve assembly. Recall from Table 1.1 in Chapter One that the state and federal governments are responsible for funding the acquisition of 56,000 acres (36.6 percent of the reserve), local permittees are expected to fund an additional 56,000 acres (another 36.6 percent of the reserve), and developers (through the real estate–approval process) or other local donors are expected to contribute the remaining 41,000 acres (26.8 percent of the reserve).

Should contributions fall short of 41,000 acres, however, local permittees will be responsible for funding the balance of acquisitions needed to complete the 153,000 acres. In other words, local permittees are, in fact, responsible for a total of 97,000 acres, though the plan envisions that developers or other local donors will contribute 41,000 of the 97,000-acre local share. Whether or not this share of contributions will be achieved is highly uncertain, as it depends on the decisions of numerous individual landowners in their negotiations with RCA and local permittees.

Evidence to date suggests that the original estimate of 41,000 acres assembled through developer contributions may be optimistic. As of October 2007, RCA had assembled a total of 35,526 acres. The state and federal governments funded or contributed 14,677 of these acres. Of the remaining 20,849, just 657 acres were received through the local development process or from other local donors, while the remaining 20,192 were purchased by local permittees (see Table 1.1).[11] In other words, just

[11] Table 2.1 in Chapter Two shows a total of 985 contributed acres as of October 2007. Of these, 328 were contributed to the state and thus are tallied as part of the state and federal government share of assembly costs. The

3.2 percent (657 of 20,849 acres) of the land that local government has obtained for the reserve has been received through contributions, while 96.8 percent (20,192 of 20,849 acres) has been purchased by local permittees. If this trend continues, local permittees would end up purchasing a total of 93,942 acres (96.8 percent of 97,000), while just 3,058 acres (3.2 percent of 97,000) would be contributed. In other words, local permittees would be responsible for funding 61.4 percent of the entire reserve (93,942 of 153,000 acres), while just 2.0 percent of the reserve (3,058 of 153,000 acres) would be assembled through contributions.

The percentage of acreage donated by developers may increase in future years, but, again, this is uncertain. To examine the influence that this factor may have on local assembly costs, we consider two alternative assumptions:

- The percentage of acreage received through the development process will remain consistent with assembly efforts to date (that is, donated acres will represent roughly 3.2 percent of the local contribution, or 2.0 percent of the entire reserve). In this case, local permittees would need to purchase 61.4 percent of the total reserve assembly.
- The percentage of acreage yielded through the development process will accelerate over time, eventually reaching 28.6 percent of the reserve acreage as envisioned in the MSHCP agreement. In this case, local permittees would end up purchasing 36.6 percent of the total reserve acreage.

With these assumptions in place, the next step is to calculate the percentage of the remaining costs that local permittees would need to fund. The calculations are shown in Table 3.8.

From the first row in Table 3.8, we see that, if developer contributions increase to the anticipated level, then local permittees will need to purchase 36.6 percent of the total reserve assembly, or 56,000 acres. Given that local permittees have already purchased 20,192 acres, they would still need to buy 35,808 additional acres to meet this share. This corresponds to 30.5 percent of the 117,474 acres that still need to

Table 3.8
Share of Remaining Acquisition Costs to Be Funded by Local Permittees

Local Contributions	Total Local Purchase Share (%)	Total Local Purchase Acres	Remaining Local Purchase Acres	Share of Remaining Costs (%)
As planned (26.8%)	36.6	56,000	35,808	30.5
Current pace (2.0%)	61.4	93,942	73,750	62.8

remaining 657 acres were received from developers and other local donors and thus count toward the local share of assembly contributions.

be assembled to complete the 153,000-acre reserve. If developer contributions fail to increase, as shown in the second row, then local permittees will end up funding 61.4 percent of the reserve, or 93,942 acres. Subtracting the 20,192 acres already funded by local permittees, they would still need to fund an additional 73,750 acres to meet this share. This corresponds to 62.8 percent of the remaining 117,474 acres needed to complete the reserve.

Leveraging this analysis, we can develop estimates of the share of remaining assembly costs that local permittees would fund under alternative assembly assumptions. Here, we focus on the lightly developed parcel–selection scenario and the partial parcel–subdivision rule, which we consider to be the most reasonable approximation of the types of parcel acquisitions that RCA would pursue in assembling the reserve.[12] For this combination, we then consider alternative assumptions regarding (1) whether developer contributions rise to the initially anticipated level, in which case local permittees will need to fund 30.5 percent of the remaining assembly value, or instead follow their current trajectory, in which case local permittees will need to fund 61.4 percent of the remaining assembly value, and (2) whether linkages can be aligned to avoid heavily developed parcels. The analysis is presented in Table 3.9.

Note that, in Table 3.9, the "153,000-Acre Cost" column values are based on data presented earlier in Table 3.7 and reflect the potential savings that could occur by constructing the linkages in a manner that avoids developed parcels. The "Remaining Cost" column values are calculated by subtracting the $320 million estimated value of parcels already acquired (see Chapter Two for details) from the total 153,000-acre cost values. These are then multiplied by the "Local Permittee Share" column values, as

Table 3.9
Remaining Assembly-Cost Estimates for Local Permittees with the Lightly Developed Parcel–Selection Scenario Under the Partial Parcel–Subdivision Assumption

Developer Contributions (%)	Linkages Realigned	153,000-Acre Cost ($ billions)	Remaining Cost ($ billions)	Local Permittee Share (%)	Local Permittee Cost ($ billions)
26.8	Yes	3.35	3.03	30.5	0.92
26.8	No	4.47	4.15	30.5	1.26
2.0	Yes	3.35	3.03	62.8	1.90
2.0	No	4.47	4.15	62.8	2.61

---

[12] While RCA may choose to purchase some large residential lots in the core areas to secure needed habitat, it is unlikely that it would choose to purchase more-expensive, heavily developed parcels. This suggests that the lightly developed scenario is the most reasonable to examine. And while RCA would benefit from subdividing all parcels at the reserve boundary line, it is unlikely that all landowners would be willing to accommodate this goal. For this reason, the partial parcel–subdivision rule is more likely than the exact parcel–subdivision rule to reflect the manner in which actual parcel-acquisition efforts unfold.

calculated in Table 3.7, to yield the remaining "Local Permittee Cost" column values. As the final column indicates, there is significant variation in our estimates of the remaining assembly costs that local permittees will need to fund. At one end of the spectrum, if developer contributions rise to the originally anticipated level and if it is possible to align the linkages so as to avoid heavily developed parcels, then the remaining cost for local permittees may be well under $1 billion. At the other extreme, if the pace of developer contributions continues to follow the current trajectory and it is necessary to purchase numerous developed properties in constructing the linkages, the cost to local permittees could easily exceed $2.5 billion.

Performance of Assembly Scenarios Against Conservation Goals

Now let us turn our attention to the performance of the assembly scenarios modeled here against the conservation goals of the MSHCP. In particular, we are interested in whether the assembly scenarios provide sufficient total acreage in the criteria cells to meet the total reserve-acreage goal of 153,000 as well as whether they provide sufficient acreage of different vegetation communities in different rough-step accounting areas to meet the enumerated rough-step goals. Table 3.10 examines these questions.

In Table 3.10, the first three columns describe the scenarios and list the total number of parcels and acres. The "Criteria Acres" column shows the number of acres in the included parcels that lie within the criteria cells and can thus be counted against the 153,000-acre total requirement. If this number is lower than 153,000, then the "Total

Table 3.10
Estimated Rough-Step Acreage Shortfalls for the Six Reserve-Assembly Scenarios

Assembly Scenario	Total Parcels	Total Acres	Criteria Acres	Total Shortfall	Vegetation Community/ Rough-Step Shortfall
Base case					
Exact subdivision	11,387	151,587	143,143	9,857	8,114
Partial subdivision	11,387	162,224	158,398	0	4,208
Lightly developed					
Exact subdivision	12,164	161,332	152,888	112	4,236
Partial subdivision	12,164	173,371	169,397	0	1,775
Heavily developed					
Exact subdivision	15,490	168,570	160,126	0	2,586
Partial subdivision	15,490	182,240	178,054	0	879

Shortfall" column lists the difference—that is, the number of additional acres that would be required to reach a total of 153,000 acres. If the number exceeds 153,000, then the "Total Shortfall" value is listed as 0. Finally, the "Vegetation Community/ Rough-Step Shortfall" column provides the combined total of any shortfalls for specific vegetation communities in specific rough-step areas. For instance, if there was a shortfall of 100 acres for coastal sage scrub in rough-step area 1 and a shortfall of 50 acres for grasslands in rough-step area 2 and these were the only shortfalls, then the rightmost column would list a value of 150.

Because portions of some of the parcels that RCA has already acquired lie outside of the criteria cells and thus would not be counted toward the total acreage goal, the acreage in the criteria area is always less than the total acreage acquired. Even so, our analysis suggests that achieving the goal of 153,000 total acres should not be difficult. In all of the partial-subdivision scenarios, which we consider to represent the more likely outcomes with respect to parcel subdivisions along the reserve boundary, the total acreage goal is achieved with a relatively comfortable margin.

In contrast, the goals for some vegetation communities and rough-step areas do present challenges within the scenarios we examined. In fact, there is not a single scenario in which all of these goals are accomplished. In the base-case scenario with the partial-subdivision assumption, which includes just open-space and agricultural parcels in the core areas, the cumulative shortfall across different vegetation communities and rough-step areas is more than 4,200 acres. (To put this number in perspective, recall from Table 3.1 that the sum of the individual goals across different vegetation communities and rough-step areas totals just less than 84,000 acres). Even in the heavily developed scenario with partial subdivision, which includes all parcels in the USFWS CRD not already under public ownership, the cumulative shortfall for vegetation-community and rough-step goals is still almost 900 acres.

This finding does not imply that RCA will be unable to assemble a reserve in the criteria cells that meets all of these goals (our scenarios were constrained to parcels in the USFWS CRD and did not include other parcels in the criteria cells). The analysis clearly indicates, however, that the USFWS CRD does not represent a potential-reserve design capable of satisfying all the plan's conservation requirements. It also suggests that careful analysis on the part of RCA in selecting parcels for conservation will be required to ensure that the reserve (1) meets all rough-step goals, (2) provides core habitat areas that are sufficiently compact and contiguous, and (3) does not grossly exceed 153,000 acres (which would drive up acquisition costs). The USFWS CRD meets the latter two goals but not the first.

Understanding Acreage Shortfalls by Rough-Step Area Using the USFWS CRD

Table 3.11 illustrates how the acreage shortfalls for each vegetative community are distributed across the rough-step areas, again using the lightly developed–parcel selection under the partial parcel–subdivision assumption as an example. The first set of rows in the table presents the initial acreage goals in the MSHCP documents for each of the vegetation-community and rough-step area combinations, while the next set of rows lists the number of acres for each combination that are provided by the parcels for the scenario. The third set of rows shows the acreage shortfall, with a positive number indicating a shortfall and zero indicating that the number of acres provided in the reserve scenario is greater than or equal to the initial goal.

For this scenario, there are 14 shortfalls for different vegetation-community and rough-step area combinations. To put this in perspective, there are 37 combinations for which the initial conservation goal is greater than 0. In other words, the assembly scenario fails to achieve more than a third of the enumerated acreage targets. Of the seven vegetation communities with goals, all but one—desert scrub—has a shortfall in at least one rough-step area. Likewise, across the nine rough-step areas, all save two— areas 2 and 9—have shortfalls for at least one vegetation community (and rough-step area 9 has no enumerated goals, so the absence of any shortfalls in area 9 is a given). Across all vegetation communities and rough-step areas, the cumulative shortfall is a bit less than 1,800 acres. The specific vegetation communities and rough-step areas that appear most problematic include playas and vernal pools in rough-step area 3, grasslands in rough-step area 6, woodlands and forest in rough-step area 7, and coastal sage scrub in rough-step area 8.

A Question of Accounting

From the data in Table 3.11, it would certainly seem reasonable to characterize the performance of the lightly developed scenario with partial subdivision as poor with respect to the individual vegetation-community and rough-step goals, since a large percentage of the goals are unmet. Yet it is quite possible that this form of accounting— examining the number of acres for different vegetation communities in different rough-step areas as required in the MSHCP agreement—may make an assembly's performance with respect to habitat conservation appear worse than it really is. Fundamental to this observation is the question of whether (or to what degree) the exact distribution of acreage for a given vegetation community across different rough-step areas matters from an ecological perspective. Stated in another way, are the rough-step areas based primarily on ecological considerations, or do they instead represent a convenient accounting tool?

To motivate this question with a practical example, consider the performance of the lightly developed scenario with partial subdivision with respect to the goals for coastal sage scrub. Across the nine rough-step areas, the total assembly goal for this vegetation community is 46,972 acres, while the scenario actually provides a total of 53,941 acres. In other words, the modeled reserve assembly provides almost 7,000 acres of coastal sage scrub beyond the amount called for in the plan, which would appear to be a desirable outcome. Yet because not enough of these acres appear in rough-step

Table 3.11
Vegetation-Community Shortfalls by Rough-Step Area for the Lightly Developed, Partial-Subdivision Scenario

Vegetation Community	Rough-Step Area									Total
	1	2	3	4	5	6	7	8	9	
Initial Vegetation-Community/Rough-Step Acreage Goals										
Coastal sage scrub	765	10,340	2,050	17,590	370	3,827	7,090	4,940	0	46,972
Desert scrub	0	0	0	3,680	0	0	0	0	0	3,680
Grassland	180	4,780	900	5,930	1,010	3,638	1,550	1,840	0	19,828
Playas and vernal pools	0	0	3,830	0	0	0	0	0	0	3,830
Riparian scrub, woodland, and forest	550	460	110	1,320	460	208	460	250	0	3,818
Riversidean alluvial-fan sage	0	1,110	100	1,099	260	0	350	130	0	3,049
Woodland and forest	0	170	0	870	1,000	98	330	0	0	2,468
Total	1,495	16,860	6,990	30,489	3,100	7,771	9,780	7,160	0	83,645
Vegetation-Community/Rough-Step Acreage in Reserve Scenario										
Coastal sage scrub	879	15,815	2,499	18,681	491	3,995	6,961	4,576	56	53,952
Desert scrub	0	0	0	4,623	0	0	0	0	0	4,624
Grassland	192	5,101	862	6,541	1,311	3,339	1,572	2,232	82	21,231
Playas and vernal pools	0	0	3,542	0	0	0	0	0	0	3,542
Riparian scrub, woodland, and forest	515	626	217	1,265	380	184	423	194	81	3,885
Riversidean alluvial-fan sage	21	1,110	106	1,050	301	30	291	138	40	3,087
Woodland and forest	0	276	40	1,960	1,120	98	68	91	38	3,690

Table 3.11—Continued

						Rough-Step Area				
Vegetation Community	**1**	**2**	**3**	**4**	**5**	**6**	**7**	**8**	**9**	**Total**
Total	1,608	22,927	7,265	34,120	3,603	7,647	9,315	7,230	297	94,010
Vegetation-Community/Rough-Step Acreage Shortfalls										
Coastal sage scrub	0	0	0	0	0	0	129	364	0	492
Desert scrub	0	0	0	0	0	0	0	0	0	0
Grassland	0	0	38	0	0	299	0	0	0	337
Playas and vernal pools	0	0	288	0	0	0	0	0	0	288
Riparian scrub, woodland, and forest	35	0	0	55	80	24	37	56	0	286
Riversidean alluvial-fan sage	0	0	0	49	0	0	59	0	0	109
Woodland and forest	0	0	0	0	0	0	262	0	0	263
Total	35	0	326	104	80	323	487	420	0	1,775

areas 7 and 8, according to the initial acreage goals, these areas are both shown as having shortfalls.

A key question, then, is whether it would be reasonable—from an ecological perspective—to allow some level of fungibility for acres of a given vegetation community between one rough-step area and another. The scope of our study has *not* included ecological considerations, and it may be the case that meeting the exact goals as enumerated *is* important to the reserve's success. If, however, the total number of acres for each vegetation community is more important than their precise distribution across different rough-step areas, the current accounting system based on rough-step areas will inevitably make the reserve's performance appear worse than it actually is.

Looking again at the data in Table 3.11, one can compare the total initial acreage goals across all rough-step areas (shown in the "Total" column in the first set of rows) with the total number of acres provided in the reserve assembly across all rough-step areas (shown in the "Total" column in the second set of rows). For each of the vegetation communities, with the exception of playas and vernal pools, the total number of acres provided in the reserve assembly exceeds the total number of acres called for in the individual rough-step goals. While playas and vernal pools remain problematic, it is less apparent from this perspective that the plan performs poorly with respect to other vegetation communities.

Conclusion

Our analysis suggests that the value of the land needed to construct the MSHCP reserve is substantially higher than originally forecast. At the time the MSHCP was adopted in 2003, the average value of land to be acquired was estimated at $13,100 per acre (TLMA, 2003, Appendix B-03). Adjusted for inflation, the 2003 projection rises to $15,200 in 2007 dollars. Our estimates of the average land value based on assembly scenarios that reflect the USFWS CRD are considerably higher. For the base-case and lightly developed parcel–selection scenarios, which we consider to be the most realistic, average value ranges from $29,200 to $29,400 for the more plausible partial-subdivision assumption (see Table 3.3). These average values are almost double the 2003 projection after adjusting for inflation. The increase is due to both a rise in per-acre land value in general and the inclusion of a significant number of developed properties in the linkages in the modeled scenarios.[13]

The average land value in our scenarios would not be nearly as large if the linkages could be shifted or realigned to avoid developed parcels. This could reduce, our estimates suggest, the overall land value for the reserve by as much as $1.12 billion, in

---

[13] As discussed in Chapter Four, the inflation-adjusted average sale price for open space and agricultural land rose 88 percent between mid-2003 and mid-2007.

which case the average per-acre values would drop to between $21,900 and $22,100 (roughly a 25-percent savings). The percentage increase over the inflation-adjusted 2003 projections would then be around 45 percent. Our analysis did not examine whether the linkages could, in fact, be aligned in a manner that avoids the need to acquire developed parcels while still meeting the plan's intended ecological goals; thus, the extent to which RCA will be able to achieve such savings remains unclear.

In addition to showing a substantial increase in the average value of land needed for the reserve, our analysis suggests that the cost of land acquired to date by RCA is much lower than the average value of the land that will be needed for the entire reserve. Recall from Table 2.3 in Chapter Two that the current value of parcels already acquired by RCA is estimated to average $9,000, a figure substantially less than our estimates for the average per-acre value of the full assembly described here. This observation is consistent with the hypothesis in Chapter Two that, to date, RCA has concentrated on purchasing the relatively cheap parcels and that these purchase costs will not be representative of those required to complete the reserve.

Estimates of the average value of land in the reserve ($29,200 to $29,400 per acre in our most realistic scenarios) can be combined with estimates of the average value of land already acquired ($9,000 per acre) and the amount of land already acquired (35,526 acres) to determine the average value of land yet to be acquired and the total value of the land still needed to complete a 153,000-acre reserve. Table 3.12 provides the results for our most plausible estimates of the average value of the land yet to be acquired in the overall reserve. If linkages cannot be rerouted, the land values average $35,300 to $35,600 for the approximately 117,000 acres yet to be acquired, with the total current value ranging from $4.15 billion to $4.18 billion. The results if the linkages can be rerouted are roughly 25 percent lower.

Our analysis of the biological aspects of the assembly scenarios shows that it is not possible to achieve all of the vegetation-community acreage goals for different rough-step areas based on the spatial configuration of the USFWS CRD. However,

Table 3.12
Estimates of Average and Total Value of Land to Be Acquired for the Reserve

Average Value of Land in Overall Reserve ($/acre)	Average Value of Remaining Land to Be Acquired ($/acre)	Total Value of Remaining Land to Be Acquired ($ billions)
Linkages not rerouted		
29,200	35,300	4.15
29,400	35,600	4.18
Linkages rerouted		
21,900	25,800	3.03
22,100	26,000	3.06

there appears to be adequate acreage for all but one vegetation community across the USFWS CRD when viewed at the aggregate level. This suggests that it may be worthwhile to revisit the form of accounting used in evaluating the reserve's biological merits. In addition, there undoubtedly is additional acreage for many of the vegetation communities inside the criteria area but outside the USFWS CRD. Thus, it is certainly plausible that RCA will be able to construct a 153,000-acre reserve that meets all habitat goals, though our analysis has not verified this.

CHAPTER FOUR

Financial Implications of Temporal Acquisition Strategies

In Chapter Three, we developed estimates of the cost of completing the reserve, given land values from mid-2007. The remaining required land will not be purchased all at once, however, and both the time frame in which the land is purchased and the future trajectory of land prices will determine the ultimate cost of assembling the reserve. In this chapter, we examine how such factors as the number of years over which RCA phases its purchases and the future trajectory of land values in the region affect total acquisition costs, expressed in terms of present value.

RCA can control or influence some of the variables that will affect long-term acquisition costs. For instance, RCA might choose to stage its parcel acquisitions relatively slowly over a period of several decades. Alternatively, RCA might seek to boost current revenue (e.g., by soliciting additional federal grants or loans or by bonding against future earmarked revenue streams) in order to complete the acquisition process in a much shorter time frame. RCA might also pursue a strategy of purchasing more parcels when land values are low and fewer parcels when land values are high.

Other factors beyond RCA's control—such as the state of the economy, future population growth in Southern California, and the resulting effects on the price of land—will also exert significant influence on the cost of assembly over time. If one could predict the future trajectory of land values in advance, it might be possible to design an optimal strategy for the phasing and timing of RCA acquisitions to complete the reserve—that is, a strategy that would minimize the present value of the acquisition costs. Yet future trends are inherently uncertain. As the recent housing-price bubble deflates, will the value of land in western Riverside County fall sharply to levels last seen in the late 1990s? Or, after a brief decline, will it flatten out, or perhaps begin to rise rapidly once again? The answer to these questions—impossible to predict—will help to determine whether RCA would be better off trying to purchase land relatively quickly or instead phasing its acquisitions over a period of many years.

Given both the importance and inherent uncertainty in the future trajectory of land prices, we pursue the following strategy in this chapter. First, we consider a range of assumptions as to how the land market may change in the coming years—for instance, whether land values will continue to follow a cyclical pattern and whether there will be positive real growth in the value of land. For each set of assumptions considered, we generate a large number of simulated land-value trajectories with year-by-year changes in the average per-acre cost over a period of decades. Finally, we evaluate the effects on present value for the total acquisition cost that would result from applying different purchase strategies for each of the simulated land-value trajectories.

The goal in this exercise is not to identify a single "best" temporal acquisition strategy for RCA to pursue, as this may well vary from one simulation to the next. Rather, it is to provide insight as to whether RCA might be better served, given the range of possible futures, by staging its acquisition activities more quickly or more slowly, as well as to examine the potential savings that might result from striving to purchase more land when costs are low and less land when costs are high. The analysis will also help to better understand the ultimate cost of assembling the reserve and, as will be examined in later chapters, how the cost measures up against current revenue sources.

Analytic Approach

The methodology for this analysis, as just described, incorporates two key elements: (1) simulating future price paths in the value of land under alternative assumptions and (2) evaluating the effects on present value for total reserve-assembly costs for different temporal land-acquisition strategies that RCA might pursue. We discuss each of these in turn and then describe their integration.

Simulating Future Land-Price Paths

Predicting future changes in the price of land presents significant challenges, as a range of local and national factors, such as interest rates, tax policy, the health of the economy, population growth, and the like, can influence the real-estate market. In combination, these factors can produce both shorter-term fluctuations and longer-term cycles in land values. These effects are illustrated in Figure 4.1, which graphs the real median home price in the Inland Empire (Riverside and San Bernardino counties) and the real average price per acre for open space–land transactions in Riverside County in the past several decades.[1]

Insights into the Behavior of Land Markets. It is extremely difficult to forecast accurately many of the underlying factors that can influence land values, let alone to predict their combined effect on the real-estate market in future years. Yet economists and other scholars have devoted considerable attention to understanding the mechanics of the real-estate market, and there are several key themes that emerge from the resulting literature that can provide guidance in efforts to simulate future land values.

---

[1]   The number of home sales during each period significantly exceeds the number of open space–land transactions; this helps to explain why there appears to be greater volatility in the average cost of open-space land than in the median home prices.

Figure 4.1
Inflation-Adjusted Median Home Price and the Average Price per Acre of Open-Space and Agricultural Land in the Riverside Region in Recent Decades

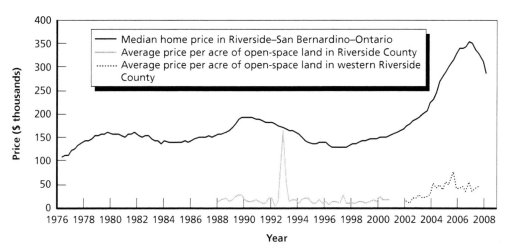

SOURCES: Quarterly median home-price data for Riverside and San Bernardino counties (Calif.) are derived from information provided by the NATIONAL ASSOCIATION OF REALTORS® and the Office of Federal Housing Enterprise Oversight. Quarterly average price per acre for open space and agricultural land from 1988 through 2001 is based on data provided by DataQuick Information Systems. Quarterly average price per acre for open-space and agricultural land from 2002 through the third quarter of 2007 is derived from data on land sales provided by the Riverside County assessor's office (described in Chapter Two).

RAND MG816-4.1

First, there is a clear link between the values of developed and open-space land. Specifically, the price of open-space land should reflect the value of developed land (assuming development to the highest and best use) minus the cost of construction (including such factors as materials, labor, permitting costs, and financial carrying costs). This linkage, often described in the real-estate literature as a *residual-value function* (Titman, 1985), can be discerned in the data in Figure 4.1. Note, in particular, the years between 1997 and 2005, when acceleration in the median home price is mirrored by acceleration in the market value for open-space land.

Second, real-estate markets often exhibit a *cyclical pattern* over time (Hoyt, 1947), in part due to cycles in the underlying drivers, such as interest rates and the state of the local or national economy. In Figure 4.1, for instance, we see cyclical peaks in median home prices around 1980, 1990, and 2006, along with cyclical troughs around 1985 and 1997. Yet to the extent that a cyclical pattern exists, it can also be difficult to predict. Consider, for instance, that the peak-to-peak cycle between 1980 and 1990 stretched approximately 10 years, while the most recent peak-to-peak cycle was closer to 16 years. The trough-to-peak percentage increase in home values was much greater in the most recent cycle as well.

A possible reason for such disparities is that the relative importance of different contributing factors may vary from one cycle to the next. In the early 1980s, for example, very high interest rates helped to trigger the decline in home values. In the early to mid-1990s, in turn, real home-price declines in Southern California were keyed to a softening economy combined with a major contraction in the aerospace industry. With the dot-com implosion in the early 2000s, the economy softened once again. Yet in this case, home prices did not decline, but rather began to rise even more quickly. This was likely due to a confluence of several factors, including significantly reduced interest rates, lax lending standards, and irrational exuberance in the real-estate market. The most recent decline in home prices, beginning in the 2005–2006 period, may be a cause rather than a consequence of the weakening economy.

A third key observation relates to the *relative magnitude of price swings in the market for open-space land.* If a residual relationship exists between the price of open-space and developed land and if construction costs remain relatively stable, then one would expect the rise and fall of open space–land values, expressed in percentage terms, to be much greater than the rise and fall in home prices. Consider the data in Figure 4.1, for instance. Between 1997 and 2006, the median home price in Riverside appreciated by roughly 170 percent (2.7 times), while the average per-acre price for open-space parcels increased by about 450 percent (5.5 times).[2] The same trend is reflected in the data presented in Table 2.4 in Chapter Two, showing that the estimated annual appreciation in agricultural and open-space parcels is, in many cases, much greater than the year-to-year percentage gains for residential properties.

A fourth theme is the *inherent uncertainty in the factors that underlie land values* and the resulting effects on real-estate investment and development decisions. As already discussed, economic conditions and interest rates can influence both the duration and amplitude of longer-term real-estate cycles. But there can be much shorter variations as well. To illustrate, Figure 4.2 graphs quarterly changes in the median home price in Riverside and San Bernardino counties in the past 30 years.

Because the future trajectory of land values is uncertain, and because development decisions are essentially irreversible, landowners may, at times, choose to defer development decisions in the hope that future economic conditions may offer the prospect for greater returns (Titman, 1985). Capozza and Helsley (1990), in examining agricultural-land values and development decisions, concluded that uncertainty in the real-estate market has the effects of delaying the development of agricultural land, imparting an option value to agricultural land, causing land at the urban boundary to sell for more than its opportunity cost in other uses, and reducing the equilibrium city size.

---

[2]   The average quarterly price was often less than $10,000 per acre in the late 1990s, increasing to approximately $55,000 per acre as of 2007. Note that the percentage change between 1997 and 2006 is based on data from two sources that may not be fully comparable. However, the fact that the second series begins in 2002 at roughly the same level at which the first series ends in 2001 (a period during which medium home values rose only gradually) provides some confidence that the two series are measuring sales on similar types of parcels.

Figure 4.2
Quarterly Percentage Changes in the Median Home Price for Riverside and San Bernardino Counties, 1977–2008

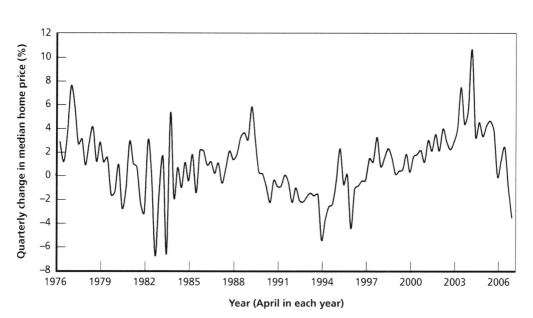

SOURCE: Median home-price data for Riverside and San Bernardino counties derived from data provided by the NATIONAL ASSOCIATION OF REALTORS and the Office of Federal Housing Enterprise Oversight.
RAND *MG816-4.2*

A fifth and final observation relates to *expected appreciation in the price of open-space land* given the opportunity cost of other investments. Although some owners of large amounts of land may be motivated by non-use values, such as the personal enjoyment they receive from their holdings, most are likely to be more concerned with the financial return yielded by land as an investment. From this perspective, expectations for the appreciation of land over the longer term should be on par with other investments of comparable risk. If the expected returns are much lower than this, many landowners will choose to sell their holdings and redirect the proceeds into more-profitable investment vehicles. This will lower the average cost of land, thereby increasing expected future returns. If, on the other hand, expected returns are greater, the demand for purchasing land will increase, raising the average price and dampening expected returns.

Referring again to the data in Figure 4.1, land values appear to appreciate considerably over the longer term, yet the appreciation is far from consistent. Between 1990 and 2000, the average real price per acre for open-space land in Riverside County remained relatively flat, while, between 2000 and 2006, it rose considerably. In short, then, while it is reasonable to expect long-term appreciation in the real per-acre value of open-space parcels, the fulfillment of this expectation is not guaranteed over any particular period.

Assumptions in Simulating Future Land Values. From the preceding discussion, it is possible to distill a set of assumptions to be considered in the simulation of future land-value trajectories in Riverside County. Key issues include the cyclical nature of the real-estate market, the relationship between home prices and open space–land values, and expectations regarding the long-term appreciation in land values. Here, we briefly describe the different assumptions considered for each of these issues.

Land-Value Cycles. From the data presented in Figure 4.1, it appears that home prices and land values follow a cyclical pattern, although the pattern is less apparent for open-space land than for homes. On the other hand, the cycles are irregular and difficult to predict, and other random factors may be at work. We therefore considered two possible cycle-related assumptions in simulating future price paths for land values:

- *Cyclical market:* In the first case, we fit a mathematical equation[3] to describe cycles in the median home price for Riverside and San Bernardino counties over the past three decades and projected that cyclical pattern forward into future years.
- *Acyclical market:* As a second option, we considered the possibility that land values are not inherently cyclical but rather reflect the outcome of other random determinants that may or may not manifest as cycles. In this case, future changes in the price of land were modeled as a *random walk*—that is, as a series of upward or downward annual changes not tied to an underlying cycle.

Relationship Between Home Prices and Open Space–Land Values. In the cyclical case, we relied on median home-price data (for which we had the longest series of observations) in modeling the cyclical pattern. The next step was to translate changes in median home prices to changes in land values. Here, we considered three alternative assumptions:

- *Residual value:* In the first case, we assumed that construction costs—that is, the gap between the median home price and the average cost per acre for open-space land—would remain constant in real dollars during the forecast period. This corresponds to a literal interpretation of residual land value and results in larger percentage swings in the price of land than in the price of housing.
- *Double percentage change for open-space land:* As a second option, we assumed that the percentage change in the price of open-space land in each period would be double the percentage change in median home prices. This value was chosen based on comparing historical annual changes in median home prices and open-space land in the period from 1988 through 2008 using the data from Figure 4.1 and again results in larger relative swings in the price of open-space land.

---

[3]   Specifically, we fit an equation of the form $\%\Delta P(t)=\alpha+\beta\cos(\delta t)+\varepsilon(t)$, where $\%\Delta P(t)$ is the percentage change in the median housing price in quarter t, $\varepsilon(t)$ is a normally distributed error term with mean 0 and standard deviation σ, and α, β, δ, and σ are parameters that we estimate via maximum-likelihood techniques.

- *Equal percentage change for open-space land:* In the third case, we assumed that the percentage change in the cost of open-space land would be equivalent to that in the median home price. Because open-space land is cheaper than housing, the net effect of this assumption is that the gap between home prices and open-space land increases during up cycles and reduces during down cycles. This is not entirely unrealistic in the sense that, as home prices rise, the demand and, in turn, the price for construction inputs, such as labor and materials, should increase as well. Indeed, careful review of the data in Figure 4.1 between the late 1990s and about 2005 reveals a widening gap between the median home price and the average cost per acre for open-space land.

Expected Appreciation in the Value of Open-space Land. The long-term real appreciation in land values should, in equilibrium, mirror that for other investments of comparable risk. As already discussed, however, there is no guarantee that this outcome will unfold during any particular period. We therefore considered two alternative assumptions:

- *Historical appreciation in median home values:* Under this option, we first assumed that the longer-term growth in median home prices would follow the same trend witnessed during the past 30 years. (Note that we chose to look at historical median home-price values rather than historical values for open-space land, given the availability of a longer series of data.) Although home prices appreciated relatively little between the mid-1970s and mid-1990s, the recent run-up in home prices during the past decade led to an average annual real rate of appreciation for the entire period of just over 4 percent. We then linked growth in median home prices to growth in the value of land using the assumptions just described. Under the assumption that percentage changes in the value of land would be equivalent to percentage changes in median home prices, this led to an average appreciation of just over 4 percent for land values as well. Under the assumption of either constant construction costs or double percentage changes for land prices, in contrast, the average appreciation in land values could far exceed 4 percent.
- *Zero real appreciation in land values:* Our second option was to assume that land values would not grow, in real terms, during the assembly time frame. Though perhaps optimistic (from RCA's perspective, given its need to acquire significant acreage), such an outcome might still be viewed as plausible. Note, in particular, that the average per-acre price for open space–land transactions in Riverside County shown in Figure 4.1 increased roughly 1,500 percent between 1997 and 2007 as a result of the bubble in housing prices. It is not inconceivable that land values could slowly unwind back to former levels, resulting in several decades of no real appreciation. Though we have no basis to argue that such an outcome is probable, it is nonetheless instructive to consider the possibility of a stagnant

market for open-space land when evaluating future acquisition strategies that RCA might pursue.

Scenarios Considered. From the possible assumptions regarding the cyclical (or acyclical) nature of the real-estate market, the relationship between home prices and open space–land prices, and the expected real rate of appreciation in land values, we constructed eight distinct scenarios intended to provide insight into the relative merits of different acquisition strategies that RCA might pursue. (Note that we examined fewer cases involving the acyclical, or random, market assumption, as we considered this to be a less likely outcome given recent trends.) Table 4.1 describes the scenarios.

Modeling RCA Acquisition Strategies

The total cost of assembling the reserve will depend not just on the future trajectory of land values in Riverside County, but also on the purchase strategies that RCA employs. We considered two key variables that RCA can either control or influence, to which we refer as the *pace* and the *timing* of purchases. In this context, the term *pace* describes the rate at which RCA acquires acreage, which, in turn, relates to the total number of years that it will take to complete the reserve assembly. For instance, in the first three years of operation since the MSHCP was adopted (2005 through 2007), RCA has assembled roughly 5,500 acres per year. Assuming that RCA continues at this same pace, it would take slightly more than 21 additional years to acquire the approximately 117,000 acres needed to complete the reserve. The term *timing* (as in *timing the market*) describes the degree to which RCA can purchase more acres of land when values are low and fewer acres of land when values are high.

Table 4.1
Land-Price Scenarios Used to Evaluate Alternative Land-Acquisition Strategies

Land-Price Scenario	Expected Appreciation in Value of Housing	Nature of Prices	Relationship Between Home Prices and Value of Open-Space Land
1	Historical (4%)	Cyclical	Residual value
2	Historical (4%)	Cyclical	Double percentage
3	Historical (4%)	Cyclical	Equal percentage
4	Historical (4%)	Acyclical	Equal percentage
5	0	Cyclical	Residual value
6	0	Cyclical	Double percentage
7	0	Cyclical	Equal percentage
8	0	Acyclical	Equal percentage

Factors Constraining the Pace and Timing of Acquisitions. Before examining the variations in pace and timing considered in our modeling efforts, it is useful to outline several factors that may constrain the choices that RCA faces across these dimensions. First and foremost is the matter of the average annual revenue that RCA receives for the purpose of funding land acquisitions. Assume, for instance, that the total current value of the acreage that RCA must still acquire is estimated at $2 billion and that RCA has an income stream of roughly $50 million per year. Assuming that land does not depreciate over this period and that RCA does not secure additional funding, this would imply that at least 40 years would be required to complete the reserve. In short, the magnitude of the annual revenue stream that RCA collects places a lower bound on the number of years required for assembly if RCA spends revenue as it is received. RCA can choose to phase purchases over a longer period if it wishes, but RCA cannot shorten the acquisition time frame without taking steps to bolster the level of revenue available in the near term or issuing bonds backed by future revenue streams.

Second is the matter of fluctuations in the annual revenue stream. Several of RCA's revenue sources, including sales taxes and developer fees, are closely tied to the state of the economy and the real-estate market. Thus, when the economy is strong and many new houses are being built, RCA has access to a greater revenue stream; when the economy and housing market soften, in contrast, RCA's revenue stream is diminished. Unfortunately, land values are likely to rise and fall with the economy and housing market. This means that RCA will have more revenue available when land values are high and fewer resources when land values fall. To the extent that RCA spends revenue as it is received, then, it will have less opportunity to time the market—that is, to target the purchase of additional acres when land is cheaper.

A third consideration, one that may also limit RCA's ability to pursue timing strategies, involves the rough-step requirements described in Chapter Three. While the reserve that RCA assembles must include at least 153,000 acres, it must also satisfy a set of individually specified acreage goals for different vegetation communities in different rough-step areas. To ensure that RCA can, in fact, meet these goals, the MSHCP specifies that any development activities in the plan area that affect the targeted vegetation communities must be offset by additional acquisitions of that same vegetation community. The practical effect of the rough-step requirements is that, as the pace of development increases, RCA is likewise required to increase the pace of acquisitions. Because the cost of land is likely to rise as development activities become more intense, this too makes it more difficult for RCA to purchase fewer acres when land is expensive and more acres when land is cheaper.

In short, then, RCA currently faces a set of constraints that may preclude its ability to assemble parcels more quickly or time purchases to correspond with down cycles in the real-estate market. However, RCA could pursue strategies to increase its financial flexibility in this regard. For instance, RCA might choose to bond against a portion of its future revenue stream to gain access to more funding up front. RCA might also seek to expand available revenues, either through local funding mechanisms or through federal sources. Given such possibilities, we model a broad range of acquisition pace and timing options, many of which might not be feasible unless RCA were to take steps to expand available resources. By examining the resulting implications for the present value of acquisition costs against alternative future land-price scenarios, it is possible to gain insight as to the potential magnitude of the benefits that might result from such steps.

Modeling the Pace and Timing of Acquisitions. We now describe our methods for modeling different acquisition strategies that RCA might pursue. We begin with the question of timing, as this has direct bearing on the manner in which we model pace.

The Timing of Acquisitions. It is difficult to operationalize the concept of timing the market in practice, given that there is always uncertainty regarding the future trajectory of land prices. We therefore considered two alternative purchasing policies that RCA could implement absent foreknowledge of the market: purchasing the same number of acres in each period and spending the same amount of revenue in each period. The first approximates current conditions under which RCA is often obliged to purchase considerable acreage even when prices are high, while the second effectively increases the percentage of acquisitions when prices are lower.

- *Buying the same number of acres each period:* If RCA purchases the same number of acres each period, it will spend more during periods when prices are high and less in periods when prices are low. This is consistent with current fluctuations in RCA's revenue stream, which rises and falls with the state of the economy and housing market and, in turn, land prices. It also reflects the fact that RCA may be obliged to purchase more parcels when prices are high in order to keep pace with rough-step requirements.

- *Spending the same amount of revenue each period:* If RCA spends the same amount of money each period, it will end up buying fewer acres when land is more expensive and more acres when land is cheaper. In other words, this strategy will approximate successful timing of the market. Note again, however, that, for RCA to implement this option, it may need to pursue steps—such as bonding against future revenue or augmenting the revenue stream—to increase its financial flexibility.

The Pace of Acquisitions. We also considered a broad range of alternatives for the pace at which RCA completes its acquisitions. Specifically, we varied the time frame in which acquisitions occur in small increments ranging between one year (acquiring all needed parcels in 2008) and 50 years (acquiring all needed parcels by 2058). For the equal-acreage-per-period timing strategy, this poses a straightforward modeling exercise. For instance, if 120,000 acres remain to be acquired, and if the goal is to complete the assembly within the next 20 years, then it would be necessary to purchase about 6,000 acres (120,000 divided by 20) each year.

For the equal-expenditure-per-period timing strategy, the matter is somewhat more complex. Here, one might begin by evaluating the current estimated cost of completing the reserve and then dividing that amount by the desired number of years for completing the reserve, to estimate an annual required expenditure. Yet, depending on future fluctuations in the real-estate market, the actual number of years may be either higher or lower than the initial calculation. Our approach, therefore, was to consider different per-period expenditure levels and calculate the number of years needed to complete the reserve under different simulations of future land-price paths. In cases in which the reserve was not fully acquired at the end of 50 years, our model assumed that RCA would purchase all remaining acres at the prevailing price in the very last year.

Integrating Land-Value Scenarios and Acquisition Strategies

To analyze the potential effects of applying different acquisition strategies, we combined alternative assumptions regarding the future trajectory of land prices and the pace and timing of acquisitions in the following manner. First, for each of the eight sets of assumptions regarding the future behavior of the real-estate market, we performed regression analysis based on the historical home-price and land-value data from Figure 4.1 to estimate a model that included (1) an equation for the underlying trajectory of land prices that could be projected forward into the future and (2) an expected distribution of error around the underlying price equation (that is, the degree to which one might expect actual prices to vary above or below the modeled trajectory in each period, given inherent uncertainty in the real-estate market).

Next, for each of the eight sets of assumptions, we employed the corresponding model to simulate 10,000 future price paths. Note that each of these paths was initialized with an average cost of about $35,000 per acre; this corresponds to the average estimated price of land for the remaining parcels needed to complete the reserve under one of our midrange assembly scenarios from Chapter Three (specifically, the lightly developed parcel–selection scenario, with partial-parcel subdivision at the reserve boundary, and with linkages not realigned to avoid developed parcels; refer to the first set of data in Table 3.12). Each price path was then simulated based on the underlying modeled trajectory over the next 50 years, with random fluctuations added in each period based on the modeled error distribution. Examples of the simulated price paths under a number of different scenarios are provided in Appendix B.

After simulating 10,000 price paths for each set of assumptions, we evaluated the effects of employing different acquisition strategies (in terms of the pace and timing of the assembly) for each simulation run. The evaluation for each strategy against each simulated price path was conducted as follows. During each period, beginning in 2008, we determined the number of acres that would be purchased and the amount of money that would be expended according to both the simulated price path and the purchase strategy under consideration. This evaluation continued, period by period, until the reserve was completed (reaching a total of 153,000 acres purchased). The amount of money spent in each period was then discounted to determine the present value of the acquisitions over time. For each purchase strategy and each simulation run, we could thus compute both (1) the time to complete the reserve and (2) the discounted value of assembling the reserve.

Because we included 10,000 simulated price paths for each set of future real estate–market assumptions, we were also able to identify both an expected value and a confidence interval for the discounted cost of completing the reserve for each temporal acquisition strategy in the context of a given set of assumptions about the future trajectory of land prices.

Discount Rate Used to Calculate Present Value

The discount rate is used to discount future expenditures to the present. The real rate of interest, or the borrowing cost, is considered to be the appropriate discount rate for cost-effectiveness analysis (see OMB, 1992). Discount rates are typically based on U.S. Treasury borrowing rates (net of inflation) because the treasury securities are virtually risk free. The most recent estimates of the real interest rates on U.S. Treasury notes and bonds run from 2.1 percent for three-year notes to 2.8 percent for 30-year bonds (OMB, 2008). Because of the long life of the MSHCP, the higher interest rates are more relevant, and we use a 3-percent discount rate in our analysis.

It is appropriate to base the discount rates on federal interest rates in part because federal sources partly fund the cost of the reserve. Local funding is also important, however, and because local securities are more risky than federal securities, the real interest rate on local securities is likely somewhat higher than rates on federal securities.[4] To examine the sensitivity of our results to a higher discount rate, we also ran the analysis using a 5-percent discount rate.

Results

By examining the results of several purchasing strategies in many simulation runs for different sets of assumptions about the future trajectory of land values in the county, it is possible to develop insights about the relative risks and rewards for alternative pacing and timing strategies. In this section, we summarize the results for different pacing and timing strategies.

---

[4] Local bonds are often tax exempt, and the implicit subsidies due to the tax exemptions should be backed out for the purpose of calculating the real interest rates. Coupon rates on recent Riverside County bonds run between 3.5 and 4.5 percent (Porr, 2008). These rates overstate the real interest rate because they include expected inflation but understate the real rate because they are tax deductible.

Effects of Pacing Strategies

For any set of assumptions about the future trajectory of land values, the present value of the cost of assembling the reserve may vary considerably depending on the pace at which the land is acquired. Table 4.2 illustrates this variation, using a 3-percent discount rate and focusing specifically on the strategy of acquiring a fixed number of acres during each period.

In Table 4.2, each row corresponds to a particular combination of assumptions about future land values, as described in the leftmost column. The next four columns present the expected present value and 95-percent confidence interval (shown in brackets) for completing the reserve within five, 10, 20, and 30 years for each set of assumptions (values are shown in billions of 2008 dollars). Finally, the last three columns describe the optimal pace of acquisitions to minimize present value for the corresponding set of assumptions.[5]

Careful review of the data in Table 4.1 leads to several helpful insights. The first four scenarios in the table include the assumption that appreciation in the housing market will continue to follow the rate observed for the past three decades (just over 4 percent starting from the historically high levels in 2007), while the latter four assume that no appreciation will occur in the acquisition time frame. This sequencing is deliberate and helps to highlight an important observation related to future growth in land values. If the average rate of appreciation in land values—that is, the underlying growth trend—exceeds the real discount rate used in computing the present value of future purchases (as it does in the first four cases), RCA will, in every case, be better off completing the reserve in a relatively short time frame. For the first three scenarios, all of which assume a cyclical market pattern, the present value is lowest when RCA stages the acquisitions over a six- to nine-year period to take advantage of the current down cycle. If there is no underlying cyclical pattern and land values appreciate more quickly than the discount rate, as in the fourth scenario, RCA will be best off buying all parcels in a few years.[6]

If, on the other hand, there is no appreciation in real land values, as in the latter four scenarios in Table 4.1, then the ideal pacing strategy is somewhat more complicated.[7] If, as in the fifth and sixth scenarios, the market cycles and changes in land values are more extreme than changes in the median home price, then RCA can still reduce the present value by acquiring all parcels in the next seven or eight years, given the current down cycle in the market. If the market cycles but the changes in land values are

---

[5] For the equal-acreage-per-period strategy, we considered 2,000 acres per year, 4,000 acres per year, 6,000 acres per year, and so on up to 50,000 acres per year.

[6] The optimal pacing option for the fourth scenario in Table 4.2 is listed as 50,000 acres per year, resulting in completion by 2011. We did not include a scenario allowing the purchase of more than 50,000 acres; had we done so, the optimal completion pace would have been even faster.

[7] As discussed, no real appreciation moving forward may be plausible, given that the price scenarios start at the historically very high levels in 2007.

Table 4.2
Present Value for Completing the Reserve in Different Time Frames by Purchasing an Equal Number of Acres per Year Under Various Assumptions About Future Land Values

Future-Land-Value Scenario	Time Frame for Completing Reserve (years)			Optimal Time Frame (among options modeled)		
	Approx. 5 (24,000 acres/year) ($ billions)	Approx. 10 (12,000 acres/year) ($ billions)	Approx. 30 (4,000 acres/year) ($ billions)	Present Value ($ billions)	Acres Acquired per Year	Number of Years Over Which Reserve Assembled
Historical appreciation						
1. Cyclical market, residual value	1.9 [0.7, 4.7]	3.3 [0.8, 7.9]	13.4 [4.9, 24.5]	1.8 [0.6, 4.7]	20,000	5.9
2. Cyclical market, double percentage	0.9 [0.5, 1.5]	1.4 [0.5, 3.2]	10.3 [3.7, 19.7]	0.7 [0.5, 1.2]	16,000	7.3
3. Cyclical market, equal percentage	3.5 [3.1, 3.9]	3.5 [2.9, 4.1]	4.0 [2.9, 5.3]	3.4 [2.9, 4.0]	14,000	8.4
4. Acyclical market, equal percentage	4.2 [3.7, 4.8]	4.3 [3.6, 5.1]	4.6 [3.4, 6.1]	4.2 [3.8, 4.6]	50,000	2.3
Zero appreciation						
5. Cyclical market, residual value	1.1 [0.6, 2.2]	0.9 [0.5, 2.5]	1.6 [0.4, 5.7]	0.9 [0.5, 1.8]	16,000	7.3
6. Cyclical market, double percentage	0.7 [0.5, 1.1]	0.6 [0.4, 1.0]	1.3 [0.3, 4.1]	0.6 [0.5, 0.8]	14,000	8.4
7. Cyclical market, equal percentage	3.2 [2.9, 3.6]	2.9 [2.5, 3.4]	2.4 [2.8, 3.6]	1.7 [1.2, 2.3]	2,000	50[a]
8. Acyclical market, equal percentage	3.9 [3.4, 4.3]	3.6 [3.1, 4.2]	2.8 [2.1, 3.6]	2.0 [1.4, 2.7]	2,000	50[a]

NOTE: Brackets contain 95-percent confidence intervals.

[a] Each year for 50 years, 2,000 acres are purchased. At the end of the 50th year, all remaining acres needed to assemble the reserve are purchased.

less extreme (as in the seventh scenario) or if the market does not cycle at all (as in the eighth scenario), then RCA can reduce the present value by staging its purchases over as long a period as possible.[8]

In short, for the first six scenarios, each of which involves either a positive growth trend in home values that exceeds the discount rate or a cyclical market pattern with significant swings in the price for open-space land (or both), RCA can minimize the present value by staging acquisitions over the relatively short time frame of less than 10 years. For the latter two scenarios, in contrast, for which there is no assumed appreciation in home values and the future trajectory of land prices exhibits either shallow cycles or no cycles, RCA can minimize present value by staging its purchases over a much longer period (essentially taking advantage of the discount factor in reducing the present cost of purchases made far in the future).

The analyses so far have all been done using the baseline 3-percent discount rate. Repeating the analysis with a 5-percent discount rate shifts the optimal acquisition time frame to a much longer period. For the first four scenarios, which assume historical appreciation rates, the optimal pacing strategy with a 5-percent discount rate is to acquire the land over as long a period as possible (for scenarios 3 and 4) or over roughly 30 years (for scenarios 1 and 2). This shift occurs because the 5-percent discount rate now exceeds the historical 4-percent upward trend in land values. In scenarios 1 and 2, the benefits of delaying purchases with a larger discount rate are offset to some extent by the benefits of taking advantage of the current downturn in land values. For the last four scenarios (5 through 8), all of which have zero appreciation in land values, the optimal pacing with a 5-percent discount rate is always to stage the purchases over as long a period as possible.

Effects of Timing Strategies

Directly comparing purchasing the same number of acres during each period and spending the same amount of money during each period proved to be somewhat challenging. With the equal-acreage strategy, the time to complete the reserve for a particular purchase option (e.g., 10,000 acres per year) will always be the same regardless of the simulated price path; only the present value will vary. With the equal-expenditure option, on the other hand, variations in the simulated price paths could affect not only the estimated present value but also the number of years required to complete the reserve. As a result, the expected completion years for the purchase options considered under the two timing strategies did not always align, and this made it more difficult to compare them to one another.

---

[8] The underlying model considered acquisition periods of up to 50 years in length. The 2058 completion in the seventh and eighth scenarios in Table 4.2 thus represents the maximum allowable time in which to complete the reserve subject to the model's parameters.

To overcome this obstacle, we extrapolated continuous present value and confidence-interval curves for each of the timing strategies based on the specific set of equal-acreage and equal-expenditure values evaluated in the model. We then aligned these curves according to the expected year of completion and compared the results. This approach is illustrated in Figure 4.3, which compares the equal-acreage and equal-expenditure strategies with a 3-percent discount rate under the assumptions that the market will cycle, that the percentage change in land values will be equivalent to that for home prices, and that the housing market will appreciate at just over 4 percent per year on average.

The results of this analysis suggested three general observations on the utility of alternative timing strategies. First, as a general rule, the equal-expenditure strategy will tend to outperform the equal-acreage strategy (i.e., result in a lower expected present value) for any given acquisition time frame. Second, the benefits of the equal-expenditure strategy are rather negligible if the reserve is assembled quickly but become more pronounced when acquisitions occur over a longer period (see the latter years in Figure 4.3). Third, the benefits of the equal-expenditure strategy also depend on the relative degree of swings in the price of open-space land. In cases in which there is a deeper cyclical pattern resulting in greater price differences between the peaks and

Figure 4.3
Comparison of Equal-Acreage and Equal-Expenditure Timing Strategies for Different Acquisition Time Frames

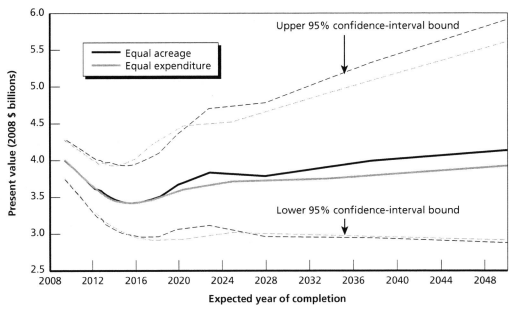

NOTE: Assumes a 3-percent discount rate under the assumptions of a cyclical market, equal percentage change in the housing and land markets, and historical appreciation rates.
RAND *MG816-4.3*

troughs (such as occur with the residual value or double percentage change assumptions), the benefits of the equal-expenditure timing strategy will be magnified. When cycles are either shallow (as with the equal percentage change assumption) or nonexistent, in contrast, the benefits of the equal-expenditure timing strategy diminish. In Figure 4.3, for example, which involves shallower cycles, the percentage savings in present value resulting from the equal-expenditure strategy are only about 5 percent over the longer acquisition time frames.

Policy Implications for RCA

In this section, we discuss the implications of these results with respect to the temporal acquisition strategies that RCA might pursue. Before doing so, however, it is worth noting two important points with respect to the total present value cost figures presented in this chapter. First, the initial per-acre value used as a starting point in the simulations—roughly $35,000—is based on the assumption that RCA will not reroute the linkages to avoid already-developed parcels. As discussed in Chapter Three, RCA stands to lower the total assembly costs by about $1 billion at current market values— roughly 25 percent of the total remaining acquisition costs under alternative assembly scenarios—if it can avoid the purchase of developed parcels in constructing the linkages. This would translate to additional savings for local permittees with respect to the values shown in Table 4.2 and Figure 4.3.

Second, the total present-value figures presented in this chapter represent estimates of the cost to assemble all of the remaining acres (roughly 117,000) needed to complete the reserve. Depending on the share of acreage contributed by local developers through the real estate–approval process, as discussed in Chapter Three, local permittees will likely need to fund between roughly 30 and 60 percent of the remaining cost of assembling the reserve.

Pacing Strategies

As discussed earlier, if the housing market continues to appreciate at historic rates in the coming decades or if the market for land exhibits a deep cyclical pattern (or both), RCA can minimize present value (using a 3-percent discount rate) by acquiring all acres over a relatively short period of approximately six to nine years. If the housing market does not appreciate in the longer term and if land-value cycles are either shallow or nonexistent, then, in contrast, RCA can reduce present value by staging its acquisitions over a much longer period.

Which course, then, should RCA pursue? Prior to answering this question, we repeat that our future price-path scenarios were intended to be illustrative rather than predictive, as the future is inherently uncertain. We have little basis for arguing, for example, that the market will continue to exhibit a cyclical pattern in the future, that price swings will tend to be deeper or shallower, or that the real rate of appreciation in home values will exceed or fall short of the real discount rate. Uncertainty regarding such outcomes makes it difficult to recommend with confidence that RCA pursue either a faster or slower pace of acquisition.

It is possible to view the question from a different perspective, by considering the issue of risk. In examining the results in Table 4.1, the very worst outcome (in terms of the magnitude of the present value as well as the percentage difference between the best-case and worst-case present values) would occur if the market exhibits a positive growth trend along with a strong cyclic pattern in land values (the first and second scenarios) and RCA chooses to pace its acquisitions over a period of many years. This would result in a present value in the range of $10 billion to $13 billion (see fourth column of Table 4.2).

To protect against this possibility, RCA can instead attempt to assemble the reserve much more quickly, ideally over a period of less than 10 years. Should it turn out that home values do not appreciate and that market cycles, if they occur, prove to be shallow (the seventh and eighth scenarios), then RCA would have lost the opportunity to save perhaps $1.5 billion to $2 billion in present value by acquiring the purchases over a longer period.[9] If, on the other hand, RCA chooses to pace its acquisitions more slowly and the market trajectory unfolds in the least favorable manner, then RCA would not only face a staggeringly large present value; it also would have lost the opportunity to save between about $9 billion and $11 billion in present value by acquiring the land more quickly. From the perspective of minimizing risk, then, the strategy of pacing acquisitions relatively quickly over a period of six to nine years appears to be clearly superior.

There are a number of issues to consider in translating the implications of our analysis on the optimal pace of land purchases into reality.

First, the evaluation of alternative land-acquisition strategies has not considered the impact of RCA purchases on the land market in western Riverside County. Concentrating purchases over a short period could put upward pressure on land prices, increasing overall acquisition costs.[10] If RCA sought to acquire the remaining 117,000 acres in six years, for example, it would have to purchase 19,500 acres per year. Total annual sales of open space and agricultural land in western Riverside County ranged from approximately 22,000 to 43,000 acres between 2003 and 2007.[11] Thus, if RCA assembled the reserve in six years, its annual purchases could easily result in a 50-percent increase in the demand for open space and agricultural land at a given price. The

---

[9]   Compare results for the optimal acquisition time frame with results in the second column of Table 4.2.

[10] Expectations that RCA will buy the land needed for the reserve may already be incorporated in the price of land. The impact on land prices of acquiring land more rapidly will be muted to the extent that this is the case.

[11] Acreage sales figures derived from data supplied by the Riverside County assessor's office as described in Chapter Two.

potential for putting upward pressure on price argues for tempering conclusions that RCA should attempt to assemble the reserve in a six- to nine-year period.

Other considerations that argue for slowing the pace of acquisition are the staffing requirements and the possibility that the appropriate discount rate could be higher. Recall that, over the past three years, RCA has acquired 5,500 acres per year on average. Increasing the rate to 20,000 acres per year would require substantial additions of staff, and it may be difficult to efficiently build and manage (and then downsize) the required staff. If policymakers believe that the appropriate discount rate is higher than the 3 percent assumed here or that the underlying real growth rate in land prices will be lower (or negative), then a case can be made for backing away from a very quick reserve assembly.

While the issues we have raised so far serve to temper recommendations that the reserve be assembled very quickly, the potential ecological benefits of a faster reserve assembly work in another direction. For example, rapid completion of linkages between core reserve areas may enhance population mixing and improve the hardiness of some threatened and endangered species. As more parcels become developed over time, RCA may have less flexibility in assembling the reserve, reducing the ecological efficacy of the reserve that is ultimately assembled.

It is not obvious how to weigh the different factors that argue in favor of faster or slower assembly of the reserve. In our view, the potential for reserve assembly in six to nine years to put strong pressure on land prices and the sheer staffing and administrative challenges of acquiring the reserve so quickly make it reasonable to stretch out the acquisition period somewhat. A reasonable period in which to quickly acquire the reserve would likely be more on the order of 10 years. However, as it implements such a strategy, RCA should monitor indications that the pace of its purchases is still overheating the market, in addition to other factors mentioned.

Timing Strategies

Should RCA be successful in completing its acquisitions within approximately 10 years in order to minimize risk, it will matter little whether RCA employs the equal-acreage or equal-expenditure strategy. As discussed earlier, the potential benefits of the equal-expenditure option (timing the market) are negligible if the acquisitions are completed quickly (refer again to Figure 4.3). If, on the other hand, RCA cannot muster the resources needed to complete the reserve in such a short period, then it will clearly benefit over the longer term from trying to time the market by spending the same amount of money during each period rather than by buying the same number of acres each period. The only potential disadvantage of the equal-expenditure strategy is that it introduces some uncertainty in the amount of time that will ultimately be required to complete the reserve.

Conclusion

The present value of the expenditures needed to complete the reserve can vary over a wide range, depending on the future trajectory of land prices and RCA's acquisition strategy. A number of plausible land-price trajectories and purchasing strategies were examined. With a 3-percent discount rate, the present value of the purchases ranged from $0.6 billion to $13.4 billion across the equal-acreage-per-year purchase scenarios examined (see Table 4.2). Even when the purchases were made in the optimal time frame, for a given set of future land-value trajectory assumptions, the present value still ranged from $0.6 billion to $4.2 billion. These ranges compare to the roughly $4.2 billion estimate in Table 3.12 in the previous chapter for the value of the acreage needed to complete the reserve as of mid-2007 (assuming that linkages are not rerouted to avoid developed parcels).

For either of the recommended temporal acquisition strategies—assembling parcels more quickly or timing the market by purchasing more acres when prices are lower—RCA will likely need to pursue steps to increase its financial flexibility. Possible options include bonding against the future earmarked revenue stream to increase available resources in the near term, boosting local revenue sources, or seeking additional funding from state or federal government.

If such steps are not taken, the acquisition process may well stretch over several decades. Continuing acquisition at the average pace observed over the past three years means it would take more than 20 years for RCA to complete the assembly. As suggested earlier in Table 4.2, this could prove extremely costly if there continues to be significant appreciation in the housing market and if the percentage changes in land prices are larger than the percentage changes in home prices. At the same time, economically driven fluctuations in the RCA revenue stream and the need to satisfy rough-step requirements are likely to combine in such a manner that RCA finds itself needing to spend more money when land values are higher. Such considerations underscore the potential utility of pursuing strategies to increase RCA's financial flexibility and resources, though this may prove difficult.

CHAPTER FIVE

Costs of Implementing the MSHCP and Operating the Reserve

In this chapter, we forecast future RCA expenditures on habitat management, biological monitoring, and MSHCP implementation and oversight. The MSHCP implementation agreement requires that RCA pay for portions of the costs of implementing the plan and managing the reserve over the entire 75-year life of the plan.

These costs are estimated using historical data on program expenditures and qualitative information elicited from subject-matter experts. We calculate a baseline cost estimate appropriate for planning purposes. We also identify a reasonable range over which the costs could vary because the future is highly uncertain and because many factors, such as how quickly the reserve is assembled and adjacent land developed, could cause these costs to deviate from the levels observed to date. Our analysis projects the management, monitoring, and plan implementation and oversight costs for RCA but not other agencies that have responsibilities under the plan, such as CDFG.

This chapter first describes our analytic approach and data sources. We then present and discuss the results of our forecast and conclude with a summary of our most significant findings.

Analytic Approach

The general approach to estimating future annual costs for managing the reserve was to disaggregate the costs into four categories identified in the final MSHCP document:

- habitat management
- adaptive management
- biological monitoring
- plan implementation and oversight.

We identified or estimated a reasonable range of costs for each category in 2007 dollars.[1] These ranges change over time, and the factors driving the changes differ for each category. Descriptions of each of the four cost categories follow.

- *Habitat management:* The MSHCP requires that habitat be "maintained and managed to the extent feasible in a condition similar to or better than the habitat's condition at the time the lands are conveyed to the MSHCP conservation area" (TLMA, 2003, p. 5-5). This consists primarily of controlling public access to conserved land by installing and maintaining fences and gates and by regularly patrolling areas that frequently experience illegal dumping, off-highway vehicle (OHV) use, hunting, and other illegal trespass. For the purposes of this cost estimate, habitat-management costs are calculated only for the 153,000 acres that RCA will acquire.

- *Adaptive management: Adaptive management* is defined as using "the results of new information gathered through the monitoring program of the plan and from other sources to adjust management strategies and practices to assist in providing for the conservation of covered species" (TLMA, 2003, p. 5-1). In practice, this program will most likely be integrated into, and administered through, the habitat-management program. However, the costs of the adaptive-management program are estimated separately because the activities it entails are presently unknown. For the last 50 years of the MSHCP, these management activities will be funded entirely from an endowment fund to be established by 2029 (year 25 of the MSHCP).

- *Biological monitoring:* There are two phases to the monitoring program. The first, which is still ongoing in 2008, is a baseline inventory to confirm the initial population, locations, and health of the 146 covered species. Once the baseline has been established, annual monitoring programs will routinely determine the statuses of the species, groups of species, and habitat types in the MSHCP conservation area. Monitoring is comprehensively conducted across the entire 500,000-acre reserve, and RCA is responsible for paying "for a portion" of the cost (RCA, 2004, p. 39).

- *Plan implementation and oversight:* These costs are the day-to-day operational expenses that RCA incurs to support and coordinate land acquisition and the management and monitoring programs. These activities include typical business functions, such as accounting, public relations, legal services, administrative support, and travel. In addition, RCA negotiates the purchase of habitat, prepares a number of reports required by the MSHCP and the RCA Board of Directors, maintains the GIS database for the reserve, and manages various consulting con-

---

[1]   All dollar amounts are in 2007 dollars. Historical values have been inflated using the CPI for Southern California, and future values have typically been deflated using a real discount rate of 3 percent. For the purposes of comparison, some future values are presented in nominal 2007 dollars.

tracts required for implementing the MSHCP. It should be noted that many of these necessary costs were not anticipated in the original cost estimate prepared for the MSHCP.

Estimating costs in each of these four categories followed a straightforward approach. We first collected quantitative data on historical expenditures in each program and, when available, similar programs at other reserves. We also interviewed RCA executives, program administrators, and subject-matter experts for qualitative information that we used to form assumptions about how costs could change over time. We analyzed this information and estimated a baseline cost and a range into which the costs could reasonably be expected to fall. These parameters and the underlying data and assumptions were assembled in a set of spreadsheets. These spreadsheets estimate costs in each category and forecast those costs through 2079. The results are summarized into tables to aid analysis. All of the data and the assumptions are transparent in the model and can be changed in the event that another analyst wishes to update the data or test alternative assumptions.

Habitat-Management Costs

At many habitat reserves, management and monitoring are integrated activities. According to the MSHCP implementation agreement, RCA is responsible for implementing the monitoring program for the entire 500,000-acre area protected under the MSHCP but is responsible for managing only the land that it owns or leases (RCA, 2004, pp. 41–57). For this reason, we forecast management and monitoring costs separately.

As discussed, habitat management consists primarily of controlling public access to conserved land by installing and maintaining fences and gates and by regularly patrolling areas that frequently experience illegal dumping, OHV use, hunting, and other illegal trespass. The habitat-management program explicitly excludes the potential costs of providing programs to the public, such as educational programs, hiking trails, or interpretive centers (TLMA, 2003, p. 8-5).[2] PQP lands are managed primarily by other agencies and organizations in accordance with the MSHCP implementation agreement (RCA, 2004, pp. 41–57). RCA does manage a modest number of PQP lands; however, in our analysis, we ignore the costs of managing these lands.

We rely on two data sources to estimate future habitat-management program costs: historical costs of managing the RCA-owned habitat and a management cost–analysis report prepared for the U.S. Environmental Protection Agency (EPA). We also interviewed RCA staff and the current reserve manager in charge of the RCA-owned

---

[2] We acknowledge that RCA could face public pressure to open the reserve to the public for educational and recreational activities but caution that such activities could exacerbate habitat disturbances. The reserve managers will determine whether allowing public access to the reserve is consistent with MSHCP goals, and the funding to support these activities should come from the county's general funds or user fees and not from RCA's operating funds.

habitat. In addition, we interviewed researchers from the Center for Conservation Biology (CCB) at the University of California, Riverside—one of whom had previously managed habitat reserves in Riverside County—to learn about the underlying scientific factors that could affect management costs.

For the baseline estimate, we used the historical cost per acre for managing RCA-owned habitat. The Riverside County Regional Park and Open Space District provides rangers and maintenance workers to patrol and manage the land that RCA owns and leases. Riverside County Regional Park and Open Space District submits monthly invoices to RCA for reimbursement for its management services. We reviewed invoices for June 2006 through December 2007. In 2007, the number of acres owned by RCA and managed by Riverside County Regional Park and Open Space District increased from 15,220 to 22,697, with an average annual cost of approximately $44 per acre.[3] We use $44 per acre as our baseline estimate of RCA's habitat-management costs.

Habitat-management costs may vary substantially based on many factors that affect the intensity with which the land must be managed. These factors affect management decisions regarding staffing, vehicle and equipment acquisition, infrastructure and building maintenance and construction, fencing and signage replacement, and habitat restoration.

One aspect that poses a major challenge to estimating habitat-management costs is that the reserve is still being assembled. The intensity of management that will be required on RCA-managed lands remains uncertain, and it is unlikely that habitat-management costs will remain at $44 per acre. (Management costs were expected to be $55 per acre in the cost analysis done when the MSHCP was adopted.) To address this uncertainty, we bound the possible future habitat-management costs within a reasonable range and explore the underlying factors that could drive average costs toward the high or low end of that range. Neither acquisition speed nor the order in which parcels are added to the reserve will likely affect the per-acre habitat-management cost. To estimate total costs over the life of the MSHCP, we assumed that habitat would be acquired at a constant rate over 25 years.

We used estimated management costs at other reserves to bound our estimate of future costs. The source of this information is the Center for Natural Lands Management (CNLM) (2004). The CNLM report contains 28 detailed case studies for a heterogeneous set of habitat reserves in Arizona, California, and Oregon. Management costs per acre ranged from a low of $8 to a high of $1,604, and the median was $91.[4]

---

[3] The monthly cost per acre varies between $2.31 and $6.45 and can vary strongly with the quantity of supplies and equipment purchased in any month as well as seasonal variation in spending on labor. To reach a consistent result, we calculated the annual average cost per acre in two ways: (1) multiplying each monthly average by 12 and taking the average of the total ($43.51) and (2) taking the average of running 12-month totals from May to December 2007 ($44.30).

[4] In calculating management costs from the CNLM case studies, we excluded costs listed as biotic surveys, water management, or contingency or administration multipliers. Values were inflated to 2007 dollars.

Many of the 28 reserves differed from the MSHCP in important ways that influenced cost, such as in the habitat type or conservation purpose. We selected a subset of nine reserves that we thought were most similar to the western Riverside County MSHCP reserve. Of course, none of these was identical to the reserve, but we thought that they represented a plausible range of management intensities and management activities under somewhat similar conditions.[5] Average management cost per acre for the subset of cases ranged from a low of $15 to a high of $92. We thus set the lower and upper bounds for management costs at $15 and $92 per acre, respectively. As shown in Table 5.1, the current cost of managing the RCA-owned habitat falls near the middle of this subset.

Our range of possible future habitat-management costs is large. It also does not provide information regarding how costs will change over time. Projecting how the per-acre cost would change over time is difficult, but important factors drive management costs. Trends in these factors will cause realized costs to trend toward the low or high end of the range.

Table 5.1
Management Costs for Selected Habitat Reserves and RCA-Owned Habitat (2007 dollars)

Reserve	Annual Management Cost ($)	Acres	Annual Management Cost/ Acre ($)
Bryte Ranch Conservation Bank (Calif.)	8,769	573	15
Tortolita Preserve (Ariz.)	38,955	2,400	16
Blind Slough Swamp Preserve (Oreg.)	19,052	928	21
McDowell Mountain Regional Park (Ariz.)	627,629	21,099	30
Buenos Aires National Wildlife Refuge (Ariz.)	3,621,689	117,000	31
RCA-owned habitat (Calif.)[a]	725,000	16,500	44
Sycamore Canyon Ecological Reserve (Calif.)	94,046	1,500	63
Laguna Wildlife Area (Calif.)	34,162	539	63
Upper Verde River Wildlife Area (Ariz.)	70,220	796	88
Skyline Ridge Open Space Preserve (Calif.)	148,639	1,612	92

[a] The number of acres is approximate because the reserve grew from 15,200 acres in December 2006 to 22,700 acres in December 2007.

---

[5]   Every reserve is different, and it was challenging to apply strict criteria, but, in general, we excluded reserves smaller than 100 acres, reserves with farming or hunting operations, reserves that primarily existed for public recreation, coastal habitat, and reserves that practiced extremely minimal management.

Factors that will affect the evolution of habitat-management costs over time include the following:

- *Economies of scale:* Larger reserves tend to cost less to manage on a per-acre basis. We see such a pattern in the 28 CNLM case studies, although few reserves are as large as the western Riverside County MSHCP reserve. As RCA acquires land, holding all else equal, management costs per acre will likely fall (but total costs will continue to rise) because some costs are fixed. RCA management costs to date have displayed such a pattern. Historical data show that, month over month, barring large expenditures on equipment, the cost per acre to manage the reserve has been falling and annualized costs per acre are currently less than $44 per acre.

- *Proximity to residential development:* One of the most significant factors that increase habitat-management costs is proximity to residential development. Rangers need to spend more time preventing and mitigating human disturbances near development, more time patrolling, and resources to install signs and gates across roads. In addition, residential development increases edge effects, in which numerous factors lead to the degradation of habitat along the edge of a reserve.[6] As RCA buys habitat close to residential development and as land adjacent to the reserve is developed, these effects will cause management costs to increase.

- *Accessibility to trespassers (and rangers):* Habitat near roads or accessible over flat land unimpeded by trees and boulders is at risk of being used as an illegal dump or recreation area. Increased patrols and management resources are required to limit access and mitigate disturbances. On the other hand, some habitat, because of a steep slope or dense vegetation, is not accessible to trespassers or to rangers; in such cases, the management cost per acre approaches zero. To the extent that RCA purchases habitat that is poorly accessible to humans, management costs per acre will fall.

- *Habitat health:* If the health of acquired habitat falls below a certain threshold, then the MSHCP specifies that certain management measures need to be taken to restore it. RCA anticipates that the habitat left alone will remain healthy, but, if the condition of the habitat worsens over time, management costs will increase.

Given that these factors can work in different directions, it is not clear how RCA's management costs will evolve over time. We keep management costs at $44 per acre throughout the life of the MSHCP and allow the upper and lower bounds of the reasonable range for management costs to span trends in the pre–acreage management costs over time.

---

[6] The literature does not agree on a distance defining the edge of a habitat, but it is known that proximity to residential development can increase the distance. Current reserve managers report that they observe most disturbances occurring within a quarter-mile of roads and adjacent residential development.

Adaptive-Management Costs

The adaptive-management program provides a separate source of money to specifically conduct habitat-management activities in response to the findings of the monitoring program (TLMA, 2003, p. 5-1). Adaptive management is fundamentally different from the habitat-management program, which is concerned primarily with applying well-understood practices to known disturbances. In the event that the monitoring program reveals that the health of a covered species or species community has declined past the threshold specified in the MSHCP, the Reserve Management Oversight Committee (RMOC) will meet and decide what management actions should be employed to restore the unhealthy habitat to a condition similar to, or better than, when it was acquired. While this could involve measures that are relatively well understood today—like seeding, mowing, and hand-weeding—it could also involve measures that will be developed in the future. The MSHCP specifically suggests that research scientists and their students may be involved in the development of adaptive-management activities (TLMA, 2003, p. 5-36).

Section 8.3.5 of the MSHCP states that the adaptive-management program will be funded from a $70 million endowment that is built up during the first 25 years of the plan. That money and the interest it generates will be used to fund the experimental and scientific adaptive-management activities. We assume that the size of this fund will ultimately determine the scope of the adaptive-management program.[7]

It is difficult to assess how the rate at which habitat is acquired will affect spending on adaptive management. It is possible that the sooner the reserve acquires land, the less likely it is that it will be subject to anthropogenic degradation by another landowner, but that is purely speculative. It is also possible that rapidly assembling the reserve could increase the size of the adaptive-management fund if money is added to the fund more rapidly as well. The earlier money is added to the fund, the more interest will be earned.

The $70 million balance specified in the plan, written in 2004, is equivalent to $78.7 million in 2007 dollars.[8] A $78.7 million endowment will generate more than $4.3 million per year for the adaptive-management program, assuming that the fund can earn a real interest rate of 5 percent (as is assumed in the MSHCP; see TLMA, 2003, p. 8-6) and that the balance of the fund reaches zero in 2079. We consider that rate to be overly optimistic because the county will invest in low-risk assets.[9] A more

---

[7]   It may be possible to use these funds to leverage other sources of scientific research funding, such as federal or private grants.

[8]   We have learned that, to date, RCA has not contributed any money to the adaptive-management fund. The source of these funds and the amount necessary to build this fund will be discussed in Chapter Six forecasting RCA revenues.

[9]   Historical returns on municipal bonds over the past several years have been approximately 4.5 percent and inflation in Riverside County in the past 10 years averaged 2.9 percent. This suggests that the real rate of return may be lower than 3 percent.

realistic long-term rate of return is 3 percent, however, or even 1 percent if the money is conservatively invested. Table 5.2 shows the annual amount available for adaptive management given different assumptions about future interest rates.

At a conservative 1-percent real interest rate, the adaptive-management program appears to be large enough to undertake many projects each year. It is a challenge to determine objectively whether $2 million to $4 million annually will be adequate to fund a sufficient amount of adaptive management because the future needs and costs are so uncertain. A nearby habitat reserve in Orange County, the Starr Ranch Sanctuary, exists for scientific research and other educational purposes (CNLM, 2004, p. 117). The annual cost for conducting all the educational and scientific programs at this 4,000-acre reserve is about $960,000. The annual budget available to RCA's adaptive-management program is two to four times larger than that for the Starr Ranch Sanctuary, although the 153,000 acres that RCA will ultimately manage is more than 35 times larger. Assessment of whether the RCA's budget for adaptive management is adequate for a reserve of this size is beyond the scope of this study.

Biological-Monitoring Costs

The monitoring program determines the population, locations, and health of the 146 species covered by the MSHCP throughout the 500,000-acre reserve that is ultimately assembled. The monitoring program also verifies whether the species objectives specified in the plan are being met.[10] Responsibility for administering and paying for the biological-monitoring program is currently shared between RCA, CDFG, and USFWS. RCA currently contracts with the Santa Ana Watershed Association (SAWA) to hire and manage field staff needed for the monitoring program. For the first eight years of the plan, CDFG provides some resources and staffs the program administrator position (RCA, 2004, p. 21). Currently, CDFG is also providing vehicles for the monitoring program and paying for its fuel and maintenance. Based on our interviews

Table 5.2
Adaptive-Management Costs, 2029–2079

Cost	Estimate		
	Low	Baseline	High
Real interest rate (percent)	1	3	5
Costs (millions of 2007 dollars)			
Annual cost	2.0	3.1	4.3
Cumulative cost (2029–2079)	100.5	153.0	215.7

---

[10] See Section 5.3 of the MSHCP for a detailed description of the monitoring program.

with RCA and CDFG staff, we assume that CDFG involvement will end in 2012 and that RCA will then have to assume the entire cost of the monitoring program.

The primary source of cost data for the MSHCP biological-monitoring program is the annual work plans and cost estimates developed by the monitoring-program administrator at CDFG. RCA's annual budget contains additional quantitative cost data. To provide contextual information and important qualitative information about the biological-monitoring program, we interviewed the program administrator and senior RCA staff about MSHCP monitoring costs to date. We also interviewed researchers from CCB at the University of California, Riverside, to learn about the underlying scientific factors that could affect monitoring costs.

An important result of our investigation is that the number of species monitored is a more important driver of the annual cost than the land area to be monitored. While counter to our expectations, this finding is reasonable because every species covered by the plan requires developing and implementing a separate monitoring protocol. This further implies that the pace of reserve assembly will not affect biological-monitoring costs. Monitoring staffs are specialized (for instance, there are separate field crews that survey the populations of mammals, birds, plants, and so forth), and the number of staff needed in any given year is dependent on the annual monitoring work plan.

The total cost of the biological-monitoring program in 2006–2007 was $1,960,419 with the cost to RCA being $1,520,419, approximately 78 percent of the total. For 2007–2008, CDFG estimated that the total program cost would be $2,108,000 with RCA again bearing a 78-percent share, or $1,545,000.

To estimate future biological monitoring–program expenses, we disaggregated historical costs into the following five components:

- staff salaries and benefits
- rent
- training by the U.S. Geological Service (USGS)
- vehicles and vehicle fuel and maintenance
- equipment and supplies.

We developed an understanding of the underlying trends, calculated the average historical costs for each of these components, and modeled each cost component separately.

Staff Salaries and Benefits. There are currently about 40 total staff members in the monitoring program, but not all are employed full time throughout the year. Seasonal staff are typically hired and trained in the winter and then go out into the field in the spring. Most of the monitoring-program employees are hired through a contract with SAWA. In addition, CDFG currently employs the monitoring-program administrator and one full-time biologist. CDFG also provides a five-person field crew, which is not employed full time during the year. USFWS employs another manager, the monitoring-program coordinator, but RCA pays for that person's salary and benefits. We assume that these arrangements end in 2012 and that RCA will bear the full expense of staffing the program from then on. RCA will employ the monitoring-program administrator and coordinator, and their salaries and benefits are estimated in the plan implementation and RCA oversight–cost model accordingly.[11] The additional field-crew members and the biologist will be hired through the SAWA contract.

To estimate the future cost of staffing the program, we calculated average expenditures on salaries and benefits using the historical costs of the SAWA contract and CDFG staff. For estimates of per-person costs before 2012, we divided the $1.375 million SAWA contract by 32, the approximate number of employees hired through that contract, for an average of $42,969 per year per position.[12] For estimates in 2012 and afterward, we added the amounts that CDFG spends on the salaries and benefits of the biologist and the five-member field crew to the SAWA contract and divide by 38 for an average of $41,737 per position. Field crews are employed part time, and their work is seasonal, so the cost per position is relatively low compared to that for a full-time employee. The staffing levels will vary each year based on the requirements of the work plan between a low of 35 and a high of 40.[13]

Rent. The SAWA contract currently includes rent, which was $81,146 in 2006 and 2007. We forecast rent separately and reasonably bound future estimates between a low of $80,000 and a high of $85,000.

USGS Training. The amount that USGS has historically spent on training has varied from $10,000 to $20,000 per year. When interviewing the monitoring-program staff, we learned that this will be an ongoing expense that RCA will fund and that the cost could go as high as $50,000. We used $10,000 and $50,000 per year to bound estimated training costs, with $20,000 as the baseline.

Vehicles and Vehicle Fuel and Maintenance. Vehicles are necessary for the monitoring staff to travel out into the field to conduct habitat and species surveys. The program currently has a pool of 10 vehicles that CDFG provides and maintains. In our interviews, we learned that 12 vehicles will be needed. When RCA takes over vehicle costs in 2012, it will need to buy or lease 12 vehicles in order to continue the monitoring program. The cost of fueling and maintaining the vehicles will also shift from CDFG to RCA.

---

[11] A relevant issue is how to divide administrative costs among management, monitoring, and plan implementation. Ultimately, we decided to model costs as RCA incurs them. This is realistic because these administrative staffing positions perform cross-cutting roles within RCA in practice. In addition, this analysis will better aid RCA in budget planning when it reflects future costs as they are most likely to occur.

[12] The actual number of employees varies throughout the year, so this is a rough estimate of the costs per person per year.

[13] Based on interviews with the monitoring-program administrator, the acting program administrator, and RCA staff.

We based the cost of acquiring the vehicles on the Kelley Blue Book® price of the 10 most popular sport-utility vehicles (SUVs).[14] The baseline estimate is the median price of the 10 vehicles, and their low and high prices bound the range. We assume that either the vehicles are leased or they are replaced, on average, every eight years. To calculate the annualized cost, we divided the low, median, and high prices by eight years.[15] The resulting annual cost per vehicle ranges from $2,688 to $4,611.

Average CDFG expenditures to date for fuel and maintenance are $6,500 per year per vehicle, and we use this value as our baseline estimate. Because the future cost of fuel is so volatile, we assume that the annual costs could vary by 40 percent in each direction to calculate our low and high estimates. This parameter can easily be changed in the model to see how total costs change with greater volatility in fuel and maintenance costs.

Equipment and Supplies. In addition to standard office equipment, computers and software, and telecommunication services, the monitoring program must purchase a variety of field surveying equipment and scientific equipment. These include such items as binoculars, handheld Global Positioning System (GPS) receivers, and remote weather stations. Some of these items are disposable, and others must be replaced periodically as they break or are superseded by more-advanced technology. Both RCA and CDFG currently purchase field equipment and office supplies, and, in fiscal year (FY) 2006–2007, they together spent $100,631 on equipment and office supplies. That increased to $138,854 in FY 2007–2008. Currently, RCA pays for only some equipment, but it will be responsible for the entire amount beginning in 2012. To calculate the baseline estimate for equipment and supplies, we average expenditures in 2006–2007 and 2007–2008 (because some equipment is not replaced every year) and divide by 40 to calculate an average per position. Because the actual number of staff positions changed throughout the year, it is not possible to know how many positions were in mind when the monitoring staff purchased their equipment. We thus divide these expenditures by 45 to calculate the low estimate of per-person equipment costs and by 30 to calculate the high estimate. We consequently estimate that total equipment costs may range from approximately $2,600 to $4,000 per position after 2012.

Plan Implementation and RCA Oversight Costs

The primary source of data on RCA's operating costs is the annual budgets prepared by RCA's accounting staff. We also reviewed other publicly available financial documents and the salary-range information for RCA staff positions. We interviewed RCA management to understand which costs were recurring and how costs and staffing

---

[14] New, 2007 model, four-wheel drive, and automatic transmission, as of May 10, 2007.

[15] This parameter is from CNLM (2004). Vehicles are annualized using eight years in 16 of the case studies and 10 years in four of the case studies. If more-accurate information is available, the parameter can easily be changed in the model.

levels are expected to change over time. All the relevant data are embedded in our cost-estimation model.

Plan implementation and oversight costs have historically consisted of staff salaries and benefits, supplies and services, and contracts. Interviews with RCA management suggest that supplies and rent are closely tied to staffing levels and that staffing levels are only loosely tied to the acreage in the reserve. We thus base our plan implementation and oversight cost estimates on actual expected costs instead of on an explicit relationship with the number of acres that RCA owns. As with monitoring costs, we disaggregate plan implementation and oversight costs into categories and estimate each separately. For convenience, we follow the classification used in RCA's annual budgets:

- staff salaries and benefits
- equipment and supplies
- service contracts.

Staff Salaries and Benefits. The total estimated salaries and benefits depend on the current organizational structure and current salary ranges. From our interviews with RCA management, we assume that staffing levels do not change when land acquisition ends and that the salary ranges will stay the same in 2007 dollars.[16] In 2012, RCA (not CDFG) will employ the monitoring-program administrator, and we assume that that position will receive the same salary range and benefits as an administrative manager I. Positions that are currently unfilled do not have associated salary ranges, so we assumed that they would have the same salary ranges as other positions with similar levels of responsibility. We calculated that, on average, RCA staff are currently paid at 97 percent of their maximum salary and that benefits total approximately 43 percent of the paid salary. We estimated the salary and benefits for each position by multiplying the maximum of the salary range by 1.3871 (0.97 × 1.43).

We estimate total future salaries and benefits by bounding staffing levels with a low and high for each position (see Table 5.3). These ranges are based on interviews with RCA management and analysis of historical RCA staffing levels. The baseline estimate is what RCA will look like when fully staffed according to the most recent approved budget, which shows the number of positions filled and authorized. We multiply the estimated salary and benefits for each position by the number of employees in each position, depending on our optimistic, baseline, and conservative assumptions.

Supplies and Services. Supplies include computers, software, office equipment, furniture, and various other items. Monitoring equipment that RCA purchased is included in the monitoring costs just discussed. Services are a broad category and the

---

[16] In interviews with RCA personnel, we learned that they believe that staff positions previously oriented toward land acquisition would transition to supporting the management and adaptive-management programs.

Table 5.3
Historical and Projected RCA Staffing Levels

Position	FY 2006–2007	FY 2007–2008	Fully Staffed	Low	High
Executive director, RCA	1	1	1	1	1
Deputy executive director, RCA	1	1	1	1	1
Director of administrative services	1	1	1	1	1
Director of land acquisition and property management	1	1	1	1	1
Monitoring-program administrator	0	0	1[a]	1[a]	1[a]
Monitoring-program coordinator	1	1	1	1	1
Administrative manager I	1	1	1	1	1
RCA administrative-services officer	0	1	2	1	2
Secretary II	1	1	2	1	3
RCA information-technology officer	1	1	2	1	3
RCA chief of technical information	1	1	1	1	1
Principal development specialist	0	1	1	1	1
Supervising real-property agent	0	0	1	0	1
Office assistant III	0	0	1	0	1
Accounting technician I	0	1	2	1	3
Executive assistant I	0	0	1	0	1
Staff analyst I	0	0	1	1	1
System administrator	0	0	1	1	1
GIS specialist II	0	0	1	1	1
Staff analyst II	2	0	0	0	0
Total RCA staff	11	12	23	16	26

[a] Starting in 2012.

distinction between *services* and *contracts* is not always clear. We are consistent in following the categorization used in RCA's financial reports. Service categories include legal services, travel, telecommunications, RCA Board of Directors and commission expenses, and printing services.

We categorized every supply and service expense as fixed, consumable, or durable. Fixed expenses recur every year and are independent of staffing levels; these include legal services, RCA Board of Directors and commission expenses, and travel.[17] Fixed supplies and services are the largest component of plan implementation and oversight costs after contracts, averaging just over $2 million per year. Durable-equipment expenses, such as for computers, furniture, and other office equipment, vary with staff levels and are annualized over three years. They average approximately $4,500 per employee per year. Consumable expenses recur every year and vary with the number of staff. These include such items as mobile phones, insurance, books, office supplies, postage, accounting services, photocopying, and training. RCA spends approximately $34,000 annually per employee on consumable supplies and services.

Contracts. Contracts include rent, environmental and professional services, public relations, and land management. We exclude the contracts RCA has with SAWA and Riverside County Regional Park and Open Space District because they are captured in the monitoring and management models. In estimating future expenditures on contracts, we exclude nonrecurring contracts as specified by RCA staff. One relatively small contract, the Impact Fee Nexus Update Study is not an annual expense but is conducted twice every five years. We annualize that contract by multiplying by 2/5. We estimate that RCA will spend between $1.7 million and $2.8 million per year on contracts, with a baseline estimate of $2.3 million per year.

Results

Our projection of RCA's total management, monitoring, and plan implementation and oversight costs in 2007 dollars over the remaining life of the MSHCP is shown in Table 5.4. The baseline estimate is the value we calculate using assumptions that we consider most reasonable and is typically a continuation of historical values. The high and low estimates are calculated using a reasonable set of optimistic and conservative assumptions. They bound our baseline estimate by values that we believe will not be exceeded unless there are unforeseen or unlikely changes in the reserve's health; the MSHCP scope; RCA's organization and its agreements with federal, state, and local agencies; or an economic or technological shock to certain prices or salaries underlying these costs.

---

[17] While travel costs could, in principle, vary with the number of staff, travel at RCA is done primarily by senior management, and the number of senior managers is not expected to change.

Table 5.4
Annual Reserve Operating Costs, by Component (millions of 2007 dollars)

Year	Habitat Management			Adaptive Management			Biological Monitoring			Plan Implementation and Oversight			Total		
	Low	Baseline	High	Low	Baseline	High	Low	Baseline	High	Low	Baseline	High	Low	Baseline	High
2007	—	1.0	—	—	0.0	—	—	1.5	—	—	11.0	—	—	13.5	—
2008	0.4	1.2	2.6	0.0	0.0	0.0	1.4	1.5	1.8	6.0	6.6	7.2	7.8	9.4	11.6
2009	0.5	1.5	3.1	0.0	0.0	0.0	1.4	1.5	1.8	6.0	6.8	7.5	7.9	9.9	12.4
2010–2019	1.0	2.8	6.0	0.0	0.0	0.0	1.6	1.9	2.2	6.4	7.8	8.6	9.0	12.4	16.8
2020–2029	1.9	5.3	11.2	0.0	0.0	0.0	1.7	1.9	2.3	6.5	8.1	9.0	10.0	15.3	22.5
2030–2039	2.3	6.7	14.1	2.0	3.1	4.3	1.7	1.9	2.3	6.5	8.1	9.0	12.5	19.7	29.7
2040–2049	2.3	6.7	14.1	2.0	3.1	4.3	1.7	1.9	2.3	6.5	8.1	9.0	12.5	19.7	29.7
2050–2059	2.3	6.7	14.1	2.0	3.1	4.3	1.7	1.9	2.3	6.5	8.1	9.0	12.5	19.7	29.7
2060–2069	2.3	6.7	14.1	2.0	3.1	4.3	1.7	1.9	2.3	6.5	8.1	9.0	12.5	19.7	29.7
2070–2079	2.3	6.7	14.1	2.0	3.1	4.3	1.7	1.9	2.3	6.5	8.1	9.0	12.5	19.7	29.7
Cumulative (2008–2079)[a]	146.6	417.0	883.6	100.5	153.0	215.7	117.5	137.0	161.8	465.8	575.0	641.8	830.4	1,282.0	1,902.9

[a] Not discounted back to the present.

Habitat-management and biological-monitoring costs are projected to total $1.3 billion in 2007 dollars over the remaining 72-year life of the MSHCP (see last row of Table 5.4). The reasonable range over which the costs could vary runs from $0.8 billion to $1.9 billion.[18] Plan implementation and oversight costs account for the largest proportion of total costs (45 percent) because RCA staff provide support to all the other activities, assemble the reserve, and implement the MSHCP.

The width of the cost range varies a great deal across the different cost components, reflecting, in part, the size of the baseline estimate as well as the amount of uncertainty in underlying parameters. For example, the range for biological monitoring ($44.3 million in Table 5.4) is relatively narrow, reflecting less uncertainty about the future cost of the biological-monitoring program. In contrast, the range for habitat management is quite large ($737 million). This reflects the considerable variation in management costs observed for other reserves and the large degree of uncertainty for projecting the cost of managing land that has not yet been acquired or surveyed.

The components of total biological-monitoring and plan implementation and oversight costs are broken out in Figure 5.1. The figure shows that we expect the staffing contract to comprise more than 80 percent of the total cost of the biological-monitoring program. It also shows that we expect the cumulative cost of RCA staff salaries and benefits to be nearly equal to the cost of professional services and supplies.

As shown in Table 5.4, total operating costs increase over time, starting at $9.4 million in 2008 and reaching $19.7 million in 2030. Outlays are not projected to change after 2030. Our habitat-management estimates do not explicitly consider changes in the proportion of the reserve that is close to residential development. As discussed, proximity to residential development is one of the most significant factors that increase habitat-management costs. As population and the reserve grow (and particularly as the linkages between core areas are acquired), it is reasonable to expect that more of the reserve will be near urban areas. Thus, management costs may move upward within the reasonable range over time.

Our baseline estimate exceeds the original total cost forecast in the MSHCP planning documents by nearly $350 million (TLMA, 2003, p. 8-3).[19] Table 5.5 compares our estimated cumulative program costs with the original estimates. Our baseline estimates for habitat-management and adaptive-management costs are lower than those made when the MSHCP was adopted and are roughly the same for monitoring costs.[20]

---

[18] The cost range for the combined management, monitoring, and plan implementation and oversight costs should be interpreted with care because it is calculated by summing the lower and upper bounds, respectively, of the ranges for the individual cost components. Thus, it compounds extreme values and is a more cautious estimate of a reasonable range than the ranges for the individual components.

[19] Adjusted for inflation; the amount in 2003 was $805.8 million.

[20] The original estimate for adaptive management was calculated incorrectly. The final MSHCP (TLMA, 2003, Table 8-2) shows a cumulative expenditure of $44.5 million for the first 25 years—but no money is spent on

Figure 5.1
Reserve Operating Costs from 2008 to 2079 with Breakdown of Cost Components (millions of 2007 dollars)

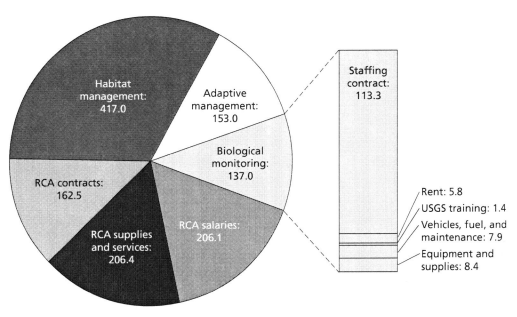

Table 5.5
Comparison of the 75-Year Forecast of Management, Monitoring, Implementation, and Oversight Costs in MSHCP Planning Documents with Our Forecast (millions of 2007 dollars)

Cost Category	Initial Forecast	Our Baseline Forecast[a]
Habitat management	493	417
Adaptive management	249	153
Biological monitoring	130	137
Plan implementation and oversight	64	575
Total	937	1,282

[a] Not discounted back to the present.

However, our estimate of implementation and oversight costs is more than $0.5 billion greater than originally planned. The original implementation and oversight cost estimate had no budget for legal services, rent and utilities, public relations, or environmental consulting services. It also underestimated salaries and benefits by $800,000

adaptive management until year 26. As well, an overly optimistic 5-percent real rate of return was used in the calculation.

per year. Exacerbating the shortfall, the original estimate assumed that implementation and oversight costs would fall from $1.2 million per year to $500,000 per year once all the habitat had been acquired. It is now believed, as discussed, that RCA will not be able to reduce implementation and oversight costs at that time.

The projected present value of managing, monitoring, and administering the habitat reserve from 2008 through the end of the 75-year life of the MSHCP is $473.5 million. Table 5.6 shows how each category of ongoing costs contributes to the overall expense incurred by RCA. Present value is calculated using a 3-percent real discount rate to account for inflation and interest rates.

Caveats and Risk Considerations

The ranges for our cost estimates incorporate myriad uncertainties about the underlying factors that drive costs. However, some events are not likely enough to build into our estimates but should be kept in mind when assessing cost projections. These events could, in principle, cause reserve operating costs to exceed (or, conceivably, fall below) our estimated ranges.

- *Pace of reserve assembly:* The speed at which the reserve is assembled will not affect constant or per-acre costs. However, if the reserve is assembled much more quickly than in the 25-year period that we assumed in this analysis, then the total 75-year costs will increase, because annual habitat-management costs will increase more quickly than estimated. This would increase total costs by only a small amount.
- *Increasing the scope of habitat management:* While the range we estimate for habitat-management costs is already large, it should be recognized that habitat reserves can be extremely expensive to manage. Adding facilities for education and recreation will add to the costs of managing the reserve. The most expensive reserves of the cases studied by CNLM spent large amounts of money on visitor centers, parking lots, trail maintenance, interpretive signs, and additional staff to

Table 5.6
Present Value of Plan Implementation and Reserve Operating Costs Through 2079 (millions of 2007 dollars)

Cost Category	Low Estimate	Baseline Estimate	High Estimate
Habitat management	51	146	309
Adaptive management	27	41	58
Biological monitoring	47	55	65
Plan implementation and oversight	189	232	258
Total	314	474	690

deal with public visitors. Adding such activities could cause habitat-management costs to exceed even the upper bound of the range constructed here.

- *Future social behavior toward the reserve:* Our management cost estimates take as given existing impacts of neighboring residential development on the reserve. However, the behavior of local residents could change over time in ways that either reduce or increase management costs. On one hand, increased concern about the reserve and private vigilance against damaging activities could dramatically reduce the cost of managing the reserve. On the other, increased OHV use, illegal dumping, or extensive criminal activity that makes patrolling and monitoring the reserve unsafe could dramatically increase the cost.

- *Anthropogenic nitrification:* Increasing concentrations of nitrogen in the soil due to increasing use of automobiles and fertilizers favors nonnative species over some protected species. Biologists at CCB warn that continued nitrification, a process that RCA cannot directly control or influence, can significantly degrade habitat quality over time. This could prevent RCA from meeting conservation goals, endangering the existence of the permit or requiring intensive habitat restoration at very high cost.

- *Inadequate management by other agencies:* If other agencies allow the quality of habitat in the PQP lands to degrade and species populations to decline, RCA may have to take responsibility for managing the PQP lands at additional cost, or it may require renegotiating the terms of the MSHCP.

- *Constructing and maintaining infrastructure and buildings:* RCA is acquiring land with existing structures that RCA management and monitoring programs may use. The cost of refurbishing and maintaining these is unknown but likely large. It is also plausible that one or more buildings might be constructed and roads and parking lots paved and graded.

- *Natural or anthropogenic disasters:* After major disruptions, additional monitoring must be conducted. This can typically be achieved within the existing budget by rescheduling monitoring activities or by reallocating resources. It is possible that postdisturbance monitoring could require one-time additional expenditures. Some major disturbances could also result in higher management costs if significant habitat management were required to respond to a major disturbance.

Assessment of Findings

Our estimates of reserve operating costs are substantially higher than those in MSHCP planning documents. The primary difference between the original estimates and actual costs is in plan implementation and oversight costs. The original estimate did not anticipate, or failed to calculate, the number of people required to implement the plan and to support and coordinate the management and monitoring activities. Since the plan was enacted, RCA has had to hire many more people than originally forecast, and it relies heavily on legal services, public-relations services, and environmental consulting services in order to implement the plan; none of these costs was included in the original estimate. While these plan implementation and oversight costs seem high relative to the habitat-management and monitoring costs, it is important to remember that RCA provides critical support and coordination functions to both of those activities, without which its costs would likely be much higher. These include maintaining the GIS database, financial and habitat accounting, recordkeeping, and reporting. RCA staff are also heavily involved in the purchase of habitat.

RCA's habitat-management costs to date compare favorably both to the original MSHCP estimate of $55 per acre and to habitat-management costs for other reserves. The RCA reserve is large and growing, and the growth of the reserve will likely lower management costs per acre, other things equal, due to economies of scale. However, much of the land that RCA has purchased is farther from residential development than is the land it still needs to acquire. Thus, as RCA acquires land closer to residential development and as land adjacent to the reserve is developed, management costs per acre may well begin to rise and could get quite high over the next 72 years.

The adaptive-management fund will pay for a substantial amount of adaptive management, but we have not attempted to assess whether it is a reasonable size for a reserve of this magnitude. It is important that RCA begin to endow the fund, or the fund may fall short of its intended size. If the fund is ultimately insufficient to pay for the necessary adaptive-management activities, it is unclear how the wildlife agencies will respond. The most plausible result is that additional funds will be needed to avoid losing the permit.

While there may be opportunities to reduce costs, many risk factors exist that could cause management and monitoring costs to increase further. It will be important for RCA to consider these risk factors and attempt to mitigate or prevent them. It will also be prudent to consider ways to reduce costs, such as by using volunteers to help staff the management and monitoring programs in ways that do not reduce the effectiveness of those programs.

CHAPTER SIX

Projected Revenue for RCA

RCA receives revenue from the local funding program (LFP) and uses it to fulfill the obligations of local permittees for reserve acquisition and reserve operation costs. Apart from the local funding sources, RCA also receives funds from federal and state entities. RCA uses these funds—mainly ESA Section 6 (Cooperative Endangered Species Conservation Fund, or CESCF) grants—to acquire land to satisfy the federal and state obligations for reserve acquisition (56,000 out of 153,000 acres).

This chapter describes the various sources of revenue for RCA and forecasts revenue for October 2007 through December 2079. It also examines revenue over the shorter term—from October 2007 through December 2035. Forecasting RCA revenue is a difficult task, as the funding program is new and changing and the analysis relies on uncertain assumptions. Therefore, projections are made for a range of assumptions about underlying economic and demographic conditions. The present value of the revenue projections are then compared with the estimates developed in the preceding chapters of the cost of assembling and operating the reserve.

Sources of Revenue

RCA receives revenue from several sources, which either are part of the LFP or come from federal and state sources. The LFP includes the following sources of revenue:

- Local Development Mitigation Fee (LDMF)
- Measure A sales taxes
- Transportation Uniform Mitigation Fee (TUMF)
- other transportation fees
- other infrastructure fees
- landfill tipping fees (TLMA, 2003, section 8.5.1).

The two sources of RCA's revenue that are not part of the LFP are grants and California Department of Transportation (Caltrans) funds. As the Caltrans funds were transferred via RCTC to RCA prior to October 2007, they do not appear in the revenue forecast.

Local Development Mitigation Fee

The LDMF is the major part of the LFP. These fees are levied on new residential and commercial development projects to mitigate their impacts on habitat. The fees must be paid "in full at the time a certificate of occupancy is issued for the residential unit or development project or upon final inspection, whichever occurs first" (Riverside County, Ord. 810.2 §10[a]). Developers face the fee rates shown in Table 6.1 for construction in western Riverside County.

RCA has been collecting the LDMF only since November 2004, so just three years of data exist from which to construct an estimate of future fee revenue. LDMF revenue is directly tied to the amount of residential, industrial, and commercial development. It is reasonable to expect that the amount of development would, in turn, be related to population growth in the region. The Southern California Association of Governments (SCAG) completed population projections for Riverside County in 2007, which extend out to 2035. To project LDMF revenue into the future, we established a relationship between LDMF revenue and housing starts and then based projections of housing starts on population forecasts by SCAG. Various assumptions about population growth and the relationship between LDMF revenue and housing starts were used to generate three scenarios for LDMF revenue from October 2007 through 2079: baseline, low revenue, and high revenue.

Figure 6.1 shows the relationship between annual housing starts in Riverside County and revenue from the LDMF. The figures for annual housing starts are based on monthly data that have been lagged by five months because the LDMF is collected

Table 6.1
Amount of the LDMF

Type of Unit	Amount of Fee ($)
Residential	
Density < 8.0 DU/acre	1,651/DU
Density < 8.1 to 14.0 DU/acre	1,057/DU
Density > 14.0 DU/acre	859/DU
Commercial	5,620/acre
Industrial	5,620/acre

NOTE: DU = dwelling unit.

Figure 6.1
Lagged Housing Starts and LDMF Revenue (by year)

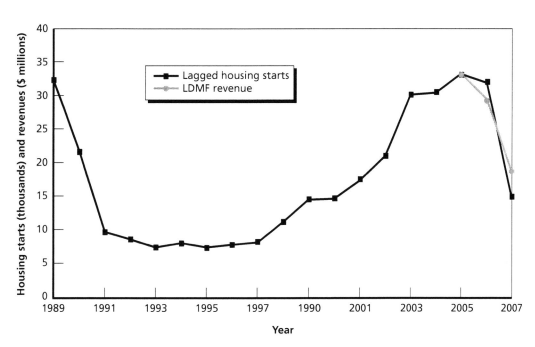

only once the housing unit is occupied.[1] The LDMF revenue tracks housing starts fairly closely for the three years in which it has been collected.

To predict future LDMF revenue for the long term, we tied its level to that of projected countywide housing starts using the relationship between the two figures observed between 2005 and 2007. On average, annual LDMF revenue has exceeded, by roughly $0.5 million, the number of housing starts multiplied by $1,000. Most recently (in 2007), LDMF revenue exceeded that same calculation by about $3.8 million. We used both of these relationships in predicting future LDMF revenue for RCA. Based on conversations with RCA personnel, who were expecting only a 10-percent decrease in LDMF revenue in 2008, the $0.5 million relationship seemed too low for the baseline scenario. We used it instead for the low-revenue scenario. We used the $3.8 million relationship between LDMF and housing starts for the baseline scenario.

To project the number of housing starts, we examined the relationship between housing starts and population in Riverside County. New housing units accommodate an increasing population. Thus, housing starts should be correlated with the popula-

---

[1] Housing units take different amounts of time between being registered as a housing start and reaching a point at which RCA collects the fee. RCA staff estimated that LDMF revenue is received roughly four to six months after the residential unit would be registered as a housing start.

tion increase in Riverside County. Figure 6.2 shows a plot of housing starts and population change since 1988.

With a few exceptions, the general trend for both population change and housing starts was a decline in the early 1990s that bottomed out in 1996–1997, then increased again until 2004, when another decline began. The first point at which the two plots followed noticeably different trends was in 1989–1990, when the numbers for population increase grew larger while those for housing starts declined. Second, the population-change figures showed a dramatic one-year jump in 2000, followed by a steep drop in 2001. Regardless of the discrepancies, an initial examination of the data suggested a relationship between the two sets of data. Indeed, an ordinary least squares (OLS) regression analysis indicated that the relationship was statistically significant.[2]

There is uncertainty in the relationship between population and housing starts. Though the SCAG population projections were made in 2007, the recent economic downturn suggests that housing starts will not follow the population projections for the near term. For example, in November 2007, there were 378 housing starts in the

Figure 6.2
Population Change and Housing Starts, 1988–2007

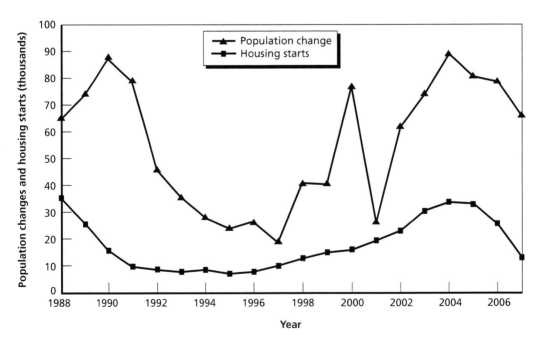

RAND *MG816-6.2*

---

[2]   OLS regression analysis was used to estimate the relationship between housing starts (in DUs) and population increase (in people). Based on annual data between 1988 and 2007 (20 observations), the estimated relationship is housing starts = 3111.4 + 0.261 × (population growth). The standard error of the coefficient for population growth is 0.0737, and the R-squared is 0.41.

county, the lowest monthly total since February 1991. To inform our predictions of near-term housing starts in Riverside County, we consulted a regional economic expert and member of the RCA staff. Regional experts generally expected that near-term housing starts would bottom out in 2008, then start a modest recovery in 2010 toward normal levels, such as those seen in 2001. To account for uncertainty in future housing starts and the relationship between housing starts and LDMF revenue, we present three scenarios for LDMF revenue.

Baseline Scenario. Housing starts reach a near-term low in 2008, similar to the 1995 level, then recover modestly from 2009 to 2013. Beginning in 2014, we tie housing starts to SCAG population projections, as described earlier. For LDMF revenue, we assume that its relationship to housing starts in 2007 holds over the long term (LDMF revenue = lagged countywide housing starts × $1,000 + $3.8 million). Figure 6.3 illustrates the baseline scenario, with projections represented by dashed lines. (Note that Figure 6.3 shows *actual* housing starts; Figure 6.1 shows lagged housing starts.)

High-Revenue Scenario. LDMF revenue shows no significant near-term downturn, remaining flat until increasing again in 2010 to eventually reach a level close to 2006 revenue by 2015. Calendar year 2006 is assumed to be a high-revenue year, and sustained revenue near this level should represent a reasonable upper bound for LDMF revenue. For this scenario, the housing-start projection is the same as the baseline

Figure 6.3
Baseline LDMF Revenue Scenario

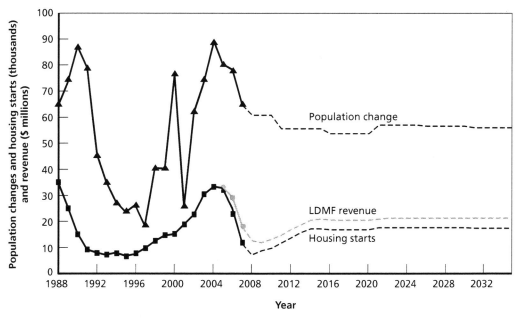

scenario, but, in order to approach 2006 levels, yearly LDMF revenue must exceed, by $10 million, the number of housing starts multiplied by $1,000. (This revenue stream is $6.2 million per year higher than the baseline scenario.)

Low-Revenue Scenario. As described, LDMF revenue is tied to housing starts, which remain depressed until 2011—longer than the baseline scenario—and then increase modestly from 2012 to 2018, after which the housing-start numbers are tied to SCAG population projections. LDMF revenue is tied to housing starts as described earlier (LDMF revenue = lagged countywide housing starts × $1 million + $0.5 million).

Each of these three scenarios lasts only until the year 2035. From 2035 onward, projections are highly uncertain, and the forecast makes several assumptions. The population growth rate projected by SCAG in 2035 is 1.57 percent, and we assume that this rate gradually drops to 1.0 percent between 2035 and 2054, remaining at 1.0 percent through 2079. This assumption reflects the approximately 1-percent average yearly growth in Los Angeles County from 1970 to 2007, an area that had already been extensively developed. This constant growth rate after 2054 would result in a steady increase in numbers of new residents per year. However, the increase in LDMF revenue that this situation would otherwise cause is dampened by build-out in western Riverside County. Build-out occurs in an area when all of the zoned land has been developed. We estimate that build-out will likely occur in western Riverside County by 2035.

Interviews with local officials reveal that roughly 75 percent of current LDMF revenue is due to residential development and that this portion of LDMF revenue is the only one that will generate revenue after build-out occurs. The commercial and industrial portion of the fees, which are assessed on a per-acre basis, will no longer generate revenue. Thus, after build-out occurs in 2035, the revenue forecast assumes that LDMF funds will decrease to 75 percent of their pre–build-out level. Figure 6.4 shows each of the revenue scenarios from 2008 to 2079 (in 2007 dollars).

The total LDMF revenue for the three scenarios from October 2007 to December 2079 is (in 2007 dollars):

- low revenue = $1.029 billion
- baseline = $1.241 billion
- high revenue = $1.617 billion.

Measure A

Measure A is a $0.005 sales tax in Riverside County that funds major highway improvements, as well as local street and road improvements, throughout the county. Voters first approved Measure A in 1988 to be in effect from 1989 to 2009. In 2002, they extended Measure A until 2039. An RCTC estimate from 2006 projects total revenue over the 30-year life of the sales tax to be $10.4 billion (Trevino, undated), but the estimate may be revised to reflect the current economic downturn. A portion of

Figure 6.4
Three LDMF Revenue Scenarios, 2008–2079

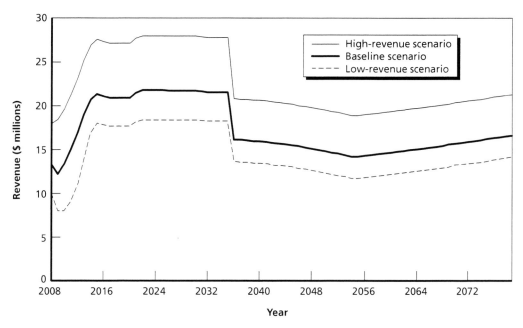

RAND *MG816-6.4*

the total Measure A revenue—$121 million—is designated for the mitigation of infra-structure projects.[3]

Under the terms of the MSHCP, RCTC will contribute $121 million (in nominal dollars) to RCA over the life of the plan. The funds are mandated only in the renewed Measure A, which becomes effective in 2009. However, the MSHCP portion of the funds has actually been available for RCA acquisitions for some time, due to higher-than-expected revenues from the original Measure A. RCTC deposits these funds into escrow for land acquisition. As such, they are not cash revenue but are considered revenue for accounting purposes. The MSHCP part of the Measure A money is independent of economic growth and not adjusted for inflation. As of October 2007, RCA had collected $51.8 million (in 2007 dollars). We assume that the remaining Measure A funds will be paid out (spent on land acquisition) evenly over the three years between 2008 and 2010.

---

[3] The $121 million figure does not include $32 million in Caltrans funds that were passed to RCA through RCTC. As discussed at the beginning of this chapter, these Caltrans funds were transferred before October 2007 and thus are not included in our revenue forecast.

Transportation Uniform Mitigation Fees

RCA receives a portion of the revenue from the Western Riverside Council of Governments (WRCOG) TUMF program. The program, begun in 2003, is the nation's largest multijurisdictional fee program for transportation improvements (WRCOG, 2007). WRCOG levies the fees on new development in western Riverside County and uses the funds to provide infrastructure improvements to accommodate the new development. By 2003, WRCOG expects that the TUMF will generate $5 billion in revenue and will fund improvements to arterial roads, bridges, intersections, and interchanges (WRCOG, 2007). The TUMF rates for July 2007–June 2008 are shown in Table 6.2.

A portion of TUMF revenue—$64 million—is being set aside to mitigate the costs of infrastructure projects. These funds will be transferred to RCA for assembling the additional reserve lands.

The first TUMF payment was for $750,000 and was received in January 2008. The forecast assumes that a similar amount in 2007 dollars will be received each year until a total of $64 million in nominal dollars is reached (RCA, 2008). Based on these assumptions, RCA receives the final TUMF payment in 2050. Due to inflation, the $64 million nominal amount is equivalent to $32 million in 2007 dollars.

Other Transportation Fees

In general, Measure A and the TUMF cover highway construction and arterial improvements for new development. In September 2007, the RCA Board of Directors adopted Resolution 07-04, which, among other actions, established contribution rates for city and county roads. The resolution states that permittees shall contribute 5 percent of the facility construction cost for city and county roadways covered by the MSHCP. The contribution applies to "new facilities, or the widened portions of existing facilities for capacity enhancement" (RCA, 2007a, §1.0 A1). (However, "maintenance and

Table 6.2
TUMF Rates, July 2007–June 2008

Land-Use Type	Amount of Fee ($)
SFH	10,046/DU
MFH	7,054/DU
Industrial	1.84/sq. ft. GFA
Retail	9.99/sq. ft. GFA
Service	5.71/sq. ft. GFA
Class A or B office	2.19/sq. ft. GFA

NOTE: sq. ft. = square foot. GFA = gross floor area.

safety projects," as defined in Section 7 of the MSHCP, are exempt from the 5-percent contribution (RCA, 2007a, §1.0 A2). The resolution does not cover Measure A or TUMF projects (RCA, 2007a).

Various sources of uncertainty make estimates of the amount of revenue that Resolution 07-04 will generate problematic. City and county roadway projects may be funded from a number of sources that often change right up to the awarding of the construction contract. In addition, the availability of funds influences the time at which projects may be built but is, in turn, influenced by the state of the economy. When the MSHCP was adopted, planners anticipated that the total contribution from local transportation projects would be $371 million (in nominal dollars) over the first 25 years of the plan (TLMA, 2003, §8.5.1). This figure was based on the need for $12 billion in new transportation infrastructure (as identified in the RCIP) over the first 25 years of the MSHCP and on the assumption that more than half of the projects would be funded locally and pay 3–5 percent of project costs for mitigation (TLMA, 2003, §8.5.1). Of the $371 million, $121 million was to come from Measure A and $64 million from the TUMF. The remaining amount, $186 million, was expected to come from non–Measure A and non-TUMF transportation projects over the first 25 years of the MSHCP.

Absent any revenue history or updated projections for this new revenue source, we used the original $186 million figure as the revenue projection for the high-revenue scenario, 80 percent of it ($149 million) as the baseline scenario, and 50 percent ($93 million) as the low-revenue scenario. These figures are in nominal dollars. RCA was originally to collect the $186 million over the first 25 years of the MSHCP, but we assume that it will do so before the estimated build-out date of 2035. After 2035, revenue from other transportation decreases by 75 percent, mirroring the assumption in the MSHCP that this would occur after the first 25 years.

The total other transportation revenue for the three scenarios from October 2007 to December 2079 is as follows (in 2007 dollars):

- low revenue = $59.8 million
- baseline = $95.9 million
- high revenue = $119.7 million.

Other Infrastructure Fees

The MSHCP also covers nontransportation infrastructure, which we divide into three main categories.

- *Regional utility projects:* As stated in the MSHCP, the utilities are not permittees under the MSHCP but are expected to "contribute to the implementation of the MSHCP and provide an additional contingency should other revenue sources not generate the projected levels of funding or should implementation costs be higher than projected" (TLMA, 2003, §8.5.1).

- *Local nontransportation facilities:* Resolution 07-04 calls for local permittees who develop parks and civic buildings to contribute under the same acreage fee rate as LDMF for commercial and industrial development ($5,620 per acre).
- *Riverside County Flood Control and Water Conservation District:* The MSHCP calls for a contribution of 3 percent of the project cost for both new capital construction and the maintenance of existing and new facilities (TLMA, 2003, §8.5.1). As a fixed percentage of project cost, these fees have an implicit CPI adjustment.

When the MSHCP was written, no attempts were made to estimate revenue from utility or local nontransportation facilities (the first two categories just described). Based on an approximate annual budget of $15 million for Riverside County Regional Park and Open Space District (the third category), the yearly estimate for this contribution was $450,000–$750,000.

As of December 31, 2005, RCA had collected $375,317 in other infrastructure fees from the three categories combined. From January through December 2006, it received $379,167. In calendar year 2007, according to preliminary figures, RCA recorded $180,000 in contributions from utilities and $378,878 from flood-control and water projects, for a total of $558,878 in other infrastructure fees.

Revenue for this category of funds will depend on whether RCA can collect the required amounts from eligible projects. RCA has indicated that some infrastructure projects may be funded without knowledge of the fees due the agency. However, it anticipates that revenue from other infrastructure should increase somewhat due to RCA proactively ensuring that covered projects contribute the required amount.

Anticipating an increase over current revenue levels ($558,878 in 2007) from this effort, the baseline estimate for other infrastructure is $650,000 per year in 2007 dollars with a modest yearly growth rate of 2 percent through 2035. We project the growth in revenue due to the fact that 3 percent of the project cost is paid not just for new construction, but also for maintenance of existing projects, which should increase in number as the population in western Riverside County increases. The high and low revenue projections for other infrastructure, respectively, are $500,000 and $800,000 per year in 2007 dollars, also with a 2-percent growth rate. We assume that these fees continue to grow at 2 percent per year after build-out, as the projects up to that point will need regular maintenance and repair and also eventual replacement.

The total other infrastructure revenue for the three scenarios from October 2007 to December 2079 is as follows (in real 2007 dollars):

- low revenue = $71.1 million
- baseline = $94.8 million
- high revenue = $118.5 million.

Tipping Fees

The Riverside County Habitat Conservation Agency (RCHCA) receives tipping fees from county landfills to fund not only the western Riverside MSHCP, but also Riverside County Regional Park and Open Space District, the Coachella Valley MSHCP, and other obligations (King and Gifford, 2005).[4] In addition to other per-ton charges for waste disposal at landfills, the tipping fees for RCHCA are $1.50 per ton for out-of-county waste received at the El Sobrante Landfill and, at other landfills, $1 per ton for in-county and out-of-county waste. RCA receives revenue from the $1.50-per-ton out-of-county fee at El Sobrante and a portion of the fees from other landfills. Tipping fees constitute the most significant portion of unrestricted revenues for RCA, meaning that the funds are not limited to land acquisition.

The MSHCP states that the revenue from fees from other landfills will continue for 25 years at $400,000 per year (nominal), then decrease to $200,000 per year for the remainder of the 75 years. The total revenue through 2079 for this portion of the tipping fees is $9.2 million (in 2007 dollars). This amount is the same for all three revenue scenarios.

The out-of-county $1.50 per-ton fee at El Sobrante will continue for 25 years at a total estimated $90 million (nominal). Growth projections for tipping fees net of inflation vary from 2 percent (recent estimate by Riverside County Waste Management Department [RCWMD]) to 3.5 percent (earlier growth forecast by RCWMD and the county executive office).

In 2005, 2006, and 2007, RCA received roughly $1.9 million, $1.7 million, and $1.6 million, respectively, in tipping fees from El Sobrante. The low-revenue scenario assumes that the 2007 revenue will grow at a 2-percent rate net of inflation until the 25-year obligation is fulfilled. The total for the 25 years in dollars that have not been adjusted for inflation is $73.7 million ($42.7 million in 2007 dollars), which is short of the $90 million estimate. The baseline scenario assumes that the real growth rate is 3.5 percent, yielding total nominal tipping-fee revenue of $86.7 million ($51.1 million in 2007 dollars)—close to the original $90 million estimate.

Recent estimates indicate that the El Sobrante Landfill could remain open and accept waste until 2037 (King and Gifford, 2005). Although the plan stipulates only a 25-year tipping-fee contribution, the high-revenue scenario assumes that the contribution is extended until El Sobrante closes. This assumption puts a reasonable upper bound on the amount of revenue that El Sobrante tipping fees could generate for RCA. With a 2-percent real growth rate, this would generate a nominal amount of $122 million ($65.2 million in 2007 dollars).

---

[4] Tipping fees are fees levied on the waste sent to landfills and are usually based on weight.

The total tipping-fee revenue—including both El Sobrante and other landfills—for the three scenarios from October 2007 to December 2079 is as follows (in 2007 dollars):

- low revenue = $51.9 million
- baseline = $60.3 million
- high revenue = $74.5 million.

Interest

The average cash balance for RCA over the past three years has been roughly $30 million to $35 million. The average interest earned on this principal was 3.8 percent in FY 2005–2006 and 4.2 percent in FY 2006–2007, yielding $1.1 million and $1.6 million, respectively. RCA has no formal liquidity requirements, and several revenue sources (e.g., Measure A) act as on-demand de facto liquidity reserves.

On September 30, 2007, the date on which land-acquisition scenarios begin, the cash balance was $22,039,915. Following standard financial-forecasting practice, it was added to the present value of the future stream of projected revenue at the baseline, and no interest earnings were included in our forecast.

Federal and State Grants

Grants offer the only current source of revenue for federal and state acquisitions. CDFG applies for the grants on behalf of RCA. If approved, the state receives the money and subgrants it to RCA to acquire habitat. Similar to Measure A funds, the grants are noncash revenue, and the funds are deposited directly into escrow. Many of the grants require local matching funds. In these cases, the grant amount counts toward the federal or state share, and RCA uses revenue from local permittees to match this amount. The portion matched by RCA counts toward the local share of reserve assembly.

Between 2001 (prior to plan approval) and 2005, RCA received four CESCF grants totaling roughly $25 million and requiring RCA matching funds of $22 million. Approximately $8.7 million remains from these funds. From 2006 to 2007, RCA received two CESCF grants totaling $17 million and requiring $17.4 million in matching funds; $11.3 million remains from these grants. RCA has also received three state grants totaling $1.9 million and requiring $2.5 million in matching funds. Two of these grants came from California State Parks in 2004 and 2007, and the third was from the State Water Resources Control Board in 2005.

The estimated grant budget for FY 2007–2008 was $5.8 million. For the baseline, we assume the same grant level for future years until 2079, or $6 million per year in 2007 dollars. For the high- and low-revenue scenarios, the forecast assumes that

$8 million and $4 million, respectively, will be received each year over the same time horizon.[5]

Grants are the only source of revenue for federal and state acquisitions, and it seems unlikely that CDFG will stop applying for grants before the acquisitions are completed. It is likely that there will be changes to the CESCF grant program—or changes in the amount that RCA receives over the years. Rather than state with certainty that grant amounts will remain at this level for the life of the MSHCP, this analysis simply provides the total amount in real and present value terms that grants would yield at these levels.

The total grant revenue for the three scenarios from October 2007 to December 2079 is as follows (in 2007 dollars):

- low revenue = $291.9 million
- baseline = $435.9 million
- high revenue = $577.9 million.

Density Bonus Fees

The MSHCP outlines a DBF program, which was intended to facilitate denser development within the municipalities involved while providing additional revenue for the MSHCP. To date, this program has not been developed, so none of the projected $66 million has been realized. The program's future is uncertain. The county may develop a DBF program at some point in the future, but no plans currently exist. We did not forecast any revenue from this source.

Total Projected Revenue

Figure 6.5 shows our baseline forecast of revenue from the local funding program in 2007 dollars from October 2007 through the end of the plan in 2079. Measure A funds deposited into escrow from 2008 to 2010 cause annual revenue to roughly double, from approximately $20 million to just over $40 million. Assuming that Measure A funds are depleted after 2010, annual revenue will drop to roughly $22 million in 2011 and then increase to approximately $30 million in the second half of the 2020s. It then falls to roughly $15 million in the 2050s before returning to nearly $20 million at the end of the plan.

As can be seen in Table 6.3, a large majority of the revenue in the baseline forecast comes from the LDMF, both over the remaining life of the plan and through 2035. Over the long term, LDMF revenue accounts for more than three-quarters of

---

[5] The 2008 estimate for grant revenue was slightly higher than these amounts to account for the expectation that the majority of grant revenue for FY 2007–2008 would come in the second half of the fiscal year.

Figure 6.5
Baseline Forecast for the Local Revenue Program in 2007 Dollars

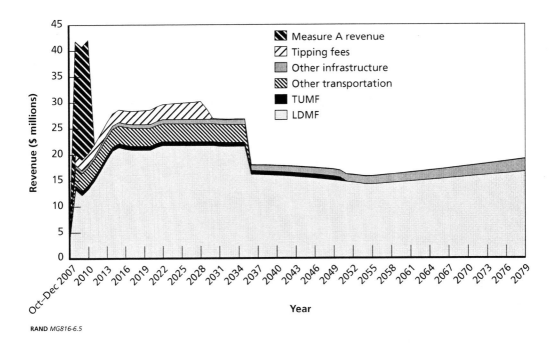

RAND *MG816-6.5*

Table 6.3
Total Local Revenue Sources, by Revenue Source in Baseline Forecast (millions of 2007 dollars)

Revenue Source	October 2007–2079		October 2007–2035	
	Revenue	Percentage of Total	Revenue	Percentage of Total
LDMF	1,241	78	565	68
Measure A funds	65	4	65	8
TUMF	32	2	21	3
Other transportation revenue	96	6	96	12
Other infrastructure revenue	95	6	22	3
Tipping fees	60	4	58	6
Subtotal	1,589	100	827	100
Cash balance	22	—	22	—
Total	1,611	—	849	—

the $1.6 billion in local RCA revenue, and, by 2079, the only sources of projected revenue that will remain in place are the LDMF, fees from nontransportation infrastructure projects, and a small amount of tipping-fee revenue from landfills other than El Sobrante. Between October 2007 and 2035, other sources of revenue figure more prominently, but the LDMF still accounts for approximately two-thirds of RCA funds from local permittees.

Revenue from federal and state sources will augment revenue from local sources. In the baseline forecast, projected revenue through 2079 from federal and state sources adds $436 million to the $1.611 billion in 2007 dollars from local sources (see Table 6.4). Table 6.4 also reports the total projected revenue using the high and low projections for each of the individual revenue sources. The low-revenue scenario, for example, represents a scenario in which the lowest estimate for each revenue source will be received over the life of the plan. For each scenario, the table shows revenue estimates in 2007 dollars and in present value using a 3-percent discount rate.

If the baseline-scenario estimates hold for all of the revenue sources, the LFP will generate $1.6 billion in revenue in undiscounted 2007 dollars for RCA. The low- and high-revenue scenarios give a range around this number of $1.3 billion to $2.0 billion. The present value of this revenue stream with a 3-percent discount rate is roughly $770 million. For state and federal sources, which are currently only grants, the revenue range is $292 million to $578 million in undiscounted 2007 dollars with a baseline-scenario estimate of $436 million. In present-value terms, the baseline-scenario estimate is $180 million with a range of $121 million to $237 million.

Gap Between Local Costs and Revenue

In this section, we combine estimates of the cost of the MSHCP from previous chapters with the projections of revenue in this chapter to estimate the funding gap. Our

Table 6.4
Present Value of Local, State, and Federal Revenue Sources (millions of dollars)

Source	Low-Revenue Scenario	Baseline	High-Revenue Scenario
Local			
2007 dollars, undiscounted	1,331	1,611	2,050
Present value (3% discount rate)	635	770	962
State and federal			
2007 dollars, undiscounted	292	436	578
Present value (3% discount rate)	121	180	237

analysis focuses on the gap between local expenditures and revenue from local sources, or the local funding gap. It ignores costs of the plan to federal and state government and any gap between these costs and potential revenue sources. Because future land prices are impossible to predict with any confidence, we do not attempt to make a point estimate of the local funding gap. Rather, we provide estimates of the local funding gap under favorable and then unfavorable outcomes for land acquisition, MSHCP operating costs, and revenue. Our analysis does not allow us to assign a probability to each outcome, but it does allow policymakers to consider policies that address the range of possible outcomes.

Table 6.5 begins with favorable and unfavorable outcomes for the present value of the acquisitions of the remaining land for the reserve. The $0.6 billion in the favorable scenarios is the lowest outcome in Table 4.2 in Chapter Four. The $4.3 billion in the unfavorable scenario is the highest present value when RCA follows the purchasing strategy recommended in Chapter Four and purchases land within 10 years (see second and third columns of Table 4.2). There are less favorable outcomes if RCA spreads purchases out over a long period and land prices evolve in a particularly unfavorable way (scenarios 1 and 2 in Table 4.2), but we assume that RCA will avoid the purchasing strategies that produce these most unfavorable outcomes. For comparison, the last two columns of Table 6.5 present the base-case estimates of the different quantities needed to calculate the local revenue gap. For the present value of the land needed to complete the reserve, we use the land value as of mid-2007 (from Chapter Three).

Table 6.5
Projected Local Revenue Gap (billions of 2007 dollars)

Source	Assumption Developer Contribution	Favorable		Unfavorable		Baseline Estimate	
		Target	Low	Target	Low	Target	Low
(1) Present value of land needed to complete reserve		0.60	0.60	4.30	4.30	4.16[a]	4.16[a]
(2) Local share of remaining reserve acreage		0.31	0.63	0.31	0.63	0.31	0.63
(3) Present value of local land-acquisition costs (1) × (2)		0.19	0.38	1.33	2.71	1.29	2.62
(4) Present value of operating cost		0.31	0.31	0.69	0.69	0.47	0.47
(5) Present value of local costs (3) + (4)		0.50	0.69	2.02	3.40	1.76	3.09
(6) Present value of local revenue sources		0.96	0.96	0.64	0.64	0.77	0.77
(7) Local revenue gap (5) – (6)		−0.46	−0.27	1.39	2.76	0.99	2.32

[a] Value of land as of mid-2007. Using this value assumes, in effect, that all land is purchased immediately.

Using this value assumes, in effect, that RCA buys all the land immediately (and thus does not discount future purchases to the present) and can do so at mid-2007 prices.

These estimates of land-acquisition costs cover all additional land for the reserve, but, as discussed in Chapter One, the plan calls for federal and state agencies to fund some of the acquisition and for a substantial amount of acreage to be conserved through the entitlement and authorization processes for private development. In Chapter Three, we developed estimates of the proportion of the remaining acreage that will need to be purchased by local permittees. As shown in the second column of Table 6.5, the share ranges from 0.31 to 0.63, with the level depending on the amount of land ultimately conserved through the entitlement and authorization processes for private development. If developer contributions to the reserve reach their target levels, then local permittees will need to acquire roughly 31 percent of the remaining acreage. If, on the other hand, developer contributions to the reserve remain at the low rates observed to date (see Table 1.1 in Chapter One), the local permittees will need to make up the shortfall and will end up acquiring roughly 63 percent of the remaining acreage. The remaining local land-acquisition costs that result from multiplying the estimates for the present value of the remaining acquisitions and the local share of remaining acreage are presented in the third row of Table 6.5.

The favorable scenarios in Table 6.5 then add in the low estimate of the operating cost from Chapter Five and subtract out the high local revenue estimate from this chapter to produce a favorable estimate of the local funding gap. The other end of the ranges for operating cost and revenue are used in the unfavorable scenarios.

As shown in the last row of Table 6.5, the present value of current revenue streams is more than enough to cover costs in the favorable scenario. In the unfavorable scenario, the present value of revenue is $1.39 billion and $2.76 billion short of the present value of costs in the target-developer-contribution and low-developer-contribution scenarios, respectively. The upshot of this analysis is that there are conceivable futures in which a number of factors line up in a fortuitous way and current RCA revenue streams are enough to cover local permittees' costs of the plan. Conversely, there are also conceivable futures in which local revenues are several billion dollars short of what is required. And, as shown in the last rows of the rightmost two columns, when base-case estimates are matched up with the mid-2007 value of land needed for the reserve, the revenue gap runs from approximately $1 billion to $2.32 billion. Policymakers will need to closely monitor developments in land prices, operating costs, and revenue to determine whether a budget surplus or budget deficit is more likely. Potential additional revenue sources are discussed in the following chapter, should they be needed.

CHAPTER SEVEN

Additional Local Revenue Options

The analysis in the preceding chapters shows that the revenue sources currently in place for the MSHCP may not be sufficient to fund the local share of the reserve-assembly and operation costs. Current revenue streams may fall several billion dollars short of costs in present-value terms. In this chapter, we investigate different options for raising revenue from local sources. Ten options are considered, listed in Table 7.1.

We begin by providing a brief review of the sources of funding for other HCPs. We then describe our approach for evaluating the 10 options for increasing local revenue for western Riverside County's MSHCP and then present our findings for each of the options. The chapter concludes with a summary of the relative attractiveness of the different options.

Table 7.1
Potential Local Sources of Revenue

Source Type	Source
Property based	1. Ad valorem property tax
	2. Parcel tax
	3. Special property assessment
	4. Mello-Roos tax
	5. Documentary transfer tax
Development based	6. LDMF
Transportation based	7. Highway tolls
	8. Vehicle-license fee (VLF)
	9. Vehicle-registration fee
Sales based	10. Sales tax

Sources of Revenue for Other HCPs

To ensure that the experiences of other HCPs informed policy recommendations for RCA, we examined revenues collected by 19 HCPs that each had an area of 1,000 acres or greater. We collected the information from Web sites, correspondence, and telephone interviews with personnel involved in administering these plans. Thirteen of the 19 HCPs receive revenue from grants, development-mitigation fees, or both. The development-mitigation fees may be a flat rate per acre or unit or tiered by habitat type. Six of the HCPs are funded entirely from sales of either timber or water. Other possible local sources of funding include sales and property taxes and real estate–excise taxes. See Appendix C for a complete review of revenue sources of other HCPs.

Like the majority of the HCPs, RCA receives revenue from grants and development-mitigation fees and is not funded by timber or water sales. Some of the other funding sources, such as property taxes, may not be feasible in California as implemented for HCPs in other states. If RCA decides to pursue additional funding mechanisms used by other HCPs, consultation with the agencies that oversee those HCPs would likely be beneficial.

Analytic Approach

Analysis of Options per Billion Dollars Raised

Given the uncertainty surrounding the size of the local funding shortage, we thought it most informative to examine how each of the funding options could be structured to raise $1 billion in revenue rather than a particular estimate of the revenue shortfall. This chapter thus describes various ways to raise an additional $1 billion in present-value revenue. If more than $1 billion is needed based on the combination of cost and revenue scenarios that RCA deems most likely, then these estimates can be scaled upward or downward over a reasonable range.

Pay-as-You-Go and Borrowing Strategies

Two general strategies exist for raising funds to assemble and operate the reserve. The first is a pay-as-you-go option, in which RCA collects revenue annually for a certain amount of time. The second strategy is to borrow $1 billion using a general obligation (GO) or revenue bond, through which RCA could receive the $1 billion up front and pay it back with interest over time. Each strategy has advantages and disadvantages. The bonding alternative would allow RCA to receive funds immediately and thus acquire large amounts of land in a short amount of time. This would eliminate the concern over uncertainty in the long-term real-estate market and save money if land values were to increase rapidly over the long term. A disadvantage to borrowing is that bonds require yearly coupon payments at rates that may exceed the savings from advance land acquisitions.[1] Conversely, the no-borrowing strategy may be advantageous if the real-estate market levels off or decreases over time. If RCA were to choose this option, it would face possible fluctuations in the market and could end up paying more to acquire the reserve lands if land values increase at a higher rate than the opportunity cost of capital.

This analysis examines up to four (depending on applicability) scenarios for raising additional revenue for each of the revenue options, which vary based on the length of time for which the new mechanism is enacted. The range of time frames for the revenue mechanisms is intended to give an idea of the trade-off between the length of time for which the mechanisms are enacted and the magnitude of the tax or fee required. The four scenarios are as follows:

- implement mechanism for 10 years
- implement mechanism for 20 years
- implement mechanism for 30 years
- implement mechanism for remainder of 75-year MSHCP (until 2079).

Reach of Tax or Fee

For convenience, the analysis of the revenue options assumes that the mechanism would be levied on all of Riverside County. In reality, if the mechanism were enacted, it might be levied only on the western portion of the county. Another alternative would be to levy the mechanism on the entire county and use part of the revenue for the Coachella Valley MSHCP or other habitat conservation. According to 2006 population estimates, approximately three-quarters of the population of Riverside County lives in western Riverside County. If any of the revenue mechanisms described here are implemented only in the western portion of the county, the magnitude needed to raise $1 billion should be adjusted upward appropriately. For instance, if the revenue was expected to be generated throughout the county in proportion to the population, then its magnitude should be increased by roughly one-third if enacted only in western Riverside County.

Effect of Increased Taxes on Behavior

The imposition of a new tax or the increase of an existing tax may affect business and consumer behavior. To the extent that businesses or consumers reduce the activity taxed, the revenue raised will not be as large as projected for a given tax rate if that behavior did not change. Estimating the feedback of increased taxes on behavior is beyond the scope of this analysis. Small changes in a tax rate will not likely have large behavioral effects. However, once tax rates become large enough to have a substantial

---

[1]   Coupon rates will generally be higher for revenue bonds than for GO bonds because GO bonds are backed by the total taxable value of local property and revenue bonds are not.

effect on behavior, the revenue resulting from the taxes examined here will not be as large as projected, and scaling a tax up or down will not translate into a simple proportional increase or decrease in the revenue raised.

Option 1: Ad Valorem Property Tax

In California, counties collect annual ad valorem property taxes at the rate of 1 percent of each parcel's assessed value and apportion the revenues according to the law in each county. Proposition 13, passed by California voters in 1978, limits ad valorem property taxes to this 1-percent rate and limits the maximum yearly increase in the assessed value of parcels to 2 percent (California Constitution, Article 13A). Each time a parcel changes ownership, the assessed value is updated to the transaction amount.

Under Proposition 13, local taxing authorities may increase ad valorem property taxes above the 1-percent threshold only to pay for the interest and redemption charges for certain types of bonded indebtedness (California Constitution, Article 13A[1][b]). One such exception is for bonded indebtedness to acquire or improve real property as approved by a two-thirds majority of the electorate. Thus, to finance open-space acquisition through an ad valorem property-tax increase, the voters in western Riverside County would have to pass a GO bond measure.

GO bonds pledge a local government's general funds and its ability to levy property taxes as security for payment of interest and principal on the bonds (California Government Code, §43600). Since property-tax revenues back the bonds, they tend to have lower interest rates than do bonds backed by other revenue mechanisms. Once a GO bond is passed, it increases the annual ad valorem tax rate only by enough to repay the bond.

Increase Needed to Raise $1 Billion

With an assumed GO bond coupon rate of 5.0 percent, the county (perhaps on behalf of RCA) would pay $50 million per year in nominal dollars to service $1 billion of debt. Over 10 years, the total amount of nominal bond servicing would be $500 million, and, in the 10th year, the county would also repay the $1 billion principal. In nominal dollars, the bond payments thus total $1.50 billion, which is 50 percent higher than the bond amount. However, in real dollars, this amount is only $1.18 billion (assuming the same 2.9-percent inflation rate) and, in present value, is only $0.93 billion (assuming the same 3.0-percent discount rate).[2]

The ad valorem property-tax rate would increase by just enough to repay the principal and interest on the bond each year. In 2007, the total taxable value of property

---

[2]   The present value is less than $1 billion because the coupon rate is less than the combined inflation and discount rates.

in Riverside County was $234 billion. Property values will fluctuate from year to year, and Proposition 13 prevents taxing authorities from levying taxes on the full assessed value of every property, but, using the $234 billion figure as an estimate, a 10-, 20-, or 30-year bond-repayment schedule would require an increase of 0.04, 0.02, or 0.01 percentage points, respectively.

Table 7.2 summarizes the necessary ad valorem tax increase for the three bonding options (we leave out the fourth option, implementing the tax for the life of the MSHCP, because this is beyond the time frame for available bonds).

Option 2: Parcel Tax

Local governments or special districts may levy a parcel tax, which is a flat rate per parcel or per square foot of taxable land. Because a parcel tax is not an ad valorem tax,

Table 7.2
Increases in Revenue Source Needed to Raise $1 Billion in Present Value

Basis of Revenue Source	Duration of Tax or Fee			
	10 Years	20 Years	30 Years	Life of MSHCP
Property				
1. Ad valorem property tax (percentage-point increase)	0.04	0.02	0.01	—
2. Parcel tax ($ increase per parcel)	133	69	49	27
3. Special property assessment ($ increase per DU)	140	73	51	28
4. Mello-Roos tax ($ increase per parcel)	Similar to parcel tax			
5. Documentary transfer tax (% increase in fee)	342	178	127	70
Development				
6. LDMF (% increase in fee)	636	336	253	183
Transportation				
7. Highway tolls ($ per mile)	—	—	0.07–1.03[a]	—
8. VLF (percentage-point increase)[b]	0.62	0.32	0.23	0.13
9. Vehicle-registration fee ($ increase in fee)	63	33	23	13
Sales				
10. Sales tax (percentage-point increase)	0.26	0.12	0.08	—

[a] Depending on traffic volume and number of miles tolled. See Table 7.4 for more details.
[b] Current level is 0.65 percent.

it must not depend on the value of the property, though it may include an annual inflation adjustment. Property owners pay the tax as part of their yearly property tax bills.

While the ad valorem property tax is a general tax, a parcel tax is a type of special tax (California Constitution Article 13D[3]). Special taxes differ from general taxes in that they are levied for a particular purpose and the revenue they generate may be used only for that purpose (California Constitution Article 13C[1][d]). Prior to Proposition 13, the state constitution prohibited local agencies from levying parcel taxes. However, they became legal under a ruling that interpreted Section 4 of the proposition to include the parcel tax as a special tax and thus allowed if approved by a two-thirds majority.

The first parcel tax was levied by a school district in 1983, and it has become a common revenue mechanism for school districts. Some California cities have used parcel taxes to fund open-space acquisition. For example, the city of Davis in 2000 passed a parcel tax of $24 per house for acquisition, improvement, and maintenance of open-space projects (City of Davis Municipal Code §15.17.040). Also in 2000, the city of Monrovia passed a special parcel tax to raise $10 million for open-space acquisition (TPL, undated).

Increase Needed to Raise $1 Billion

According to the Riverside County assessor, roughly 772,000 parcels exist in Riverside County under the following zoning regulations: residential, agricultural, industrial, and commercial. For simplicity, we assume that the parcel tax is levied on all 772,000 parcels equally. We also assume that the parcel tax will be adjusted for inflation on a yearly basis and that, due to subdivision, the number of parcels will grow at the estimated rate of population increase. To raise $1 billion in present value over 10 years, RCA would need to generate $102 million in year 1, which would increase at a real rate equal to the rate of population increase. This amounts to $133 per parcel per year for 10 years. Table 7.2 summarizes the necessary per-parcel tax for each of the four scenarios.

Option 3: Special Property Assessments

While local taxes are levied on all citizens or properties in a city, county, or special district, regardless of the benefit received, special assessments are levied on each property based on the magnitude of the special benefit. A *special benefit* is

> a particular and distinct benefit over and above general benefits conferred on real property located in the district or to the public at large. General enhancement of property value does not constitute "special benefit." (California Constitution, Article 13[D][2][i])

The assessment for each property may not exceed the cost of providing the facility or service (California Constitution, Article 13). The special district responsible for the assessment provides an annual engineer's report, which justifies the assessments based on the amount of special benefit. Thus, for an agency to use benefit-assessment financing to acquire open space, the open space must provide special benefits to the properties in the proposed benefit-assessment district.

The agency proposing the assessment must follow certain procedural steps to enact it under Article 13D of the California Constitution, which was approved by the voters who enacted Proposition 218 in 1996:

1. Arrange for the preparation of an engineer's report by a registered professional engineer certified by the state of California.
2. Notify all property owners of the proposed assessment by mail at least 45 days prior to a scheduled public hearing on the assessment. The notice must include a ballot for supporting or opposing the assessment.
3. Conduct a public hearing on the proposed assessment and tabulate the ballots. The agency may impose the assessment only if a majority of the returned ballots (weighted by the assessment amount for each property) supports the assessment (California Constitution, Article 13D).

Several local agencies in California use special assessments to finance open-space acquisition, but the courts are still determining the extent of their ability to do so. The Mountains Recreation and Conservation Authority formed two assessment districts to acquire and preserve open-space land in the Santa Monica Mountains portion of the city of Los Angeles. Property owners approved the ballot measures for both districts (weighted by assessment amount) in 2002. Owners of single-family homes pay approximately $40 annually for 30 years, businesses pay roughly $120 per acre, and apartment owners pay on a sliding scale (MRCA, undated).

The Santa Clara County Open Space Authority (OSA), with the assessment it levies on property owners, is a good example of how an assessment financing mechanism might function in western Riverside County. The authority levies two benefit assessments that, together, raise approximately $12.2 million annually (Santa Clara County Civil Grand Jury, 2006). The first was established in 1994, prior to Proposition 218, and the amount of the assessment is currently $12 annually per "benefit unit" (a single-family residence is equal to one benefit unit, while multifamily and commercial units may count as multiple benefit units) (OSA, 2007a). Voters passed the second assessment in 2001, and it is roughly $20 annually per benefit unit (OSA, 2007b).

Following the passage of the assessment, a taxpayers' organization sued to prevent collection of the tax (*Silicon Valley Taxpayers v Santa Clara County Open Space Authority*, 2005). The California Sixth District Court of Appeal ruled in favor of Santa Clara OSA, but the Supreme Court of California agreed to hear the case, and a decision is expected in 2008. Two issues in front of the court have implications for whether RCA would be able, under Proposition 218, to use special assessments to acquire land for the MSHCP. The first is whether the future acquisition and maintenance of open-space land is constitutionally permissible when the particular parcels to be acquired are uncertain and therefore unspecified. The second issue is whether the acquisition and maintenance of open space confer a special benefit on the assessed properties and whether Santa Clara OSA levied the assessments in proportion to those special benefits conferred.

If a special assessment were considered for western Riverside County, it is unclear what impact the MSHCP would have on the debate over this second issue. It could be argued that the assessment would allow the region to comply with the land-acquisition requirements of the MSHCP and, thus, earn the approval for additional infrastructure and development projects. Along with the special benefits from open space, the region would also have the *ability* to develop further, which may be considered part of the special benefit conferred on the property. In the end, the issue would likely be determined by the courts.

Riverside County has voted on special assessments for open-space acquisition and maintenance in the past. In 1990 (prior to passage of Proposition 218), the county voted to create an open-space district but rejected the proposed assessment to finance its activities.

Increase Needed to Raise $1 Billion

As of 2006, Riverside County contained approximately 732,000 owner-occupied, renter-occupied, and vacant housing units. The assessment for each parcel would depend on an engineer's report relating the special benefit to a monetary amount. Santa Clara OSA has a formula for weighting parcels to determine how many benefit units each includes. The formula depends on the number of dwelling units, land use, and parcel size. For simplicity, this analysis assumes that each unit would pay the same assessment and that commercial and industrial developments would not pay the assessment. Table 7.2 shows the necessary per-unit assessment to generate $1 billion. The amounts are similar to parcel taxes because the number of qualifying parcels is close to the number of countywide DUs.

Option 4: Mello-Roos Taxes

The Mello-Roos Community Facilities Act (see California Government Code §§53311–53368.3) provides a mechanism for local public agencies to finance certain public capital facilities, acquisitions, and services—including acquisition of parks and open space. The agency may be a city, county, special district, school district, or joint-powers entity. This mechanism allows the agency to form a community-facility district (CFD), which may issue bonds backed by special taxes imposed in the Riverside County Regional Park and Open Space District. The formation of the CFD is subject to a two-thirds vote of the registered voters of the Riverside County Regional Park and Open Space District.[3]

To date, habitat acquisition on a large scale has not been a focus of CFDs. The largest open-space reserve financed by a CFD is 6,000 acres by the Solano County Farmlands and Open Space Foundation (ILG, 2008). This is not necessarily because it is impractical from a legal standpoint; it may instead be the result of several phenomena (Misczynski, 2008). First, CFDs are typically used to pay for infrastructure improvements and other community amenities that new development necessitates. When development occurs, there may be tension between the city (or other local government entity) and the developer about who will pay for the infrastructure. Mello-Roos is a way for the city to build it and the future residents of the CFD to pay the city back over time. Developers often prefer Mello-Roos to development fees because fees come more directly from developers, while the Mello-Roos special taxes are spread out over time and are paid by future residents.

The second reason that CFDs are not typically used for large-scale open-space acquisition is that, if the CFD includes large amounts of existing development, the required two-thirds vote of the residents may be an onerous burden. RCA could avoid this difficulty by forming a CFD that includes only new development and proposing an alternative, easier-to-pass mechanism for existing development, such as special assessments, which require only a weighted majority.

Increase Needed to Raise $1 Billion

Though similar to a parcel tax, Mello-Roos is more flexible than a parcel tax. While parcel taxes must be levied on a per-square-foot or per-parcel basis, CFDs do not have this limitation and may impose the special tax according to a different formula. Therefore, we did not undertake a calculation to determine the magnitude of a Mello-Roos tax needed to raise $1 billion. Instead, refer to the "Option 2: Parcel Tax" section of this chapter to see the average amount per parcel that would need to be levied.

Using Deferred Assessments to Collect Property Taxes and Special Assessments

The four revenue options considered so far rely on land-based taxes or assessments. Before moving on to other revenue options, it is relevant to discuss an approach that may soften the impact of the financing mechanisms on property owners and reduce

---

[3]   When fewer than 12 registered voters reside in a proposed CFD, the vote is weighted among landowners. In contrast to many other property taxes, Mello-Roos taxes are not always deductible for personal income-tax purposes (California Franchise Tax Board, undated).

opposition to them. If RCA pursues property taxes or special assessments on properties in western Riverside County, it could use a financing option known as a *deferred assessment* (Shoup, 1990). Assessments fund improvements to properties in a given area and, through higher property values, property owners reap the benefits. However, assessments are typically collected on an annual basis, before the property owner receives the additional cash from the sale of the property. A deferred assessment allows property owners to elect not to pay the assessment until their property is sold, at which time they receive the cash that the improvements created. When they pay at the time of sale, they pay all of the yearly assessments plus interest. Such an option would eliminate the cash-flow problem of property owners who, in principle, approve of the assessment but would find it difficult to pay immediately.

The option to defer assessments may increase the political acceptability of imposing such a measure in Riverside County. In addition, a study by Donald Shoup (1990) suggests that deferred assessments would not simply shift the cash-flow problem to RCA. Examining SFH in a Los Angeles neighborhood from 1950 through 1980, he found that the cash flow to the government would be similar regardless of whether deferred assessments were used. A precedent for such a program in California is the Property Tax Postponement for Senior Citizens, Blind or Disabled Citizens, which allows a qualified person to postpone payment of property taxes until he or she moves, sells the property, or dies. During the postponement period, individuals pay simple interest to the state. To qualify for enrollment, individuals must meet various requirements related to age (or disability), income, home occupancy, and home equity.

Option 5: Documentary Transfer Tax

California state law allows counties to tax property transfers at a maximum rate of $1.10 per $1,000 of transferred value (California Revenue and Taxation Code §§11911–11929). The purchaser pays the tax at the time of property transfer. *General-law cities*, or cities that do not have their own charters, may tax such transfers at half this rate, and this amount is deducted from the county tax.

Chartered cities operate not only under state law, but also under their own charters, adopted by the city's citizens. Depending on what is specified in the charter, these cities may charge more than the maximum rate for general-law cities. The city of Riverside, for instance, is a charter city and levies a transfer tax of $1.10 per $1,000, in addition to the county rate of $1.10 per $1,000. Though other cities in Riverside County have their own charters,[4] only in the city of Riverside do homebuyers pay more than $1.10 per $1,000.

---

[4]   The chartered cities in Riverside County are Desert Hot Springs, Indian Wells, La Quinta, Norco, Palm Desert, Palm Springs, Rancho Mirage, and Riverside.

To increase the documentary transfer tax rate, the state legislature could amend the revenue and taxation code to allow for higher county rates, city rates, or both. Alternatively, chartered cities in western Riverside County could enact the higher rates themselves and dedicate the revenue to RCA, though this would be an inequitable solution, as not all of the cities in the region are chartered.

Increase Needed to Raise $1 Billion

Table 7.3 shows the amounts of documentary transfer tax that Riverside County collected (countywide) in the past six fiscal years.

Assuming a modest baseline amount of $30 million for the tax, the state of California would need to enable the rate increases shown in Table 7.2 for Riverside County to raise $1 billion present value through documentary transfer taxes. These rough calculations assume that the real growth rate for real-estate transactions increases at the same rate as the population.

Option 6: Local Development-Mitigation Fee

As discussed in Chapter Six, Riverside County levies the LDMF on new development projects in western Riverside County to mitigate the habitat impact of the project in question. The RCA Board of Supervisors established the LDMF in 2003 and has the authority to adjust it. In past years, the fees have been adjusted for inflation.

Increase Needed to Raise $1 Billion

Using each of the three LDMF revenue scenarios, Table 7.2 shows how much the RCA Board of Supervisors would have to increase real LDMF rates to raise $1 billion in present value. The LDMF rate would have to be more than doubled for any of the durations considered.

Table 7.3
Annual Documentary Transfer Tax
Revenue in Riverside County

Fiscal Year	Tax Revenue ($ millions)
2005–2006	35.2
2004–2005	31.0
2003–2004	23.7
2002–2003	15.8
2001–2002	11.5
2000–2001	9.2

Option 7: Highway Tolls

Charging tolls on new or existing highways is a possible option for Riverside County to raise funds for RCA. Several toll-road projects already exist in Southern California. Private firms participated in the financing of two of these projects (State Route [SR] 91 in Orange County and SR-125 in San Diego County), and a private firm continues to operate SR-125 under contract to San Diego County, which now owns the road. Assembly Bill (AB) 680, which the California legislature passed in 1989, made private-sector involvement possible. It allowed the creation of four public-private partnerships (PPPs) for infrastructure projects in California. In 2006, Governor Arnold Schwarzenegger signed AB 1467, which allows two additional PPPs in Southern California. If Riverside County decided to proceed with toll roads, it would have the option to involve the private sector according to the terms of the legislation.

In addition to the toll roads involving the private sector, four public toll roads exist in Southern California—all in Orange County. The Transportation Corridor Agencies (TCA) operates SR-73, SR-133, SR-241, and SR-261. TCA raises between $0.14 and $0.17 per vehicle-mile traveled (VMT) on the toll roads (TCA, 2007c, 2007d). According to budget estimates, SR-73 will raise roughly $152 million in revenue in 2008, of which 61 percent is from tolls (TCA, 2007b). The other toll roads will raise $185 million—60 percent from tolls (other income sources are development-impact fees, penalties, and interest) (TCA, 2007a). Besides operating costs, tolls also pay mitigation costs for the projects. Orange County has an HCP, which set aside 38,738 acres of habitat for 42 species. As part of the mitigation for the toll roads, TCA set aside 2,000 acres of native habitat as permanent open space. It also funded $6 million of a $10 million endowment that provides for the management of the land in perpetuity (TCA, undated). The total cost of mitigation was $150 million, which is 5.2 percent of the $2.9 billion in bonds that were issued to pay for construction of the infrastructure in 1997 and 1999.

Increase Needed to Raise $1 Billion

We estimate the toll that would be necessary to raise $1 billion in present-value revenue based on various scenarios for both traffic volume and miles of toll facilities. Table 7.4 shows the results. The rows present scenarios for miles of toll roads in the county from 10 miles to 40 miles in increments of 10 miles. The columns show possible traffic volume.

Traffic volumes on existing Riverside County and Orange County highways form the basis for the traffic-volume characterizations in the table, which range from light to very high. *Light* traffic volume is 10,000 average annual daily trips (AADT),[5] which

---

[5] Caltrans estimates AADT figures by counting the number of vehicles that pass a particular point on a highway for a day, then extrapolating for the entire year.

Table 7.4
Thirty-Year Tolling to Raise $1 Billion (in present-value dollars per VMT)

Miles of Toll Facilities	Traffic Volume[a]			
	Light	Medium	High	Very High
10	1.03	0.51	0.29	0.21
20	0.51	0.26	0.15	0.10
30	0.34	0.17	0.10	0.07
40	0.26	0.13	0.07	0.05

[a] Light = 10,000 AADT; medium = 20,000 AADT; high = 35,000 AADT; very high = 50,000 AADT.

is roughly half of the average volume on SR-74 or SR-79 in Riverside County.[6] These amounts increase up to *very high*, which is 75,000 AADT, or approximately the traffic volume of SR-73 in Orange County.[7]

Hypothetical toll facilities in Riverside County would raise $1 billion by charging comparable rates to the $0.14 to $0.17 per mile that TCA charges in a variety of scenarios. As seen in Table 7.4, the $0.14–$0.17 per-VMT toll-rate range begins with medium traffic volume for 30 to 40 miles of toll facilities and continues for higher traffic volumes coupled with fewer miles of toll facilities. These rates are in addition to tolls raised to pay for the construction and operation of the facilities.

Option 8: Vehicle-License Fee

All citizens of California owning registered vehicles are required to pay a VLF every year as part of their registration payment to the department of motor vehicles (DMV). The revenue from the VLF goes mainly to cities and counties. It is levied at 0.65 percent of the estimated vehicle value and constitutes roughly one-third of the annual registration payments that vehicle owners pay to the California DMV. The yearly fees may also include a registration fee, weight fee, special-plate fee, county or district fees, and owner-responsibility fee, which are not based on the value of the vehicle. The VLF is levied in place of taxing vehicles as personal property, but it is not subject to the restrictions that Proposition 13 places on property taxes.

Prior to 1999, the VLF tax rate was 2 percent, and most of this revenue went to counties and cities. At that time, the state of California had ample revenue, so it began to lower the effective VLF rate for vehicle owners and offset the shortfall to counties

---

[6]   AADT figures are calculated at a particular point on the freeway, and the figures here are averages for the entire highway in the county.

[7]   For comparison, the traffic volume on I-15 in Riverside is approximately 141,000 AADT; on I-215, it is 99,000 AADT, and, on SR-74, it is 22,000 AADT.

and cities from the general fund. By 2001, the effective VLF rate was 0.65 percent (with the additional 1.35 percent offset by the state). The reductions were designed to be removed if the general fund was ever insufficient to offset the VLF. The California state controller and the director of finance made findings of insufficient revenues in June 2003, and the effective VLF was increased back to 2 percent. However, Governor Gray Davis was recalled in October 2003, and, as part of the 2004 state budget, Governor Schwarzenegger proposed to permanently lower the VLF to 0.65 percent and to pay the VLF offset with property taxes. In November 2004, the legislature placed Proposition 1A on the ballot—a constitutional amendment that voters approved in the general election. Among the provisions of Proposition 1A was a requirement that the legislature replace any revenue to cities and counties if it lowered the VLF below 0.65 percent.

Increasing the VLF would require approval by the state legislature. California Revenue and Taxation Code §§10752–10752.1 set the rate at 0.65 percent; this section of the code would need to be amended.

Increase Needed to Raise $1 Billion

In 2005, nearly 33.4 million autos, trucks, trailers, and motorcycles were registered in the state. Roughly 1.6 million of these vehicles, or 4.9 percent, were registered in Riverside County (DOF, 2007). The state of California collected approximately $2.2 billion in VLF in FY 2005–2006 (DOF, 2007). Using these figures as approximations, we can estimate that 4.9 percent of the $2.2 billion—or $108 million—comes from Riverside County. Table 7.2 shows how many percentage points over the current level of 0.65 percent the current VLF rates would have to go up to raise an additional $1 billion under the four scenarios for Riverside County. The calculations assume that the proportion of vehicles in Riverside County remains constant and that VLF revenue increases at the rate of population growth. The highest required increase, which is for the 10-year option, is 0.62 percentage points, which is 95 percent more than the current rate. This fee rate corresponds to a VLF rate of 1.3 percent, which is less than the pre-1999 level of 2.0 percent.

Option 9: Vehicle-Registration Fee

While the VLF amount varies with the value of the vehicle, a vehicle-registration fee could be imposed that would be the same for each vehicle regardless of market value. Currently, registration fees fund a variety of vehicle-related services that counties may choose to provide, such as disposing of abandoned vehicles (California Vehicle Code §9250.7) and preventing vehicle theft (California Vehicle Code §9250.14). In addition, state law gives some air quality–management districts the authority to request that the DMV levy fees, which they use to reduce air pollution from motor vehicles (California Vehicle Code §§9250.2, 9250.11, and 9250.16). The authority for the legislature to enact the program comes from the California Constitution:

> Revenues from fees and taxes imposed by the State upon vehicles or their use or operation, over and above the costs of collection and any refunds authorized by law, shall be used for the following purposes:

> (a) The state administration and enforcement of laws regulating the use, operation, or registration of vehicles used upon the public streets and highways of this State, including the enforcement of traffic and vehicle laws by state agencies *and the mitigation of the environmental effects of motor vehicle operation due to air and sound emissions.* (California Constitution Article 1 §2[a]. Emphasis added.)

As the state constitution states, vehicle-registration fees may be used only to mitigate "air and sound emissions." If the legislature were to create a program to allow counties to levy a fee to fund conservation activities, state voters would probably first have to amend the constitution to allow for it to include the mitigation of habitat destruction as well.

Increase Needed to Raise $1 Billion

Table 7.2 shows the magnitude of vehicle-registration fees that would need to be added to current fees in each scenario to raise $1 billion in present-value revenue. The estimates use the same assumptions as the "Option 8: Vehicle-License Fee" section: There are 1.6 million fee-paid vehicles in Riverside County. The revenue from the fees grows with the number of vehicles, which we tie to population growth. Registration-fee increases under the various scenarios range from $13 annually per vehicle—if the fees are levied until 2079—to $63 per vehicle if the fees are levied for only 10 years.

Option 10: Sales Tax

The state of California levies statewide sales and use taxes at a rate of 7.25 percent.[8] Besides the uniform statewide rate, special taxing districts may impose taxes on sales in the Riverside County Regional Park and Open Space District. District tax rates currently range from 0.1 to 1.0 percent. Areas in two or more taxing districts face a maximum combined rate of 1.5 percent. Thus, the total maximum sales-tax rate is 8.75 percent. The 0.5-percent Measure A tax in Riverside County falls under this category, and other counties in California have also passed tax measures to pay for transportation projects. (See Chapter Six for information on the portion of Measure A revenue that

---

[8] Most of this revenue goes to the state's general fund. The remaining is divided between specific state funds and local funds.

goes to RCA.) With Measure A, citizens making purchases in the county face a total tax rate of 7.75 percent on each transaction.

To levy an additional dedicated sales tax, voters would need to approve the measure with a two-thirds majority, as they did in 1989 and 2002 with Measure A and its renewal.[9]

Increase Needed to Raise $1 Billion

RCTC projected Measure A revenue from 2009 to 2038 using a study that the UCLA Anderson Forecast completed for it. It estimates that Measure A will raise $10.7 billion in 2007 dollars,[10] though the estimate may be revised in the near future to reflect the decline in sales due to the economic downturn.

To estimate sales-tax revenue from an additional countywide tax, this analysis assumes that the sales tax would raise revenue proportionate to the revenue raised by Measure A. In reality, an increase in the sales tax would likely result in a less-than-proportionate increase in revenue because the higher tax rate would, at the margin, inhibit some sales from occurring. Table 7.2 shows the level of tax that would be needed for three of the four scenarios (we do not consider the scenario for a tax over the life of the MSHCP because Measure A revenue projections exist for only 30 years). Measure A is $0.005 per dollar—or 0.5 percent—so a 10-year additional sales tax would require roughly half of the Measure A rate if all of the countywide revenue were to go to RCA. If the county levies the tax for 30 years, the required additional tax is only $0.008 per dollar—or a 0.08 percentage-point increase—for $1 billion in present-value revenue.

Political Acceptability of Revenue Mechanisms

Politicians generally consider raising taxes, fees, and assessments to be undesirable, but voters in California have passed numerous such measures in the past decade to support open-space preservation and transportation. While obtaining voter approval for new revenue sources in Riverside County would require polling and an organized campaign, an analysis of past measures can lend insights into what types of revenue mechanisms may be most politically feasible. This section briefly describes the transportation and open-space ballot measures brought before the electorate and the results of studies to determine what factors influenced their passage.

Between 1988 and 2008, 86 open-space financing measures were brought to the ballot in California. Thirteen of the measures were at the state level, 21 at the county

---

[9] Measure A passed in 1989 with 78.9 percent of the vote and in 2002 with 69.0 percent.

[10] The actual estimate was $10.4 billion in 2006 dollars. The $10.7 billion figure uses an inflation rate of 2.9 percent.

level, 40 at the municipal level, and 12 in special districts (TPL, undated). Fifty of the 86 measures passed (58 percent), with approval of either a simple or two-thirds majority. Passage rates for the state, county, municipal, and special-district measures were 69 percent, 57 percent, 58 percent, and 50 percent, respectively (TPL, undated). Only one ballot measure appeared in Riverside County during this period: a measure to increase the parcel tax in the city of Moreno Valley, which failed by a 41- to 59-percent margin (the measure needed 67 percent to pass) (TPL, undated). Table 7.5 shows the number of measures that passed and failed during this period for revenue mechanisms considered in this chapter. The table includes state, county, municipal, and special-district measures. Benefit assessments had the highest pass rate, while parcel-tax measures were the only type that had more fail than pass votes when put before voters.

Studies have been undertaken to determine why some measures pass and others fail. Kotchen and Powers (2006) analyzed national data on open space–conservation measures from 1998 to 2003. At the state, county, and local levels, they found that voters are more likely to vote in favor of an open space with bond financing than with a straight tax increase, including property taxes, sales taxes, and income-tax surcharges. Other factors that increased voter support on a national level included higher income, lower tax rates at the local level, higher tax rates at the state and county levels,[11] and holding the referendum outside of the regular November election cycle (Kotchen and Powers, 2006). Kline (2006) examined the factors that influenced the prevalence of open-space referenda in U.S. counties between 1999 and 2004. His study found that the presence of open-space ballot measures was positively correlated with increasing population density, income, and education. Notably, the average population density for counties that voted on open-space referenda was 753 people per square mile, versus

Table 7.5
Open-Space Ballot Measures in California, 1988–2008

	Measure	
Revenue Mechanism	Passed	Failed
Benefit assessment	10	3
Bond	19	15
Parcel tax	7	10
Sales tax	6	4

SOURCE: TPL (undated).

---

[11] The author explains this phenomenon by postulating that, when the taxing jurisdiction is large enough (state or county), the benefits of the additional revenue generated by all taxpayers outweigh the personal cost to any one taxpayer of a higher rate.

195 people per square mile for counties that did not vote on referenda; the population density of Riverside County was roughly 283 people per square mile in 2007.

California residents have also voted to tax themselves to pay for local transportation projects. In the past 25 years, 20 California counties have passed local transportation sales taxes, including twice in Riverside County (Measure A) (Crabbe et al., 2005). These measures have been part of a nationwide trend in the past two decades that has seen a shift in transportation funding away from user fees, such as fuel taxes, toward more general taxes (Hannay and Wachs, 2007). Crabbe et al. (2005) attributed the popularity of sales taxes to four factors. First, the measures require direct voter approval as opposed to passage by elected representatives. Second, voters experience benefits directly, as the funds are spent in the counties that raise them. Third, most of the measures expire automatically unless voters renew them. Fourth, most measures specify the particular projects to be financed. Another desirable aspect of local transportation sales taxes is their broad tax base (Wachs, 2003). Because sales taxes are collected from more transactions than fuel taxes, a smaller rate increase in the sales tax will generate the same amount of revenue as a larger increase in the fuel-tax rate.

Although this has been the trend for funding transportation, revenue sources other than sales taxes are, of course, available if public opinion should shift and make other options more politically feasible. A recent study examined the amount of support in California for transportation funding options (Dill and Weinstein, 2007). The most popular options were truck-only toll lanes, which received support from 64 percent of respondents, and opening underused carpool lanes to solo drivers willing to pay a toll (55 percent). Several of the revenue mechanisms discussed as potential sources for RCA were addressed in the survey: toll roads (47 percent support), increasing the sales tax by $0.005 (40 percent), raising the VLF from 0.65 percent to 1 percent (40 percent), increasing the vehicle-registration fee by an average of $31 (32 percent), and using GO bonds (30 percent).[12]

A new revenue mechanism could fund some combination of transportation and conservation. (Appendix D examines the degree to which existing federal transportation grants may be used for conservation and vice versa.) The results from Dill and Weinstein (2007) suggest that this could increase the popularity of funding measures among voters. Support for higher vehicle-registration fees increased from 32 percent to 44 percent when the fee was tied to environmental impact, making it higher for vehicles that emit more pollution or get lower gas mileage. In addition, the study found that changing a transportation tax or fee from a flat-rate version to a "green" version can increase support by more than 20 percent.

---

[12] The survey asked about the state of California using GO bonds—thus, the bond would be repaid with general-fund revenue and not increased property taxes.

Conclusions

Various potential funding sources exist to supplement RCA's revenue and close the revenue gap. In general, these revenue mechanisms could be based on property, transportation, or sales transactions. Table 7.2 details the magnitude of each mechanism necessary to raise $1 billion.

Sales taxes, ad valorem property taxes (through a GO bond), and a VLF increase could raise $1 billion with relatively small percentage-point increases to current rates, as these mechanisms levy the value of large amounts of property (real estate and vehicles) and large numbers of sales transactions. Parcel taxes, special assessments, and Mello-Roos are not levied directly on property value, but the yearly amounts that property owners pay could be comparable to an ad valorem tax, depending on the formulas that taxing authorities choose to implement. The vehicle-registration-fee increase would likely be a flat rate for all vehicles and therefore differ from the VLF for many people. The LDMF and documentary transfer tax would both need significant increases from their current levels to raise $1 billion. Increasing the LDMF could be difficult politically for RCA due to the slowing real-estate market and requests from developers to lower the current fee rates. For the documentary transfer tax, procedural hurdles for raising the maximum tax rate may not be easy to overcome. With toll facilities, comparable rates to those on Orange County toll roads could raise $1 billion if traffic volumes were high enough and toll roads long enough. However, these rates would have to be in addition to tolls charged to pay for the construction and operation of the facilities.

Apart from the effectiveness of each revenue mechanism in raising $1 billion, which Table 7.2 reflects, other criteria should be considered when deciding which (if any) mechanism should be implemented. First, efficiency is the ratio of monetary benefits to the cost of implementing the mechanism. Factors that may increase the cost of a mechanism include revenue-collection administration and infrastructure for collection (e.g., toll facilities). Second, procedural simplicity is a measure of the procedural hurdles that a revenue mechanism must overcome to be implemented. For example, an LDMF increase would require a vote by the Board of Supervisors, while a sales tax would require a countywide ballot measure. Third, political feasibility must be considered. A mechanism that is procedurally simple may also be politically unpopular and therefore unlikely to be passed.

Finally, equity with respect to both use and income should be examined. If those who pay the tax also receive the benefits of the transportation, development, and open space that the MSHCP facilitates, then equity with respect to use would be high. With respect to income, progressive taxes require the rich to pay a greater proportion of their income than the poor pay. Taxes that require each group to pay similar absolute amounts are regressive, causing the poor to pay a higher percentage of their income than the rich do.

Considering the potential for revenue generation together with these criteria will help RCA to develop a strategy for closing the projected revenue shortfall. Such a strategy may consist of a single revenue mechanism, but RCA could also use a combination of measures to raise the appropriate funds. While the mechanisms in this chapter focused mainly on the county level, it is possible that new revenue for local conservation could come from the state or federal level. Appendix D addresses existing sources of federal and state conservation and transportation funding, as well as possibilities for expanding their scope.

CHAPTER EIGHT

The MSHCP's Effects on the Permitting Process for Transportation and Development Projects

An important expectation of the MSHCP is that it accelerate the permitting process for transportation and well as commercial-, industrial-, and residential-development projects in western Riverside County. In previous chapters, we have examined the costs of setting up and operating the reserve that the plan requires and the revenue sources to pay for it. In this chapter, we investigate the extent to which the MSHCP has, in fact, shortened the time needed to obtain the permits required to undertake road transportation and development projects. We examine the effects observed during the approximately four years since the MSHCP was adopted as well as expected effects during the next 10 years.

The MSHCP is also expected to have important ecological benefits. Rather than a patchwork assembly of uncoordinated habitats that can result from the project-by-project mitigation of impacts on threatened and endangered species, the MSHCP creates a well-integrated conservation area. The ecological benefits of such a reserve will presumably exceed the benefits of a collection of unconnected conservation areas that sum to the same area. In this monograph, however, we do not examine the magnitude of this or other potential environmental benefits of the MSHCP.

This chapter begins with a discussion of our analytic approach and then provides an overview of the features of the MSHCP that can either speed up or slow down the permitting process for transportation and development projects. Based on interviews with and a detailed questionnaire filled out by stakeholders familiar with the permitting process in western Riverside County and the MSHCP, we examine

- the MSHCP's impact to date on projects to build new or expand existing roads
- the MSHCP's impact to date on road safety and maintenance projects
- the MSHCP's impact to date on development projects
- the MSHCP's effect to date on lawsuits
- the MSHCP's expected future effects on transportation and development projects.

Analytic Approach

Our analysis of the effects of the MSHCP on permitting for transportation and development projects is based on interviews with people thought to have important experience with and insights into the MSHCP and its implementation as well as a questionnaire completed by most of those interviewed and other knowledgeable stakeholders. The interviews helped us to better understand habitat-conservation planning and permit processes[1] and to identify major issues related to implementation of the MSHCP. The interview results aided us in developing the questionnaire. The questionnaire allowed us to systematically capture the perceptions of those interviewed and others whom we could not interview.

Neither the interviewees nor other stakeholders asked to complete the questionnaire were randomly selected from a large underlying population of potential respondents. A relatively limited number of people have experience with the permitting process under the MSHCP to date. The interviews and returned questionnaires capture the perspectives of many different interests that the MSHCP affects. Even though the numbers of completed questionnaires and interviews are not particularly large, we believe that they provide a reasonably accurate overall picture of the perceived impact of the MSHCP on the permitting process.

Considerable care was taken to design the questionnaire so that responses would accurately reflect reality. For example, as discussed later in this chapter, respondents were asked to identify specific road projects that have been active in the planning process since the MSHCP was adopted and to answer questions about each project so identified. Respondents were also asked whether they were familiar with the subject addressed by a particular section of the questionnaire and told to skip to the next section of the survey if they were not. Respondents frequently did skip particular sections of the survey (with the sections skipped related to stakeholder group), providing some evidence that they restricted their attention to topics with which they were familiar.

In spite of these precautions, stakeholders' perceptions of the MSHCP's impact on the permitting process are subject to error, and it would be desirable to validate stakeholder perceptions with data on the time needed to complete the permitting process with and without the MSCHP. We thus considered two additional analytic approaches: (1) a comparison of projects in western Riverside County before and after the establishment of the MSHCP and (2) a comparison of projects in counties that have HCPs with those in counties that do not have such plans. We did not pursue the first approach because the project-approval process and legal environment have changed

---

[1] *Permitting process* describes collectively the steps to secure one or more of the authorizations required for a project to proceed in western Riverside County. These may include obtaining a dredge-and-fill permit from the U.S. Army Corps of Engineers (USACE) or a streambed alteration agreement from CDFG, certification of the relevant California Environmental Quality Act (CEQA) (codified at California Public Resources Code §§21000–21177) document, a grading permit, or determination of consistency with the MSHCP.

over time and past projects may not be meaningful controls for projects initiated after the MSHCP. We did not pursue the second approach because the MSHCP has a number of features that make it very different from other HCPs, including multiple-species HCPs.[2] Further work is warranted on the feasibility and cost of using administrative data on the time needed to complete the permitting process.

As shown in the second column of Table 8.1, 22 people were interviewed, with the perspectives of seven stakeholder groups represented. Interviews were conducted in person or by phone on a confidential basis between January 2007 and March 2008 using an interview protocol that identified several topics to be covered. Most of the interviews were conducted with at least two researchers (interviewers) present and with one interviewee. In some cases, two interviewees were present; for those, both are counted in Table 8.1. Interviewees belonging to more than one stakeholder group were assigned to the group that best reflects their primary role (e.g., a city attorney was included in the Cities group, not the Lawyers group).

The questionnaire asked stakeholders to identify transportation projects for which various permits have been sought since the MSHCP was adopted and to answer a

Table 8.1
People Interviewed and Filling Out a Detailed Questionnaire

Stakeholder Group	People Interviewed[a]	People Asked to Fill Out Questionnaire	Questionnaires Completed
Cities	3	13	7
Transportation agencies	4	3	3
Resource agencies	6	4	2
Consultants	3	5	3
Lawyers	1	4	2
Environmental organizations	3	1	1
Developers	2	8	1
Total	22	38	19

[a] Multiple individuals may have participated in the same interview.

---

[2] We did explore data on the length of the environmental review for transportation projects available from California's CEQAnet database. The State Clearinghouse and Planning Unit of the Governor's Office of Planning and Research manages the CEQAnet database, which contains information from all CEQA documents submitted to the unit for state review since 1990. We attempted to compare the time needed to complete the environmental-impact report (EIR) or environmental-impact statement (EIS) process for road projects in counties with HCPs and those without HCPs. However, the data available were inadequate to come to any statistically significant conclusions.

number of questions about the permitting process for each one.[3] In particular, those who received the questionnaire were asked to provide an estimate of the time needed to complete various steps of the permitting process with the MSHCP in place compared to their best estimate of the time the various steps would have taken for the same projects had the MSHCP not been adopted.[4] Stakeholders were also asked to characterize the MSHCP's effects to date on development projects and lawsuits intended to stop or modify transportation or development projects. Our interviews indicated that the number of transportation projects that have completed the review process since the MSHCP has been in place is still rather limited. For this reason, respondents were asked to provide their best estimates of the MSHCP's effect on the average time needed to complete the permitting process for projects expected in the next 10 years.

In January 2008, the questionnaire was mailed to 48 potential participants, including planning directors, community-development directors, city managers of all cities in western Riverside County, and staff of the transportation and resource agencies that are involved in planning and development activities in western Riverside County. The questionnaire was also sent to consultants, lawyers, developers, and senior staff of environmental organizations who were identified during the course of the study as being knowledgeable about the permitting process and the workings of the MSHCP. Those who received the questionnaire were asked to complete it and return it by mail. Repeated follow-up phone calls and emails were made through May 2008 to those who did not return the questionnaire urging them to do so. Five recipients explicitly declined participation, generally stating that they were unqualified to respond meaningfully. Five more recipients, all of them developers, became unreachable, possibly due to the severe housing-market downturn that occurred in Riverside County during that period. These 10 questionnaire recipients were removed from the target sample. In the end, 50 percent of the 38 remaining recipients completed and returned the questionnaire. The breakdown of respondents by stakeholder group is shown in Table 8.1.

Features of the MSHCP That May Speed or Slow the Permitting Process

The MSHCP affects the permitting processes for transportation and development projects in a number of different ways, some of which may shorten the time needed and

---

[3]   The questionnaire is available from the authors on request.

[4]   Respondents were first asked whether they were familiar with the topic covered by a particular set of questions and to skip to the next set of questions if they were not. For example, respondents were first asked whether they were familiar with projects to expand existing roads or build new roads that had completed major steps in the permitting process since the MSHCP was adopted. Those who were familiar with such projects were asked to name the projects with which they were familiar and to answer a number of questions about each one. Those who were not familiar with such projects were asked to skip to the next topic.

some of which may increase the time needed to obtain the required authorizations. Next, we summarize potential effects of the MSHCP on the three basic aspects of the permitting process:

- the assessment of environmental impacts
- project siting and design
- the mitigation of environmental impacts.

We also examine how the MSHCP may affect litigation intended to stop or modify projects. MSHCP procedures for transportation projects differ in some respects from procedures for development projects. The discussion in this section focuses on transportation projects, but we highlight the most important ways in which MSHCP effects may differ for development projects.

The permitting process is complex and involves many components. Many factors contribute to whether a project proceeds through the permitting process quickly or is instead delayed.[5] Given the rich diversity of species found in western Riverside County,[6] it is not surprising that securing an incidental take permit is often the determining step in how quickly a project will proceed and, often, whether the project will proceed at all.[7] We therefore focus our attention on the MSHCP's effect on the permitting process.

Potential Effect on the Assessment of Project Environmental Impacts

The MSHCP can, in principle, reduce the time and cost of the biological assessments required for road or development projects. In the absence of the MSHCP, detailed biological assessments are typically required, and these can cause considerable delay.[8] With the MSHCP in place, however, project assessments can draw on the comprehensive biological assessments that were done in preparing and implementing the MSHCP. The ability to reference this information can save both time and money.

The environmental-review process typically requires that field surveys be conducted for sensitive species that a project may affect, and these surveys can add considerable time and expense to a project. The MSHCP reduced some survey requirements—namely, for species afforded protection by the ESA—but added survey requirements for other species that are currently not threatened or endangered. The result is that, in some cases, applicants may need to conduct fewer surveys with the MSHCP in

---

[5] See FHWA (undated) for a review of reasons that road projects in the United States are most often delayed during the environmental-review process.

[6] See Stein, Kutner, and Adams (2000) for a national perspective on biodiversity hot spots in the United States.

[7] Several of those interviewed as part of this study held this view.

[8] Assessments are often species-specific and can require repeated surveys over multiple seasons or years.

place than would have been required without the MSHCP but, in other cases, may be required to do more surveys. The MSHCP also provides guidance on the survey protocols that should be followed. These guidelines may reduce the time and cost of negotiations among applicants and resource agencies regarding the biological-survey efforts required.

Potential Impact on the Project Siting and Design Processes

The MSHCP can, in principle, substantially accelerate project siting and design. As one transportation planner interviewed during the study pointed out, a fundamental benefit of the MSHCP is the right to build projects covered by the MSHCP.[9] In the absence of the MSHCP, detailed analyses would be required of the biological impacts of various project alternatives, including no project. Without the MSHCP, lengthy discussions between applicants and resource agencies about the biological effects of project alternatives and the design features required to reduce impacts could ensue. With the MSHCP, on the other hand, the roads listed in the general circulation plan can more easily be approved, and planning discussions can move on to how to design and build projects to be consistent with the MSHCP.[10]

The MSHCP delineates project-specific considerations that must be addressed in the design process, and the enumeration of project-specific requirements can also reduce the scope of debate over what design features will be required. It details requirements that all projects must meet regarding riparian areas, certain endemic species, and the interface between urban and wildlife areas. Prior to the MSHCP, in contrast, it was often not clear what design features were adequate. According to transportation planners interviewed for this study, prior to the MSHCP, a resource agency might deny a permit but give little guidance on what modifications would address their concerns. Applicants were then left to come back with another design, not knowing whether it, too, would be found inadequate. Considerable time and expense accompanied each such iteration. By expressing project-specific design requirements up front, the MSHCP better defines expectations for project design, thus potentially reducing the time and cost of the permitting processes.

While the MSHCP can, in principle, shorten the siting and design processes, some aspects of the MSHCP can reduce or reverse any time or cost savings. Chief among these is the joint project-review (JPR) process. The JPR process requires RCA and the wildlife agencies to confirm that a project in the criteria area is consistent with the requirements of the MSHCP. The resource agencies may determine that a project is not consistent, triggering further negotiations between the applicant and the resource

---

[9]   The MSHCP establishes the right to build the roads that were in western Riverside's County's general circulation plan when the MSHCP was adopted.

[10]   An exception to agreement on route is the Mid County Parkway. When the MSHCP was adopted, a specific route had not been settled on, and negotiations over the route are ongoing.

agencies. Resource agencies expressed real concern that RCA is not implementing the MSHCP as initially agreed upon, prompting USFWS in particular to find many projects to be inconsistent with the plan. According to those interviewed, USFWS has rejected on the order of 15 to 25 percent of the approximately 400 JPR submissions under the MSHCP to date.[11] It is important to note that such a finding by the resource agencies does not block a project; ultimately, the local permittee has the discretion to accept or reject guidance coming out of the JPR process. However, frequently exercising this authority could conceivably result in revocation of the take permit.

A second aspect of the MSHCP that can reduce its ability to shorten permitting processes is the potential for the wildlife agencies to be involved again when applicants seek required permits from USACE, which is not a party to the MSHCP; under the Clean Water Act (CWA) (Federal Water Pollution Control Act, Pub. L. 845), applicants must receive a dredge-and-fill permit for projects that affect waters of the United States, including jurisdictional wetlands. Before issuing such a permit, USACE is required to consult with USFWS regarding species and habitat issues. Thus, even though a project can formally proceed even if USFWS has not found it consistent with the MSHCP during the JPR process, USFWS can raise issues with the project during the consultation with USACE. When the MSHCP was adopted, it was hoped that a special area management plan (SAMP) would be developed that resulted in an areawide dredge-and-fill permit under CWA, much like the MSHCP does for the incidental take permit required under ESA. A SAMP could further accelerate the permitting processes for projects in western Riverside County. A SAMP, however, has yet to be completed.

Potential Impact on the Process of Determining Adequate Mitigation

In the absence of the MSHCP, the project applicant and wildlife agencies must agree on how to mitigate the biological effects of the project that remain once siting and design issues have been resolved. The parties must come to an agreement on what the impacts are worth in terms of land that must be conserved or other mitigation measures.[12] For example, applicants may have to set up and fund a separate HCP for each project with substantial biological effects. These project-by-project negotiations can be contentious and lengthy. The MSHCP removes much of the negotiation over mitigation issues, as it is an established mitigation mechanism available to applicants. The 500,000-acre habitat reserve is the agreed-on mitigation for transportation and development projects in western Riverside County, and further mitigation is not required. Some areas for negotiation over mitigation remain, however. For example, projects built in the criteria

---

[11] This discussion does not imply that the JPR process is not critical to MSHCP performance from a habitat-conservation standpoint. Rather, it identifies a factor that may limit the MSHCP's effectiveness in accelerating the permitting processes.

[12] If the project has a federal nexus—that is, if a federal agency funded, authorized, or carried it out—the project applicant consults with USFWS under Section 7 of the ESA (so-called Section 7 consultations). If there is no federal nexus, the applicant negotiates the required mitigation under Section 10 of the ESA.

area must replace the habitat values of the project footprint, and wildlife agencies must concur that they indeed do so. Nevertheless, the MSHCP would seem to offer considerable time savings for many projects.

Commercial, industrial, and residential projects must go through an additional step in the mitigation process that road-transportation projects do not. The HANS process requires applicants for projects in criteria areas to negotiate with their local jurisdictions over what portion of the property should be donated to the reserve in return for development entitlements. As discussed in Chapter Two, however, little land has been added to the reserve through the HANS process, and it would appear that the HANS process has not been a major factor in slowing the permitting process for development projects to date.

Potential Impact on Litigation

Lawsuits that attempt to block or substantially modify a proposed project can add substantial cost and time to the permitting process. In some cases, they can halt the process altogether. The MSHCP would seem to remove one of the key allegations made in such lawsuits—namely, that the mitigation plan does not address the project's cumulative and growth-inducing effects.[13] By setting up a conservation plan for western Riverside County, project applicants would be able to argue that a mitigation plan has been put in place to address all effects of the transportation and development projects identified in the MSHCP. Indeed, some of the project applicants interviewed during this study viewed the MSHCP as insurance against litigation on these grounds. In their view, the MSHCP would allow applicants to argue that they had made a good-faith effort to address cumulative and growth-inducing effects, thus reducing the likelihood that such suits would prevail or be brought in the first place.

A broad array of stakeholders participated in developing the MSHCP, including wildlife agencies, environmental groups, and leading conservation biologists. The fact that the plan was formulated through this collaboration would arguably also reduce the likelihood of lawsuits, as varied interests were represented. The sense of several of those interviewed was that it was unlikely that the MSHCP itself would be challenged. Failure to properly implement the plan, however, might induce lawsuits.

---

[13] Cumulative effects and growth-inducing effects are called to attention during the CEQA-mandated environmental review of projects. The concern over cumulative effects derives from the possibility that, while the effect of any one project may be modest, the effects of multiple projects can be significant, and that the mitigation required for the individual projects will not accumulate sufficiently to offset the total effect of the projects. Growth-inducing effects describe the possibility that a project (particularly a road) will induce further growth and consequent environmental damage in the area.

Stakeholder Perceptions of the Features of the MSHCP That May Accelerate or Slow Permitting Processes

The questionnaire asked respondents to identify the three most important ways in which the MSHCP speeds the placement of transportation or development projects as well as to identify the three most important MSHCP attributes that reduce its effectiveness in this regard. These questions were open-ended; instead of choosing among response options, respondents were asked to write in their responses. Responses were compiled and reviewed for similarities and differences, then grouped into general categories describing attributes that enhance or reduce MSHCP effectiveness.

Given the limited sample size and the amorphous nature of the underlying population (the number of people in each stakeholder group who are familiar with the MSHCP's effect on permitting processes), it did not seem appropriate to reweight the responses to account for different response rates across stakeholder groups or to disaggregate responses by stakeholder group.[14] Thus, in interpreting the tabulations, it is best not to focus on the precise number or percentage of responses in the various categories but on the general nature of the responses.

Ways in Which the MSHCP Speeds Project Delivery

As shown in Table 8.2, the responses to the questionnaire indicate three general ways in which the MSHCP reduces the time required for permitting processes.

Provides Scientific Information. Several respondents reported that the detailed information in the MSHCP describing biological resources and environmentally sensitive areas is an important means for accelerating project delivery. As shown in Table 8.2, however, only a small share of the respondents (three of 19) identified this benefit.

Provides Administrative Structure and Procedure. About one-third of the respondents pointed to the additional administrative structure and procedural features that the MSHCP provides as being important means of speeding project delivery. Several detailed explanations for this were reported, including the following:

- The MSHCP provides additional resources and expertise to local government, thereby enhancing local planning capacity.
- The MSHCP provides a clearer framework for mitigating biological effects of projects.
- In some cases, the MSHCP improves interagency coordination and eliminates difficult negotiations.

---

[14] Even if there were solid information on the number of stakeholders in each group, it is not obvious how best to weight the responses across groups. For example, if 20 developers but only four resource agencies have been working in western Riverside County since the MSHCP was adopted, should developer responses be weighted five times as heavily as those of the resource agencies?

Table 8.2
Ways in Which Respondents Perceived That the MSHCP Affects Delivery of Transportation or Development Projects

Response	Respondents (N = 19)
A. Ways in which the MSHCP speeds delivery of projects	
It provides scientific information	3
It provides administrative structure and procedure	6
It streamlines the permitting process	11
There are no ways in which the MSHCP speeds project delivery	1
Don't know	3
B. MSHCP attributes that reduce its effectiveness	
It provides uncertain and inaccurate information	4
It creates an additional layer of bureaucracy and implementation challenges	12
It delays the permitting process by requiring additional survey work and project review	6
It increases concern for planning issues unrelated to the MSHCP	4
There are no attributes that reduce MSHCP effectiveness	1
Don't know	3

Streamlines the Permitting Process. More than half the respondents (11 of 19) described the MSHCP's ability to streamline the authorization process in one way or another. Respondents reported that the MSHCP

- clarifies the review of biological effects, especially for endangered species, by identifying species and survey requirements and, in some cases, reducing survey requirements
- eliminates consistency review by CDFG per ESA Section 7 if MSHCP requirements have been met
- reduces dredge-and-fill permitting delays
- redirects the CEQA and National Environmental Policy Act (NEPA) (Pub. L. 91-190) processes from requiring more-extensive to requiring less-extensive analysis and mitigation, especially by providing mitigation for growth-inducing and cumulative effects related to endangered species.

In these ways, the MSHCP ensures a clearer, more certain overall authorization process, which shortens permit processing. One notable response highlighted the importance of reducing the time and effort previously needed to permit the small but numerous safety and maintenance projects that are required across western Riverside

County. As described later, these projects are exempt from review for consistency with the MSHCP.

Attributes of the MSHCP That Reduce Its Effectiveness

While respondents reported important ways in which the MSHCP speeds project delivery, they also identified important attributes of the MSHCP that reduce its effectiveness in the placement of transportation or development projects. The attributes that respondents reported, in four general categories, are as follows.

Provides Uncertain and Inaccurate Information. While some respondents praised the scientific information that the MSHCP provides, others identified several ways in which the additional information provided under the MSHCP reduces the plan's effectiveness in speeding project delivery. Four of the 19 respondents cited this reason for reduced effectiveness of the MSHCP. Uncertainties about and inaccuracies of information on linkage and core areas and burrowing-owl habitat were specifically raised.

Creates Additional Layer of Bureaucracy and Implementation Challenges. The most frequently reported attribute that reduces MSHCP effectiveness is the additional administrative structure and process that the plan requires, cited by nearly two-thirds of the respondents (12 of 19). Respondents specifically called attention to the HANS and Determination of Biologically Equivalent or Superior Preservation (DBESP) processes. Respondents identified the additional bureaucracy as increasing complexity, confusion, and disagreement among parties, often resulting in inconsistent implementation of the MSHCP.

Delays the Permitting Process by Requiring Additional Survey Work and Project Review. Six of 19 respondents reported that the MSHCP has increased permit-processing delays or that permit delays are still common, notably those associated with ESA Section 7 interagency consultation to conserve federally protected species.

Increases Concern for Planning Issues That Are Unrelated to MSHCP. Four respondents commented that the MSHCP exacerbates political problems in and among jurisdictions and calls attention to issues of land scarcity in western Riverside County, thereby intensifying the competition for land among transportation and development interests.

Synthesis of the MSHCP's Perceived Strengths and Weaknesses

The results suggest that the MSHCP features that can speed project delivery are associated with features that can also reduce the MSHCP's effectiveness. The MSHCP provides additional scientific information that some perceive to speed project delivery. Yet, others find that debates over the accuracy of the information can delay projects. Likewise, the administrative structure and procedural requirements of the MSHCP can speed project placement in certain circumstances and delay it in others. While some respondents believe that the MSHCP has streamlined the overall permitting process, others cite new requirements for additional survey work and permit-processing delays that remain even with the MSHCP in place.

The results suggest that the MSHCP's effect on the permitting process will vary across projects, with the effect depending on the project's particular features and setting. The effects may vary, for example, by project size, whether the project is located inside or outside the criteria area, and whether the project affects a threatened or endangered species. The results also provide no assurance that the MSHCP's net effect across all projects will be positive or negative.

We now turn to the best information currently available on the direction and magnitude of the MSHCP's effect on the length of the permitting process—the perception of the stakeholders who are very familiar with permitting transportation and development projects in western Riverside County. We start with the perceived effects to date, then turn to expected future effects. The analysis of the perceived effects to date begins by examining effects on projects to build new roads or expand existing ones. Effects to date on the permitting process for road safety and maintenance projects, development projects, and litigation are subsequently discussed.

The MSHCP's Effect to Date on Projects to Build New or Expand Existing Roads

Stakeholders who received the questionnaire were asked to identify projects to build new roads or expand existing ones that (1) had completed one or more major steps in the permitting process and (2) had been active in the planning process since the MSHCP was adopted but had not yet completed a major step in the permitting process.[15] For projects in the first category, the MSHCP's effect can be examined for discrete components of the permitting process that have been completed subsequent to the MSHCP's adoption. Transportation projects can take many years to permit, however, and the experience with projects that have completed some or all of the major steps of the permitting process to date may not represent the MSHCP's full effects. For example, as suggested earlier, larger and more-complex road and highway projects may not yet have made substantial progress through the permitting process, but it may be these larger projects that the MSHCP benefits. It is thus also important to examine perceptions about how the MSHCP has affected the permitting process for the second group of projects. We list the projects that respondents identified in each category and then report the perceived effect on the time needed to complete the permitting process.

---

[15] A project to expand existing or build new roads was considered to have completed a major step in the permitting process if it had completed any or all of the following: (1) satisfied the requirements of the MSHCP, (2) obtained a dredge-and-fill permit from USACE or a streambed alteration agreement from CDFG, or (3) obtained all necessary permits and final approvals to proceed with project construction (i.e., completed environmental review, obtained a grading permit).

Transportation Projects Identified in the Questionnaire Responses

As shown in Table 8.3, questionnaire respondents identified 22 road projects that had completed one or more steps in the permitting process since the MSHCP was adopted in June 2004 and 11 projects that had been active in the permitting process since the MSHCP was adopted but had not yet completed a major step in the process.

Table 8.3
Transportation Projects Identified by Questionnaire Respondents

Project	Location
A. Projects that had completed one or more major steps in the permitting process since the MSHCP was adopted	
Clinton Keith Road, Antelope to SR-79	Murrieta
DePalma Avenue, Temescal Wash	Lake Elsinore
Greenwald Avenue	Lake Elsinore
I-10 bridge repair	Beaumont
I-15 interchange	Temecula
Ivy Street Bridge	Murrieta
Lincoln Avenue	Lake Elsinore
Nason Street and I-60	Moreno Valley
Nichols Road	Lake Elsinore
Nobel Creek I-10 Bridge	Beaumont
Oak Valley Parkway and Noble Creek Bridge	Beaumont
Pechanga Parkway	Temecula
Ramona Expressway widening, Bridge Street to Sanderson	San Jacinto
Rice Road and Leon Road Bridges over Salt Creek	Menifee
River Road Bridge over Santa Ana River	Northwest Riverside County
Sanderson Avenue widening, Esplanade to Ramona Expressway	San Jacinto
Scott Road, Antelope to Briggs	Murrieta
SR-79, Hunter to Thompson	Southwest Riverside County
SR-79, Thompson to Whispering Heights	Southwest Riverside County
State Street Road	Hemet
Van Buren Bridge over Santa Ana River	Northwest Riverside County
SR-243 widening	Mountain Center

Table 8.3—Continued

Project	Location
B. Projects that have been active in the planning process since the MSHCP was adopted but have not completed major steps in the permitting process	
Bundy Canyon and Scott Road, I-215 to I-15	Lake Elsinore
Clinton Keith Road/I-15 interchange	Southwest Riverside County
I-15 French Valley Parkway interchange	Temecula
Limonite Avenue/I-15 interchange	Northwest Riverside County
Mid County Parkway	Various
Murrieta Road, McCall to Ethanae	Sun City
Oak Valley Parkway/I-10 interchange	Beaumont
Potrero Boulevard interchange on SR-60 (1 mile west of I-10/SR-60 junction)	Beaumont
Scott Road/I-215 interchange	Southwest Riverside County
SR-79 realignment	Murrieta
Sunset grade separation	Banning

Projects that have completed major steps in the permitting process differ in important ways from projects that have not. Table 8.4 summarizes key characteristics of the projects that fall into each category, based on questionnaire responses.[16] Caltrans projects tend to be larger than non-Caltrans projects, and, as might be expected, Caltrans projects account for a smaller share of the respondent-project pairs for projects that have completed major steps in the permitting process than for projects that have not completed major steps in the permitting process since the MSHCP was adopted.[17]

A sizable proportion of respondent-project pairs in both road categories describe projects that widen existing roads, but projects that extend existing roads or propose to build new roads on open-space land are more common among projects that have not yet completed major steps in the permitting process. Also, a greater proportion of roads in the latter category affected federally listed species. The permitting process is often expected to be more involved for projects that extend roads or affect federally

---

[16] A single respondent may report on more than one project. Likewise, more than one respondent can report on a single project. The numbers in Table 8.4 describe the percentages of the resulting respondent-project pairs. As can be seen by comparing Tables 8.2 and 8.3, 30 respondent-project pairs address the 22 projects that have completed major steps in the permitting process, and 20 respondent-project pairs address the 11 projects that have not completed major steps in the permitting process.

[17] A Caltrans project is defined as a project to construct or expand a Caltrans facility (which includes state and interstate highways) or a transportation project for which Caltrans provides oversight (e.g., a county or local road that connects to a Caltrans facility).

listed species, so it is not surprising that projects with these characteristics are more common among roads that have not completed major steps in the permitting process. Finally, Table 8.4 shows that substantial percentages of respondent-project pairs have a federal nexus whether or not the projects have completed major steps in the permitting process.[18]

Table 8.4
Characteristics of Transportation Projects Identified by Questionnaire Respondents (percentage of respondent-project pairs)

Project Characteristic	Projects That Have Completed Major Steps in Permitting Process (N = 30)	Projects That Have Not Completed Major Steps in the Permitting Process (N = 20)
A. Caltrans facility or project with Caltrans oversight		
Yes	37	75
No	60	25
Do not know	3	0
B. Project widens an existing road		
Yes	90	75
No	7	25
Do not know	3	0
C. Project extends an existing road or proposes to build a new road on open-space land		
Yes	27	65
No	67	35
Do not know	7	0
D. Project affects a federally listed species		
Yes	20	50
No	57	45
Do not know	23	5
E. Project has a federal nexus		
Yes	63	85
No	33	5
Do not know	3	10

---

[18] A transportation project has a federal nexus if it is funded by, authorized by, or carried out by a federal agency; if it crosses lands under U.S. jurisdiction (such as U.S. waters or wetlands); or if it relates to federal projects (such as interstate highways).

The results in Table 8.4 suggest that the MSHCP's effect to date on the permitting process for road-transportation projects may not be representative of the plan's ultimate effects. The projects that have completed major steps in the permitting process since the MSHCP was adopted appear to be smaller, simpler projects; larger, more-complex projects have yet to be permitted. We thus examine the MSHCP's effects separately on roads that have completed major steps in the permitting process and roads that have not. It should be acknowledged that analysis based on experience to date provides only a partial look at MSHCP effects on the permitting process. The questionnaire did ask respondents about their expectations regarding the MSHCP's effects for the next 10 years; nevertheless, a more complete analysis will need to wait until a greater number of complex projects have completed the permitting process.

Projects That Have Completed One or More Major Steps in the Permitting Process
The questionnaire asked respondents to assess the MSHCP's impact on the time needed to complete major steps in the permitting process. In particular, respondents were asked to compare

- the time needed to satisfy MSHCP requirements with the time that would have been needed to obtain a take permit in the absence of the MSHCP
- the time needed to obtain a dredge-and-fill permit or a streambed-alteration agreement relative to the time that would have been needed to obtain these permits in the absence of the MSHCP
- the time needed to receive all required authorizations for the project to proceed relative to the time that would have been required in the absence of the MSHCP.

The perceived effects of the MSHCP on each of the steps in the permitting process are presented next.

Time Savings on Take Permit. Table 8.5 summarizes the perceived effect of the MSHCP on the time needed to obtain a take permit. Take permits are required only when a project affects listed species, so respondents were asked to compare the time needed to satisfy MSHCP requirements (and thus benefit from the take permit issued pursuant to MSHCP) with the time needed to obtain a take permit in the absence of the MSHCP for projects that affect listed species. In the absence of the MSHCP, project applicants would need to obtain a take permit either through a Section 7 consultation with USFWS (if the project has a federal nexus) or set up an HCP through Section 10 of the ESA (if the project does not have a federal nexus). As shown in panel A of Table 8.5, respondents identified only six respondent-project pairs that address federally listed species and have satisfied MSHCP requirements so far. Nevertheless, for the most part, the respondents believed that the MSHCP reduced the time needed for this part of the permitting process for these projects. Time was reduced for five of

Table 8.5
MSHCP Effect on Time Needed to Obtain Take Permit for Projects That Have Completed Major Steps in the Permitting Process (respondent-project pairs)

Effect	All Projects	Caltrans Project	
		Yes	No
A. Projects that affect federally listed species: time needed to satisfy MSHCP requirements compared to time needed to obtain take permit if there were no MSHCP			
Increased > 3 months	1	—	—
Made little or no difference	0	—	—
Reduced > 3 months	5	—	—
Reduced 3 months to 1 year	0	—	—
Reduced 1 to 2 years	3	—	—
Reduced 2 to 5 years	1	—	—
Reduced > 5 years	0	—	—
Allowed a project to proceed that otherwise would not	1	—	—
Do not know	0	—	—
Responses	N = 6	—	—
B. Projects that do not affect federally listed species: time added to project due to MSHCP requirements			
Little or none	7	3	4
4 to 12 months	2	1	1
Do not know	8	3	5
Responses	N = 17	N = 7	N = 10

NOTE: — = response not reported due to small sample size.

the six project-respondent pairs. The time savings reported varied between one and five years, and, in one case, the respondent believed that the MSHCP allowed a project to proceed that otherwise would not. The MSHCP was not thought to accelerate this part of the permitting process in all cases; one respondent identified a project for which he or she believed that it took more than three months longer to satisfy MSHCP requirements than it would have taken to obtain a take permit without the MSHCP.

Satisfying MSHCP requirements thus appears to typically take less time than obtaining a take permit through the ESA Section 7 or Section 10 processes when the project affects federally listed species. However, the MSHCP may add extra time to projects when the project does not affect federally listed species. In these cases, a take permit is not required, and satisfying MSHCP requirements adds extra steps that would not be necessary in the absence of the MSHCP. Those completing the questionnaire did identify 17 projects that had completed major steps in the permitting process and did not affect federally listed species, but the time added due to MSHCP requirements was not thought to be great. Respondents believed that the MSHCP had little or no effect on seven of the cases, versus only two for which the MSHCP was thought to have increased time by between four and 12 months. There was considerable uncertainty about whether the MSHCP added time to the permitting process for projects that did not affect federally listed species—nearly half of the respondents answered that they did not know.

Table 8.5 and subsequent tables report responses broken down by whether the project is a Caltrans project and whether the project affects federally listed species. Sample sizes are too small to support statistical analysis of whether differences in MSHCP effects are due, for example, to whether the project is a Caltrans project, holding other project attributes constant. We report these breakdowns, however, for a number of reasons. First, some of the questions discussed were asked separately for Caltrans and non-Caltrans projects, and reporting results by Caltrans status allows readers to compare responses across these questions. Second, while differences in MSHCP effects by project attribute may not be statistically significant, they do suggest several relationships that warrant future analysis. As will be seen, respondent evaluations of the MSHCP's effect differ depending on whether the project affects federally listed species. For example, Table 8.5 suggests that the MSHCP has greater benefits for projects affecting federally listed species than for those that do not. Caltrans projects are typically larger and more complex than non-Caltrans projects, and breaking down responses by Caltrans status may provide evidence that the MSHCP has greater benefits for larger, more complex projects. In the case of Table 8.5, however, the small number of responses in panel A does not support a breakdown of responses for Caltrans and non-Caltrans projects, and the differences between Caltrans and non-Caltrans projects in the bottom panel of the table are minor.[19] Sample sizes in many of the tables are larger, allowing more-meaningful comparison between larger and smaller projects and projects that do and do not affect listed species.

Time Savings on Dredge-and-Fill Permit or Streambed-Alteration Agreement. The MSHCP appears, on the whole, to have reduced the time needed to obtain a dredge-and-fill permit or a streambed-alteration agreement, although the results are mixed. As shown in the "All Projects" column of panel A of Table 8.6, there are 21 project-respondent observations for projects that have obtained a dredge-and-fill permit or a streambed-alteration agreement since the MSHCP was adopted. In one-third of the cases (seven of 21) respondents could not say whether the MSHCP increased or decreased the time needed to obtain the permit. Of the remaining

---

[19] Caltrans status and the presence of federally listed species are not correlated. For projects that have completed major steps in the permitting projects, about 20 percent of Caltrans projects affect federally listed species, and about 20 percent of non-Caltrans projects affect federally listed species. For projects that have not completed major steps in the permitting process, the percentages are both about 50 percent.

Table 8.6
MSHCP's Effect to Date on Transportation Projects That Have Completed Major Steps in the Permitting Process (project-respondent pairs)

Effect	All Projects	Federally Listed Species		Caltrans Project	
		Yes	No	Yes	No
A. MSHCP's effect on time needed to obtain a dredge-and-fill permit or a streambed-alteration agreement					
Increased > 3 months	1	1	0	0	1
Made little or no difference	5	0	5	5	0
Reduced > 3 months	8	4	4	4	4
Reduced 3 months to 1 year	4	0	4	2	2
Reduced 1 to 2 years	2	2	0	1	1
Reduced 2 to 5 years	1	1	0	1	0
Reduced > 5 years	0	0	0	0	0
Allowed a project to proceed that otherwise would not	1	1	0	0	1
Do not know	7	0	0	2	4
Responses	N = 21	N = 5	N = 9	N = 11	N = 9
B. MSHCP's effect on time needed to receive all authorizations					
Increased > 3 months	1	0	1	0	1
Made little or no difference	6	0	6	5	1
Reduced > 3 months	9	4	5	4	5
Reduced 3 months to 1 year	5	0	5	2	3
Reduced 1 to 2 years	3	3	0	1	2
Reduced 2 to 5 years	1	1	0	1	0
Reduced > 5 years	0	0	0	0	0
Allowed a project to proceed that otherwise would not	0	0	0	0	0
Do not know	0	0	0	0	0
Responses	N = 16	N = 4	N = 12	N = 9	N = 7

14 cases, respondents in about half (eight of 14) believed that the MSHCP had reduced the time. There was one case in which the MSHCP was thought to have increased the time needed to obtain this permit. Comparison of the responses for projects that affect federally listed species with those that do not suggests that MSHCP benefits in obtaining dredge-and-fill permits or streambed-alteration agreements are greater for projects that affect federally listed species, although the sample sizes are small.

Savings in Time Needed to Obtain All Project Authorizations. Questionnaire respondents identified a number of transportation projects that had obtained all necessary permits and authorizations to expand existing roads or build new roads since the MSHCP was adopted. As shown in panel B of Table 8.6, the respondents believed that the MSHCP had reduced the overall time needed to obtain all required permits and authorizations in the majority (nine of 16) of cases reported. However, the amount of time saved for transportation projects that have completed the permitting process to date was not large; the most common response describing savings was three months to one year, followed by savings of between one and two years. The MSHCP was believed to have made little difference in about one-third of the projects (six of 16) and slowed the permitting process by at least three months in one of the projects reported. Again, the time savings that the MSHCP affords appear more pronounced for projects that affect federally listed species; the permitting process was accelerated for all four project-respondent pairs involving federally listed species compared with less than half the transportation project-respondent pairs that did not involve federally listed species. Examples of such projects include Clinton Keith Road in the southern part of western Riverside County and the River Road bridge over the Santa Ana River.

Projects That Have Not Completed One or More Major Steps in the Permitting Process

The responses to the questionnaire suggest that, on the whole, the MSHCP has reduced time for permitting transportation projects that are active in the process but have *not* yet completed major steps in that process. Respondents reported 20 project-respondent pairs for such roads, and these projects were mainly Caltrans projects and mainly projects to extend existing roads or build new roads (see Table 8.4).

As reported in the second column of panel A in Table 8.7, respondents believed that the MSHCP has decreased the uncertainty of the permitting process in a majority of cases (11 of 20), even though the MSHCP was thought to have increased uncertainty in four of 20 cases.[20] Similarly, the MSHCP was thought to increase the likelihood that the project would ultimately receive all the required authorizations in the majority of cases, in contrast to only one case in which it was believed to have decreased the likelihood (panel B). As shown in panel C, the MSHCP was thought to have accelerated the

---

[20] *Uncertainty of the permitting process* describes the lack of clear understanding about what is required of the project proponent and the unpredictability of outcomes, including whether and when a permit will be granted.

Table 8.7
MSHCP's Effect to Date on Transportation Projects That Have Not Completed Major Steps in the Permitting Process (project-respondent pairs)

Effect	All Projects	Federally Listed Species		Caltrans Project	
		Yes	No	Yes	No
A. MSHCP's effect on uncertainty of authorization process so far					
Decreased	11	6	4	8	3
Increased	4	2	2	3	1
Not changed	3	1	2	2	1
Do not know	2	1	1	2	0
B. MSHCP's effect on the likelihood that the project will ultimately receive required authorizations					
Increased	12	7	4	10	2
Decreased	1	0	1	0	1
Not changed	6	3	3	4	2
Do not know	1	0	1	1	0
C. MSHCP's effect on time needed to obtain authorizations so far					
Accelerated	9	6	3	9	0
Slowed	3	1	2	2	1
Not changed	5	1	3	3	2
Do not know	3	2	1	1	2
D. MSHCP's effect on the cost of the authorization process so far					
Decreased	5	1	3	4	1
Increased	6	2	4	4	2
Not changed	2	1	1	1	1
Do not know	7	6	1	6	1
Responses	N = 20	N = 10	N = 9	N = 15	N = 5

permitting process in nine of 20 cases, substantially more than the number of cases for which it had slowed the permitting process (three cases). The Mid County Parkway and the realignment of SR-79 are examples of projects that respondents cited as having benefited from the MSHCP.

While the MSHCP, on the whole, appears to have increased the predictability of the permitting process, increased the probability that projects will receive the required authorizations, and reduced the time needed to obtain the required permits, it does not appear to have reduced the cost of the permitting process and, if anything, may have increased it. As illustrated by panel D in Table 8.7, respondents reported that the MSHCP has increased the cost of the permitting process in more cases than it had reduced (six versus five of the 20 cases). At least two caveats should be kept in mind when interpreting the responses related to cost. First, whether the MSHCP permitting cost's overall effect is positive or negative will depend on the relative size of the cost changes and the proportion of projects showing changes. Second, it is conceivable that the MSHCP has caused a higher percentage of total permitting costs to be incurred earlier in the permitting process, while savings that might accrue later are as yet undetected. Respondents were asked to assess the MSHCP's effects on the costs of the permitting process so far. Their assessment may be different once the permitting process for these projects is complete.

Consistent with our findings for projects that have completed major steps in the permitting process, the responses to the questionnaire suggest that the MSHCP's benefits in terms of time savings and certainty are greater for projects that affect federally listed species (see third and fourth columns of Table 8.7). Even so, the MSHCP still appears, on the whole, to positively affect the permitting time and certainty of projects that do not involve federally listed species.

The last set of columns in Table 8.6 suggests that MSHCP benefits are greater for Caltrans projects than non-Caltrans projects. This result suggests that MSHCP benefits may be greater for larger, more-complex projects. The sample size for non-Caltrans projects is small, however, and other factors (such as the existence of federally listed species) have not been controlled for in comparing Caltrans versus non-Caltrans projects. Thus, observations on the effect of a project's Caltrans status are only tentative.

The MSHCP's Effect to Date on Road Saftey and Maintenance Projects

Road safety and maintenance projects are exempt from review for consistency with the MSHCP and thus may move more quickly through the permitting process.[21] Even if the time saved to permit each project is modest, the overall effects may be large when accumulated over the potentially large number of safety and maintenance projects in western Riverside County.

Most of the respondents to the questionnaire were unfamiliar with safety or maintenance projects that had obtained all the required approvals since the MSHCP was adopted. Their lack of familiarity may not be surprising, considering that safety and maintenance projects are typically of limited scope and do not draw a great deal of attention. In some cases, however, the respondents were familiar with a substantial

---

[21] Road safety and maintenance projects include a variety of projects, such as clearing brush or installing culverts in the immediate area of an existing road.

number of such projects. For example, one respondent was familiar with more than 30 safety and maintenance projects on non-Caltrans facilities.

By and large, the five respondents who could assess the MSHCP's effect on the permitting process for road safety and maintenance projects believed that the MSHCP reduced the time needed to obtain all project authorizations relative to the time that would have been required without the MSHCP. As shown Table 8.8, the typical time savings was three months to one year per project.[22] One respondent reported that the MSHCP did not typically save time for Caltrans safety and maintenance projects, but no one reported time increases. It should be recognized that respondents were asked for typical time savings and that savings should be expected to vary across projects.

The MSHCP's Effect to Date on Development Projects

Our analysis thus far has focused on road-transportation projects. We now turn to the perceived effect of the MSHCP to date on development projects—namely, commercial, industrial, or residential projects for which roads may also be included but are not the primary project element. Many respondents were familiar with development projects that had obtained all the required authorizations since the MSHCP was adopted, and some respondents were familiar with a substantial number of such projects. Because

Table 8.8
Typical Effect of the MSHCP on Time Needed to Permit Road Safety and Maintenance Projects (respondents answering question)

Typical Effect of the MSHCP Relative to No MSHCP	Caltrans Projects	Non-Caltrans Projects
Increase > 3 months	0	0
Little or no difference	1	0
Reduce > 3 months	3	3
Reduce 3 to 6 months	0	1
Reduce 6 months to 1 year	3	2
Reduce 1 to 2 years	0	0
Reduce > 2 years	0	0
Allowed a project to proceed that otherwise would not	0	0
Do not know	1	2
Responses	N = 5	N = 5

_____

[22] The effect on road and maintenance projects was asked separately for Caltrans and non-Caltrans projects, and the results cannot readily be combined to produce a response for all safety and maintenance projects.

permitting requirements are often more stringent for projects that affect larger areas of land, respondents were asked for their experiences with projects on more than five acres and projects on five acres or less.[23]

Respondents were asked to provide a rough estimate of the percentage of development projects that had obtained all required authorizations since the MSHCP was adopted that fell into various time-savings categories. Table 8.9 shows the average percentage reported in each time-savings category for the respondents completing the question, separately for larger and smaller development projects.[24]

While the responses to the questionnaire suggest that, on the whole, the MSHCP speeds the permitting of transportation projects, the benefits for development projects, at least so far, appear limited. As shown in the last column of Table 8.9, respondents who were familiar with development projects that had obtained all required authorizations, on average, perceived that the MSHCP increased the time needed to do so for

Table 8.9
The MSHCP's Effect on Time Needed to Obtain All Required Permits and Approvals for Development Projects (average percentage of projects in each time-savings category)

Effect	Development Projects on 5 Acres or Less	Development Projects on More Than 5 Acres
Increase > 3 months	18	36
Little or no difference	42	30
Reduce > 3 months	39	34
Reduce 3 months to 1 year	16	3
Reduce 1 to 2 years	17	21
Reduce 2 to 5 years	5	9
Reduce > 5 years	0	<0.5
Allowed a project to proceed that otherwise would not	0	1
Do not know	2	<0.5
Responses	N = 6	N = 11

---

[23] The permitting steps required typically depend on various project considerations, including project size. For example, certain projects avoid potentially lengthy environmental review when they affect five acres or less, are within city limits, are surrounded by substantially urban uses, and do not affect habitat for protected species. Such projects are often categorically exempt from detailed CEQA review. With these regulations in mind, we set the cut-point between larger and smaller development projects in our study at five acres.

[24] This calculation weights each questionnaire respondent equally, even though one respondent may have been familiar with more development projects than others. Respondents who did not answer the question are excluded from the calculation.

larger projects more often than it reduced it. The time to obtain permits was increased by more than three months for 36 percent of the larger projects on average, was reduced for 34 percent, and showed little or no difference for 30 percent of projects reported. Results were only slightly more positive for smaller development projects. There was at least one development project that respondents believed would not have proceeded without the MSHCP (corresponding to the 1-percent average in the last column of Table 8.9). Overall, however, it appears that stakeholders perceive that the MSHCP has slowed the permitting process for a substantial proportion of development projects and has made little difference for a sizable percentage as well.

Limits on questionnaire complexity and respondent burden did not allow us to ask respondents to distinguish between development projects that did and did not affect federally listed species or to inquire about how frequently the development projects of which they were aware affected federally listed species. The responses in Table 8.9 thus may include development projects that affect federally listed species and those that do not. It is possible that the projects for which the MSHCP reduced permitting time are those that affected federally listed species and those for which the MSHCP had a negative or no impact on time savings are those that did not affect federally listed species. Additional information is needed to investigate this possibility.

The MSHCP's Effect to Date on Lawsuits

The MSHCP may accelerate the placement of road and development projects in part by reducing litigation during the project-authorization process. To evaluate the MSHCP's effect on litigation so far, respondents were asked to assess the extent to which the MSHCP has reduced the scope of lawsuits intended to stop or modify transportation and development projects that have been active since the MSHCP was adopted compared to what likely would have been the case for the same projects had the MSHCP not been in place. Respondents were asked to assess the MSHCP's litigation effects for five categories of projects:

- Caltrans projects to expand existing roads
- Caltrans projects to build new roads
- non-Caltrans projects to expand existing roads
- non-Caltrans projects to build new roads
- development projects.

The effect of any reduced (or expanded) litigation due to the MSHCP may be reflected in results presented on the MSHCP's effect on the time needed to complete the permitting process. However, in answering such questions, respondents may have ignored any contribution that the MSHCP has made to reducing litigation delays, particularly if there had been no litigation involving the project. Thus, any contributions the MSHCP makes to reducing litigation may result in the acceleration of transportation and development projects beyond effects discussed so far.

As shown in Table 8.10, sizable percentages of the respondents who answered questions on the MSHCP's litigation effect believed that the plan had reduced the number or scope of lawsuits intended to stop or modify projects; six of eight respondents who could answer the question believed that the MSHCP has either probably or definitely averted or reduced the scope of some lawsuits for Caltrans projects that expand existing roads, and five of seven believed that the plan probably or definitely averted lawsuits for Caltrans projects to build new roads.[25] The responses were somewhat less positive for the smaller, less complex, non-Caltrans projects, but the majority who responded still believed that the MSHCP had definitely or probably averted lawsuits. Consistent with previous results, respondents were less optimistic about the MSHCP's benefits for development projects. About half the respondents (six of 13) believed that the MSHCP had no effect on litigation; only about half (six of 13) thought that the MSHCP probably or definitely averted or reduced the scope of some lawsuits. One respondent believed that the MSHCP probably had caused additional lawsuits or increased the scope of lawsuits in each project category. Even so, the results still suggest that the MSHCP has, on the whole, reduced the amount of litigation for development projects.

Table 8.10
The MSHCP's Effect on Lawsuits Intended to Stop or Modify Projects Since the MSHCP Was Adopted (respondents answering question)

| Effect | Caltrans Projects | | Non-Caltrans Projects | | |
	Expand Existing Roads	Build New Roads	Expand Existing Roads	Build New Roads	Development Projects
Definitely averted or reduced scope of some lawsuits	1	1	1	2	2
Probably averted or reduced scope of some lawsuits	5	4	5	5	4
Did not avert or reduce scope of any lawsuits	2	2	3	3	6
Probably caused additional lawsuits or increased scope of lawsuits	0	0	1	1	1
Responses	N = 8	N = 7	N = 10	N = 11	N = 13

[25] This question asked respondents to check all answers that apply. However, every respondent who answered the question checked only one answer. It is likely that at least some respondents did not notice the instruction to check all answers that apply.

Expected Future Effects of the MSHCP on Transportation and Development Projects

Our analysis so far has been restricted to stakeholder assessments of the MSHCP's effect to date. The MSHCP has been in place for only four years, however, and may generate greater benefits in the future than observed to date. Future benefits may be greater as agencies and developers work through issues associated with the implementation of the MSHCP and as more projects proceed through the permitting process entirely under the MSHCP regime as opposed to partly under the pre-MSHCP regime.

To elicit expectations about the MSHCP's future benefits, the questionnaire asked respondents to forecast the MSHCP's effect on the average time needed to obtain all necessary permits for projects expected in the next 10 years relative to what the average time would have been without the MSHCP. Table 8.11 shows that nearly three-quarters of respondents expect the MSHCP to reduce permitting times for Caltrans projects that expand existing roads or build new roads (eight of 11 in each case). The responses are comparable to the responses for Caltrans projects that are currently active but have not completed major steps in the permitting process (see the penultimate column of Table 8.7) and suggest that respondents, by and large, expect the MSHCP to benefit the permitting process for Caltrans projects. Time reductions range between

Table 8.11
Expected Effect of the MSHCP on Average Time Needed to Obtain All Required Permits and Approvals in the Next 10 Years (respondents answering question)

Effect	Caltrans Projects		Non-Caltrans Projects		
	Expand Existing Roads	Build New Roads	Expand Existing Roads	Build New Roads	Development Projects
Increase > 3 months	2	2	4	5	6
Little or no difference	1	1	2	0	2
Reduce > 3 months	8	8	7	8	6
Reduce 3 months to 1 year	2	2	2	1	3
Reduce 1 to 2 years	4	2	3	5	1
Reduce 2 to 5 years	2	3	2	2	2
Reduce > 5 years	0	1	0	0	0
Allowed a project to proceed that otherwise would not	0	0	0	0	0
Do not know	0	0	0	0	0
Responses	N = 11	N = 11	N = 13	N = 13	N = 14

three months and five years, and one respondent believed that the average permitting time for Caltrans new road projects would decline by more than five years.

There is more variation in the MSHCP's perceived effects for non-Caltrans projects. Substantial proportions of respondents (four of 13 and five of 13 for projects that expand existing roads and build new roads, respectively) believe that the MSHCP will increase the average length of the permitting process for non-Caltrans projects, compared to seven and eight of 13 who think it will reduce the average time.

There is little agreement among respondents that the MSHCP will reduce permitting-process time for development projects on average in the next 10 years. As many respondents believed that the MSHCP would increase permitting time, on average, as believed would decrease it (six each). These responses are comparable to the perceived effect of the MSHCP on development projects to date (see Table 8.11).

Turning to expected effects on future litigation, questionnaire respondents, by and large, believe that the MSHCP will reduce litigation for projects that are expected in the next 10 years. Table 8.12 indicates that eight of nine respondents believed that the MSHCP will either somewhat or greatly reduce the likelihood of lawsuits concerning Caltrans projects in the next 10 years.[26] Consistent with previous findings, the share drops somewhat for non-Caltrans projects and still more for development projects. However, even for development projects, just over half (seven of 13) believe that the MSHCP will somewhat or greatly reduce the likelihood of lawsuits for projects expected in the next 10 years. Moreover, in contrast to the results for the MSHCP's

Table 8.12
Expected Effect of the MSHCP on Likelihood of Lawsuits in the Next 10 Years (respondents answering question)

Effect on Likelihood of Lawsuits	Caltrans Projects		Non-Caltrans Projects		
	Expand Existing Roads	Build New Roads	Expand Existing Roads	Build New Roads	Development Projects
Greatly reduce	3	1	4	3	2
Somewhat reduce	5	7	5	5	5
Have no effect	1	1	2	2	5
Somewhat increase	0	0	0	1	0
Greatly increase	0	0	1	1	1
Responses	N = 9	N = 9	N = 12	N = 12	N = 13

---

[26] This question asked respondents to check all answers that apply. However, every respondent who answered the question checked only one answer. It is likely that at least some respondents did not notice the instruction to check all answers that apply.

effect on average time savings, few respondents believed that that the MSHCP would somewhat or greatly increase the likelihood of lawsuits for any project type.

The MSHCP's Effect on Mobility in Western Riverside County

So far, we have presented our findings on the perceived benefits of the MSHCP on the permitting process. But this analysis can be turned around to assess what would happen if the plan were abandoned. If the plan were revoked, the permitting process for many roadway projects would likely lengthen, our research suggesting by up to five years. There would also be increased delays in the many road safety and maintenance projects that are planned for the coming years. If the plan were abandoned, the habitat-conservation process in western Riverside County would also revert to the uncoordinated, project-by-project system that existed before the MSHCP.

Delaying the placement of transportation infrastructure in western Riverside County will reduce mobility in the area. To better understand how large these reductions might be, we used a detailed computer model of the transportation network to quantify the mobility effects of delays in the completion of four major transportation corridors that resulted from the Community and Environmental Transportation Acceptability Process (CETAP) in western Riverside County. As detailed in Appendix E, our analysis suggests that delaying the four CETAP corridors will cause travel speeds in western Riverside County to decline more rapidly than they would otherwise. The effects on individual trips may not be large, but they can add up when aggregated across all trips taken in a year. Average speeds do not change by more than 1 or 2 miles per hour, but the cost to drivers can total hundreds of millions of dollars annually.

Conclusion

Overall, the findings on the MSHCP's effect on the permitting process for road-transportation projects are encouraging. Projects that affect federally listed species appear to benefit the most from the MSHCP. Stakeholders indicated that the MSHCP had accelerated the permitting process for all such projects with which they were familiar that had completed major steps in the permitting process since the MSHCP was adopted. Savings in time ranged from one to five years, and, in some cases, the MSHCP was thought to have allowed a project to proceed that would not have been allowed to proceed otherwise. The perceived benefits for projects affecting federally listed species that had not yet completed major steps in the permitting process were also substantial: Stakeholders believed that the MSHCP increased the chance that the project would receive all the required authorizations and accelerated the permitting process in substantial majorities of the cases reported.

The MSHCP's effect on road-transportation projects that do not affect federally listed species were seen, on the whole, as positive but does not appear to be large and, in some cases, is negative. For example, for such projects that have not completed major steps in the permitting process, stakeholders reported roughly equal numbers of cases in which the MSHCP had (1) accelerated the permitting process, (2) slowed the process, or (3) had no effect on the process.

The MSHCP's benefits also extend to road safety and maintenance projects. While the amount of time saved was not thought to be great for such projects (typically six months to one year), the large number of such projects can cause the aggregate time savings across all safety and maintenance projects to be substantial.

A sizable majority of stakeholders believe that the MSHCP has reduced the number or scope of lawsuits that seek to stop or modify road projects since the MSHCP was adopted. While the consequences of this reduction may be reflected, to some degree, in stakeholder estimates of the degree to which the MSHCP has accelerated the permitting process, the reduced litigation may also add to the quantitative estimates of time savings.

On the downside, our investigation suggests that the MSHCP has increased the cost of the permitting process, at least in some cases to date. Stakeholders reported that, for roads that have not yet completed major steps in the permitting process, the MSHCP increased the cost of the permitting process more frequently than it decreased the cost. The MSHCP presumably reduces the cost of obtaining the required authorizations for road safety and maintenance projects because it exempts such projects from review for consistency with the MSHCP; however, we could not investigate the magnitude of such savings or whether the MSHCP adds to or reduces project-permitting costs across all projects.

Stakeholders generally expect the MSHCP's benefits to continue for road projects for the next 10 years. The acceleration of the permitting process and the reduction in lawsuits are, by and large, expected to be somewhat greater than have been observed to date. Time savings are frequently expected to run from one to five years, and expected time savings of more than five years were reported.

While the MSHCP appears to provide benefits for many road projects, findings for the effect on development projects are not so positive. Stakeholders reported that the MSHCP has increased the time needed to obtain required permits as frequently as it has reduced it for development projects on more than five acres, and they expect similar outcomes for development projects in the next 10 years. The findings suggest that the MSHCP has, on the whole, reduced the frequency and scope of lawsuits over development projects, but the effect's magnitude is lower than for road projects.

The MSHCP is still relatively new, and the analysis in this chapter provides an early look at its effect on the permitting process. The extent to which the MSHCP actually facilitates the placement of infrastructure will be much clearer over the next three or four years, as major infrastructure projects, such as the Mid County Parkway, work their way through the permitting process. The plan's benefits may also change over time for a number of reasons. First, stakeholders will become more familiar with the process, potentially speeding it up. Second, there may be fewer points of contention between the resource agencies and permittees as the habitat-conservation goals for the plan are achieved (see Appendix F for a discussion of how permitting requirements will change once the reserve is assembled and species objectives are met). Finally, the plan's benefits may grow as economic growth continues in western Riverside County in the long term. The permitting process without the plan in place would likely become increasingly onerous as the amount of open space declines. The analysis presented in this chapter can serve as a baseline against which future assessments of MSHCP benefits can be compared.

CHAPTER NINE

Conclusion

Western Riverside County's MSHCP is an ambitious effort intended both to stream-line the approval process for transportation and development projects and to protect the habitat needed to support threatened and endangered species in a more coordi-nated way. This monograph has examined several issues related to the cost, revenue sources, and plan benefits. In this concluding chapter, we offer overall observations on the findings and identify issues that the RCA Board of Directors, RCA staff, and stakeholders should address moving forward.

Value of Land Needed for the Reserve

Our analysis shows that, as of mid-2007, the value of the land comprising a reserve of 153,000 acres was substantially higher than projected when the MSHCP was adopted. Back in 2003, the value of land needed for the reserve was put at approximately $15,200 per acre (or $2.3 billion in total in 2007 dollars). Our analysis suggests that, as of mid-2007, the land comprising the reserve was valued at about $29,300 per acre ($4.5 bil-lion), approximately double the initial estimate. This average includes the value of land already purchased as well as that remaining to be purchased. The land remaining to be purchased averages roughly $36,000 per acre. While not nearly as substantial, the projected cost of implementing the plan and operating the reserve has also increased by nearly $350 million, or about 35 percent, since the initial forecasts were made.

The substantial increase in the projected cost of assembling and operating the reserve raises concern that current revenue sources may be inadequate to fund the plan. The overall cost of assembling the reserve, however, depends not on the level of land prices in mid-2007 but on the trajectory of land value over time and the time frame in which RCA acquires the land needed for the reserve. The financial consequences of different price trajectories and purchase strategies can be enormous. For example, if the current downturn in housing prices causes land values to retreat substantially from the $35,000 average in mid-2007 and if RCA buys a substantial amount of land during the downturn, then reserve-assembly costs could be considerably lower than estimates based on mid-2007 values. If, on the other hand, RCA purchases the land over a long period and land prices continue to appreciate at historic rates, then the ultimate costs of assembling the reserve could be far greater than estimates based on mid-2007 prices.

Land-Acquisition Strategy

It is impossible to predict with certainty how the price of the land needed for the reserve will evolve over time. To address this uncertainty, we constructed a wide range of price scenarios based on economic theory and historic trends in land prices. We then investigated the consequences of different land-acquisition strategies. While it is desirable to spread purchases over a long period in some land-price scenarios, the preferred strategy overall is to acquire the land in about 10 years. Acquiring land over the next decade is desirable because the financial risks of spreading land purchases over a much longer period are substantial, while the potentially excess costs of buying land too quickly are not nearly as large.

Assembling the remaining acreage needed for the reserve over 10 years would entail a considerable acceleration in land acquisitions. Land acquisitions during the first three years of plan operation (2005 through 2007) averaged approximately 5,500 acres per year. Acquisitions would need to increase to nearly 12,000 acres per year to acquire the remaining 118,000 acres in 10 years.

Our findings also suggest that it would be preferable for RCA to set annual land-acquisition goals in terms of the dollar amount of land purchased rather than the number of acres purchased. In this way, more land will be purchased when land prices are low than when they are high. This strategy appears to be especially beneficial if RCA assembles the reserve over a period of several decades but has less effect if RCA can complete assembly activities in 10 years or less.

Our analysis suggests an additional way in which RCA may be able to substantially reduce the cost of assembling the reserve. We found that the land needed for the linkages between core habitat areas is disproportionately expensive because it runs through heavily developed areas and includes many parcels that have already been developed. Modifying the linkages to avoid existing development could reduce the total reserve-assembly costs by as much as 25 percent. In addition, rerouting linkages outside the criteria area would require an amendment to the plan, which can be a time-consuming and contentious process. Whether linkages could be modified without degrading the plan's ecological integrity would need to be investigated. However, rerouting the linkages away from already-developed parcels warrants careful consideration, given the magnitude of the potential savings involved.

The Adequacy of Revenues to Fund the Plan

Review of the sources of revenues for the plan raises two main issues: the timing of revenues relative to expenditures and the overall adequacy of revenues. Regarding the first issue, the expected receipts from revenue sources that are already in place do not line up well with a strategy of acquiring land in a relatively compressed time frame. RCA's projected annual revenues peak at approximately $40 million per year in the next few years, before falling to between $25 million and $30 million through 2035, and then to between $15 million and $20 million through 2079. To finance acquisition of the reserve in a relatively short period, RCA will need to pursue financial strategies that allow it to decouple annual expenditures from annual revenues. Strategies that would enable this include bonding against future revenue streams or borrowing funds with repayments made over time from ongoing revenues.

Regarding the overall adequacy of revenue, our analysis does not allow us to conclude with certainty whether existing revenue streams will be sufficient to finance the assembly and operation of the reserve. We project that current revenue from local sources will total between $635 million and $962 million in present value. In scenarios that combine very optimistic assumptions about land prices (from RCA's point of view) with optimistic assumptions about revenue, the present value of existing revenue streams will be adequate to cover the present value of expenditures. In less favorable scenarios in which land prices remain relatively high and revenue flows in at the low end of the projected range, the present value of revenue could fall several billion dollars short of expenditures. We cannot assign probabilities to the various outcomes but note that the factors that could lead to low land values (e.g., a drop in the housing market) could also lead to low revenues (i.e., a decline in revenue from the LDMF), decreasing the likelihood of scenarios in which current revenue sources are adequate.

To determine whether additional revenue instruments will be acquired, RCA should pay close attention to the changes in land prices over the next few years. If land prices fall substantially from the levels paid for comparable parcels in mid-2007 and RCA can purchase a substantial amount of acreage at the reduced prices, then it is conceivable that revenue from new sources will not be needed. If, on the other hand, land prices do not decline much over the next few years, it will become increasingly likely that revenue from existing instruments will be inadequate and that additional revenue sources will be required.

Additional Revenue Options

A wide range of options exists for raising additional revenue. We examined 10 additional revenue sources, including property-based revenue sources, development-based revenue sources, transportation-based revenue sources, and sales tax–based revenue sources. Estimates of the amount by which each tax or fee would need to increase to raise $1 billion on a present-value basis were provided. Each of the options considered has advantages and disadvantages in terms of equity, efficiency, and political feasibility, and policymakers will need to weigh the trade-offs in deciding what options to pursue if additional revenue is necessary.

Funding mechanisms that consider the construction of transportation facilities and habitat conservation as one integrated project offer the prospect of more-flexible funding that may reduce the cost of the overall project. For example, sources of funds that could be used both for infrastructure construction and habitat acquisition could allow RCA to accelerate reserve assembly and reduce overall land-acquisition costs. Currently, major funding sources on which RCA relies do not allow the construction of transportation infrastructure and the conservation of habitat on a fully integrated basis. Legislation at the federal or state level would be required to enable such mechanisms. Infrastructure banks could likewise offer loans that allow flexibility in the allocation of funds between construction and habitat conservation. Infrastructure banks do exist in California, but the two we identified do not provide loans large enough to make much of a difference in western Riverside County. Development of programs that integrate transportation funding and habitat conservation warrants further attention.

Prospects for Achieving the Habitat-Conservation Goals of the Reserve

To ensure the viability of species covered by the MSHCP, the plan requires that RCA conserve sufficient acreage of various habitat types spread across different regions of western Riverside County. This has been operationalized as a set of specific acreage requirements for seven distinct vegetation communities in nine subregions in the plan area, referred to as *rough-step accounting areas*.

We found that individual acreage goals cannot all be met using the USFWS CRD. That said, we found that, for all but one of the vegetation communities, the sum of the acreage in the USFWS CRD across all rough-step areas exceeded the sum of the acreage targets across all rough-step areas. In other words, while there are numerous shortfalls in specific rough-step areas, there appears to be sufficient acreage in total for most of the vegetation communities. The reserve assembled by RCA will not necessarily precisely follow the USFWS CRD. We have not examined the extent to which different reserve configurations that are consistent with the land-acquisition criteria in the MSHCP would satisfy the rough-step requirements. However, our analysis shows that one configuration, the USFWS CRD, will not meet the rough-step requirements as currently written, and it is plausible that other configurations will face similar problems. It also shows that it may be worth revisiting rough-step requirements to determine whether it is appropriate to allow some fungibility of acreage requirements across rough-step areas.

The MSHCP's Benefits for Infrastructure Construction

Our findings on the MSHCP's effect on the permitting process for transportation projects were encouraging. Stakeholders familiar with the MSHCP and the permitting process in western Riverside County indicated that the MSHCP has, so far, accelerated the permitting process in a substantial majority of the road projects that affect federally listed species and reduced the frequency or scope of lawsuits.

Our findings with respect to the MSHCP's effect on the permitting process for transportation projects, however, were not uniformly positive. First, effects appear to vary greatly across projects. For some types of projects, such as those affecting threatened or endangered species, the plan generally appears to accelerate the permitting process, but, for other types of projects, it appears to have had little impact, and, in some cases, it appears to slow the permitting process. The relatively short time since the MSHCP was adopted and the limited number of projects that have completed the permitting process under the plan make it difficult to characterize the types of projects that benefit from the plan and those that do not; further research is warranted on this subject. However, it appears that the MSHCP has so far favored permitting of transportation projects on the whole but that the gains for some projects have been offset to some extent by losses for others.

Second, while the MSHCP appears to streamline the permitting process for transportation projects on the whole, initial indications are that it has not necessarily decreased the cost of the permitting process. Attention needs to be paid to how the plan's procedures and processes might be adjusted to reduce the cost of compliance.

Finally, in contrast to transportation projects, our findings on the MSHCP's benefits for commercial, industrial, and residential projects are mixed. Stakeholders reported that the MSHCP has increased the time needed to obtain required permits as frequently as it has reduced it for development projects on more than five acres, and they expect similar outcomes for the next 10 years. It may turn out that the MSHCP's benefits for development projects will increase over time as the amount of open space in the county declines. But in any case, it is important for the RCA Board of Directors, RCA staff, and other stakeholders to examine how the MSHCP might be modified to better address development projects or at least to better communicate how the benefits of the existing plan may increase in the future.

So far, we have presented our findings on the perceived benefits of the MSCHP on the permitting process. But, this analysis can be turned around to assess what would happen if the plan were abandoned. If the plan were revoked, the permitting process for many roadway projects would likely lengthen, our research suggesting by up to five years. There would also be increased delays in the many road safety and maintenance projects that are planned for the coming years. If the plan were abandoned, the habitat-conservation process in western Riverside County would also revert to the uncoordinated, project-by-project system that existed before the MSHCP.

Delaying the placement of transportation infrastructure in western Riverside County will reduce mobility in the area. To better understand how large these reductions might be, we used a detailed computer model of the transportation network to quantify the mobility effects of delays in the completion of four major transportation corridors that resulted from CETAP in western Riverside County. Our analysis suggests that delaying the four CETAP corridors will cause travel speeds in western Riverside County to decline more rapidly than they would otherwise. The effects on individual trips may not be large, but they can add up when aggregated across all trips taken in a year. Average speeds do not change by more than 1 or 2 miles per hour, but the cost to drivers overall can total hundreds of millions of dollars annually.

Moving Forward

Our analysis has identified a number of MSHCP benefits and some areas in which improvements could be made to further the plan's goals. Based on our findings, we recommend that the RCA Board of Directors, staff, and stakeholders

- explore ways to increase the acreage obtained through the entitlement and authorization processes for private development projects
- examine how to route the linkages between the core habitat areas so as to minimize acquisition costs but meet the ecological goals for the reserve
- reexamine the rough-step requirements to determine whether they are overly prescriptive with regard to the spatial distribution of vegetative-community acreage, and explore how the rough-step accounting system could be modified to better reflect progress in achieving the plan's conservation goals
- determine the time frame in which the reserve should be completed, taking into consideration the potential financial savings of completing it within the next decade
- develop bonding or other financial strategies that allow decoupling of annual revenue and annual expenditures and that enable reserve completion in the next decade
- regularly update land-acquisition cost and revenue projections to determine whether additional revenue will be necessary
- prepare a strategy for raising additional revenue that could be implemented should additional revenue become necessary

- work with federal and state authorities to determine whether transportation and habitat-conservation funding programs could be integrated to permit more-comprehensive resource planning and investment
- investigate how to increase the plan's benefits for commercial, industrial, and residential development projects
- explore how to limit the apparent plan-induced increase in permitting costs for transportation projects.

Being proactive with respect to these issues can help ensure the plan's success and the ongoing economic and ecological health of western Riverside County.

Specification and Estimation of the Land-Value Model

Details of the methods used to estimate the land-value model and to predict parcel values are provided in this appendix.

Specification and Estimation of the Land-Value Model

The regression specification of the land-value model and the coefficient estimates and standard errors are reported in Table A.1. Note that separate models are run for each of the five land-use categories.

Because the distribution of purchase prices has a heavy right tail, we model the natural logarithm of the purchase price. Several explanatory variables are categorical (for example, year of sale or the use for which the parcel is zoned). For such variables, one category is chosen as the reference, and the categories are then specified as a series of indicator variables (variables that take on a value of 0 or 1), excluding an indicator variable for the reference category.

When developing statistical models to address problems with a spatial component—in this case, the location of parcels—it is necessary to consider potential difficulties that may arise due to the phenomenon of *spatial autocorrelation*. That is, the value of nearby parcels may be similar to one another, not just because of comparable characteristics, but also by virtue of their proximity to one another. With respect to land value, the practice of appraisers who use recent sales records for nearby parcels when estimating the value of a new parcel to be sold exacerbates the potential for correlation. Though we do not treat the problem of spatial autocorrelation in a formal manner, we do include neighborhood-level (as opposed to just parcel-specific) variables that help to mitigate the potential for error due to spatial autocorrelation (see Landis and Reilly, 2003, for a discussion of this approach).[1] We thus estimate the model using OLS without any consideration for spatial correlation.

---

[1] For instance, we include variables, such as the percentage of already-developed land within a certain radius surrounding each parcel, as well as the percentage of land that is still available for new development (these two

Table A.1
Regression Results for Land-Value Model, by Land Use (dependent variable is log of purchase price in 2007 dollars)

Characteristic	SFH		Agriculture		Other		Open Space		MFH	
	Coefficient	Standard Error	Coefficient	Standard Error	Coefficient	Standard Error	Coefficient	Standard Error	Coefficient	Standard Error
Commercial (dummy)	—	—	—	—	0.00**	0.00	—	—	—	—
Industrial (dummy)	—	—	—	—	0.38**	0.17	—	—	—	—
Owner (dummy)	—	—	—	—	—	—	—	—	-0.19**	0.02
Manufactured-home (dummy)	0.00**	0.00	—	—	—	—	—	—	-1.12**	0.04
Percentage of land within 1 mile developed	0.10**	0.01	0.71	0.54	-0.20	0.25	1.83**	0.11	0.50**	0.07
Percentage of land within 1 mile undeveloped	0.01	0.01	-0.65	0.44	-1.18**	0.24	-0.35**	0.09	-0.02	0.07
Difference in percentage of land within 2.5 and 1 miles developed	0.05**	0.01	-0.52	0.73	0.74**	0.26	1.00**	0.15	0.40**	0.08
Difference in percentage of land within 2.5 and 1 miles undeveloped	-0.25**	0.01	-0.93*	0.52	-0.34	0.27	0.06	0.13	-0.60**	0.08
Number of jobs within 30 miles (log)	0.03**	0.00	0.12**	0.03	0.00	0.02	-0.01	0.01	0.09**	0.01
Acreage (log)	0.13**	0.00	0.48**	0.06	0.00**	0.00	0.00**	0.00	0.00**	0.00
Number of bedrooms	0.13**	0.00	—	—	—	—	—	—	—	—
Slope 0–5 (dummy)	-0.02**	0.01	0.14	0.14	-0.21	0.20	0.18**	0.04	0.22**	0.06

Table A.1—Continued

Characteristic	SFH		Agriculture		Other		Open Space		MFH	
	Coefficient	Standard Error	Coefficient	Standard Error	Coefficient	Standard Error	Coefficient	Standard Error	Coefficient	Standard Error
Slope 5–10 (dummy)	-0.02**	0.01	0.05	0.18	-0.14	0.21	0.13**	0.05	0.21**	0.06
Slope 10–15 (dummy)	-0.02**	0.01	0.07	0.18	-0.17	0.21	0.16**	0.06	0.21**	0.06
Slope 15–20 (dummy)	-0.01**	0.01	-0.04	0.15	-0.12	0.20	0.18**	0.05	0.18**	0.06
Slope 20–25 (dummy)	-0.04**	0.01	0.08	0.21	-0.16	0.26	0.11*	0.06	0.14*	0.08
Slope 25–30 (dummy)	0.00	0.01	-0.08	0.25	-0.07	0.27	0.12*	0.07	0.24**	0.09
Slope 30–50 (dummy)	-0.03**	0.01	-0.09	0.15	-0.34	0.24	0.12**	0.05	0.24**	0.07
Slope 50+ (Ref)	—	—	—	—	—	—	—	—	—	—
Distance from highway (log feet)	-0.01**	0.00	-0.11	0.08	-0.09**	0.02	-0.08**	0.01	0.02**	0.01
Distance to major road (log feet)	0.03**	0.00	-0.12**	0.05	0.00	0.03	-0.10**	0.01	0.01	0.01
Distance to park (log feet)	-0.01**	0.00	0.03	0.07	0.06**	0.02	-0.07**	0.01	0.00	0.01
Distance to sewer (log feet)	0.01**	0.00	0.00	0.04	-0.03**	0.01	-0.02**	0.01	-0.02**	0.00
Within a city annex (dummy)	-0.09**	0.00	-0.38**	0.18	0.27**	0.13	-0.02	0.04	0.19**	0.03
Within city boundary (dummy)	-0.08**	0.00	-0.34*	0.19	0.5**	0.09	0.14**	0.04	0.16**	0.02
Within a flood zone (dummy)	-0.04**	0.00	0.15	0.17	-0.06	0.05	0.27**	0.04	0.03*	0.02

Table A.1—Continued

Characteristic	SFH		Agriculture		Other		Open Space		MFH	
	Coefficient	Standard Error	Coefficient	Standard Error	Coefficient	Standard Error	Coefficient	Standard Error	Coefficient	Standard Error
Presence of conserved land (dummy)	−0.02*	0.01	−0.04	0.25	−0.02	0.13	−0.29**	0.06	−0.15*	0.08
Presence of body of water (dummy)	0.15**	0.01	0**	0.00	0.94**	0.46	0.32*	0.18	0.33**	0.09
Presence of wetland (dummy)	0.44**	0.03	—	—	0.27	0.91	0.77**	0.16	0.56**	0.10
Within the USFWS CRD (dummy)	−0.02**	0.01	−0.14	0.13	0.32	0.23	−0.26**	0.04	−0.03	0.06
Year 2000 (dummy)	−0.96**	0.05	−1.39*	0.78	−0.71	0.64	0.16	0.59	—	—
Year 2001 (dummy)	−0.72**	0.05	−1.33**	0.42	−0.73	0.90	−1.72**	0.10	−1.92**	0.28
Year 2002 (dummy)	−0.49**	0.00	−1.23**	0.18	−0.82**	0.11	−1.17**	0.06	−0.57**	0.03
Year 2003 (dummy)	−0.33**	0.00	−0.61**	0.18	−0.5**	0.10	−0.95**	0.05	−0.43**	0.02
Year 2004 (dummy)	−0.1**	0.00	−0.44**	0.17	−0.29**	0.10	−0.44**	0.05	−0.19**	0.02
Year 2005 (dummy)	0.06**	0.00	0.02	0.16	−0.19*	0.10	−0.07	0.05	0.05**	0.02
Year 2006 (dummy)	0.09**	0.00	0.04	0.18	−0.19*	0.10	−0.04	0.05	0.05**	0.02
Year 2007 (ref)	—	—	—	—	—	—	—	—	—	—
Zoned agricultural (dummy)	−0.04**	0.01	0.11	0.12	−0.31	0.34	0.05	0.03	−0.46**	0.05
Zoned commercial (dummy)	0.02**	0.01	0.36	0.50	0.36**	0.10	0.51**	0.06	−0.07**	0.02

Table A.1—Continued

Characteristic	SFH		Agriculture		Other		Open Space		MFH	
	Coefficient	Standard Error	Coefficient	Standard Error	Coefficient	Standard Error	Coefficient	Standard Error	Coefficient	Standard Error
Zoned industrial (dummy)	0.09**	0.01	0.83	0.57	0.33**	0.10	0.52**	0.06	−0.39**	0.06
Zoned MFH (dummy)	0.05**	0.00	0.34	0.81	0.24*	0.13	−0.17**	0.05	0.13**	0.01
Zoned open space (dummy)	0.06**	0.00	0.00**	0.00	0.52**	0.15	−0.05	0.08	0.07**	0.02
Zoned other (dummy)	−0.14**	0.04	—	—	0.30	0.91	−0.35	0.58	0.08	0.13
Zoned SFH (ref)	—	—	—	—	—	—	—	—	—	—
Mean household income in census tract (log)	0.47**	0.00	0.20*	0.12	0.33**	0.07	0.71**	0.04	0.37**	0.02
Constant	7.27**	0.04	10.73**	1.55	10.53**	0.88	5.65**	0.42	7.81**	0.27
Observations	127,120		342		1,606		7,272		6,698	
R-squared	0.58		0.46		0.45		0.65		0.56	

NOTE: ** statistically significant at 5 percent; * statistically significant at 10 percent; ref = reference category (variable omitted from regression).

The model appears to perform fairly well. A substantial number of the estimated coefficients are statistically significant with the expected sign. The R-squared is quite high for cross-sectional data, ranging from about 0.44 to 0.66 for the different land uses. Encouragingly, the highest R-squared value is for open-space parcels, the land-use category into which the vast majority of parcels already acquired (and still to be acquired) falls.

Data Sources and Analysis Techniques

A large share of the variables used in the land-value models were derived through GIS analysis. This section provides more details on the data sources and geographic-analysis techniques used in developing variables related to different parcel characteristics. For further information, interested readers are welcome to contact the authors.

Data Sources

The data used in our analysis were drawn from several sources, including RCA, the Riverside County assessor's office, and other governmental agencies.

RCA Data. RCA maintains its own GIS database for western Riverside County, and this was the source of much of the data used in the analysis. Examples of the information we received from RCA's database include

- all parcels in western Riverside County
- parcels already assembled by RCA
- other parcels held in public trust
- parcels in designated habitat-linkage areas
- criteria-cell boundaries
- rough-step accounting area boundaries
- location and distribution of vegetation communities
- other natural features, such as bodies of water and wetlands
- legal and jurisdictional features, such as current zoning and the location of city boundaries and city annexes within western Riverside County.

Riverside County Assessor's Office Data. The Riverside County assessor's office provided other helpful data, including

- recent parcel sales in western Riverside (year and price)
- number of bedrooms (for single-family homes)
- manufactured-housing indicator (for single-family homes)

---

variables are obviously related to one another, but because permanently conserved land counts as neither developed nor developable land, there is some degree of independence).

- owner-occupied indicator (for MFH)
- current land use for each parcel in western Riverside County.

Data from Other Government Sources. Finally, we made use of data sets provided by several government agencies. Examples include

- U.S. Census Bureau: location of roads and highways (from Topically Integrated Geographic Encoding and Referencing system, or TIGER®, files), median household income, by census tract (from 2000 census)
- Federal Emergency Management Agency: location of federally designated flood zones
- USGS: digital elevation data (for parcel-slope calculations)
- SCAG: employment, by traffic-analysis zone (for job-accessibility calculations).

Geographic-Analysis Techniques

Many of the variables used in estimating the land-value models—including sale price, most recent year of sale, zoning, current land use, number of bedrooms, and the like—were available in the data sets just enumerated and required no additional processing. Rather, they could be directly linked into our parcel records based on their unique assessor's parcel number (APN) value. The derivation of other variables, however, required additional geographic analysis, including such techniques as spatial intersection, distance calculations, slope calculations, neighborhood analysis, and accessibility analysis.

Spatial Intersection. For many of the variables, it was necessary to determine whether a parcel fell within a certain area. In such cases, we performed a spatial-intersection operation, which indicates whether a parcel lies within, or at least partially overlaps, a feature of interest. Examples of variables relying on spatial intersection include

- presence within city boundaries or city annex areas
- presence within a flood zone
- presence of bodies of water or wetland features
- mean household income for the census tract in which the centroid of the parcel lies.

Distance Calculations. Other variables involved the calculation of distance from a parcel to some specified feature, such as the nearest highway. In these cases, we determined the distance from each parcel's centroid (as opposed to its boundary) to the feature in question. Examples include

- distance to the nearest highways and roads
- distance to the nearest park
- distance to sewer service.

Slope Calculations. Given digital elevation data as an input, most GIS software packages have built-in functions for computing related information, such as slope and aspect. We used these functions to estimate the slope at the centroid of each parcel, which served as a proxy for average slope throughout the parcel.

Neighborhood Analysis. The variables related to the percentage of developed and undeveloped land within a given radius of each parcel relied on neighborhood analysis. For each parcel, we first identified the set of nearby parcels whose centroids were located within the specified distance from the centroid of the parcel in question—that is, the "local neighborhood" of parcels. Based on current land-use information, each parcel in the local neighborhood was categorized as developed, undeveloped, or permanently conserved. This enabled us to add up the total number of acres for each of these categories within the local neighborhood. We could then estimate the percentage of developed and undeveloped land in the local neighborhood by dividing the total acres for each of these categories by the total number of acres across all three categories. This analysis was repeated for each parcel in western Riverside County; that is, we constructed a separate local neighborhood around each parcel in order to generate these variables:

- percentage of developed land within 1 mile
- percentage of undeveloped land within 1 mile
- difference between the percentage of developed land within 2.5 miles and the percentage of developed land within 1 mile
- difference between the percentage of undeveloped land within 2.5 miles and the percentage of undeveloped land within 1 mile.

Accessibility Analysis. Accessibility analysis was used to generate variables related to the number of jobs (or employment opportunities) that could be reached within a given travel time from each parcel. We began with a set of traffic-analysis zones (TAZs) in western Riverside County as well as in surrounding counties, such as Los Angeles, Orange, San Bernardino, and Imperial, including information about the number of jobs in each TAZ as of 2000.[2] For each TAZ in western Riverside County, we then identified the set of surrounding TAZs that could be reached within a travel time of 30 minutes.[3] We then added up the employment in all of the surrounding TAZs that could be reached within this time and recorded that sum as the *job-accessibility value* for the TAZ in question. Finally, the parcels in western Riverside County were

---

[2]   Employment data for each TAZ in Riverside, Los Angeles, Orange, San Bernardino, and Imperial counties are available from SCAG; TAZ-based employment data for San Diego County are available from the U.S. Census Bureau.

[3]   Specifically, we examined the estimated drive time from the centroid of one TAZ to the centroid of another using shortest-path analysis on the existing road network. We also assumed that the average travel speed on arterial roads is 35 miles per hour and the average travel speed on highway links is 55 miles per hour.

matched to different TAZs based on the locations of their centroids, and each parcel inherited the job-accessibility value of the TAZ in which it was located.

Predicting the 2007 Value of RCA's Current Land Portfolio

The estimated regressions were used to predict the value as of mid-2007 of the 539 parcels already acquired by RCA. To do this, the year-2007 indicator variable was set to 1 and the other year-indicator variables were set to 0. The natural logarithm of the 539 parcel values was predicted after setting the other explanatory values to their observed values. The results were exponentiated and summed separately for each land-use category.

Method Used to Develop Confidence Intervals for Land-Value Predictions

Bootstrapping techniques were used to construct 95-percent confidence intervals for the combined current value of the parcels in each land-use category. The basic idea behind bootstrapping is to generate a series of alternative estimations of the regression model in which each alternative is constructed by drawing a different random sample (with replacement) of observations from the original sales data set and using that sample to estimate the regression coefficients. Each alternative estimation is then used to develop a different point estimate for the current value of the parcels already acquired by RCA. We performed a total of 1,000 iterations of the bootstrapping process, yielding 1,000 estimates for the current value of RCA acquisitions for each land-use category. The 1,000 projections for each land-use category were then ranked by size, and the 95-percent confidence interval was bounded by the values of the 25th lowest bootstrap estimate and 25th highest estimate.

To develop a confidence interval for the estimated value of *all* parcels assembled to date by RCA (as opposed to those only in a particular land-use category), we created an expanded version of the regression that simultaneously considered all land uses. To do so, we fully interacted the explanatory variables with the land-use categories (effectively expanding the total number of terms in the regression by five (for the five land uses) and ran the regression on all 143,038 observations in the sample. With this expanded model in place, we developed a 95-percent confidence interval using the same bootstrapping techniques already described.

Examples of Simulated Land-Price Paths

In Chapter Four, we analyzed the performance of various land-acquisition strategies for eight scenarios for future land prices. For each of the eight scenarios (listed in Table 4.1 in that chapter), we generated 10,000 price paths that reflect different realizations of the error terms in the statistical equations that describe the scenarios. To illustrate the range of resulting outcomes, Figures B.1 through B.4 show 10 of the simulated price paths for four of the eight land-price scenarios.

Figure B.1
Ten Simulated Price Paths for Open-Space Land Under Scenario 1 (historical appreciation, cyclical market, and residual valuation)

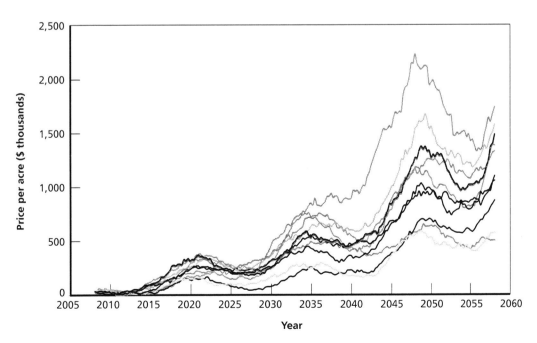

Figure B.2
Ten Simulated Price Paths for Open-Space Land Under Scenario 4 (historical appreciation, acyclical market, and equal percentage)

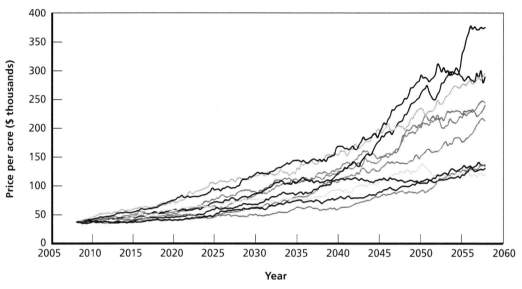

Figure B.3
Ten Simulated Price Paths for Open-Space Land Under Scenario 6 (zero appreciation, cyclical market, and double percentage)

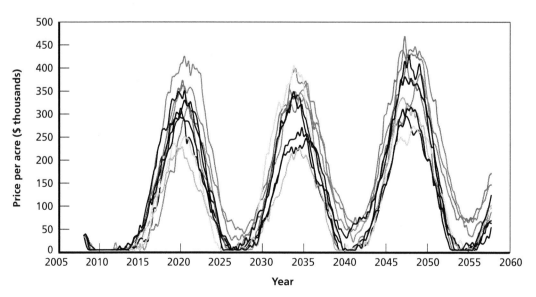

Figure B.4
Ten Simulated Price Paths for Open-Space Land Under Scenario 7 (zero appreciation, cyclical market, and equal percentage)

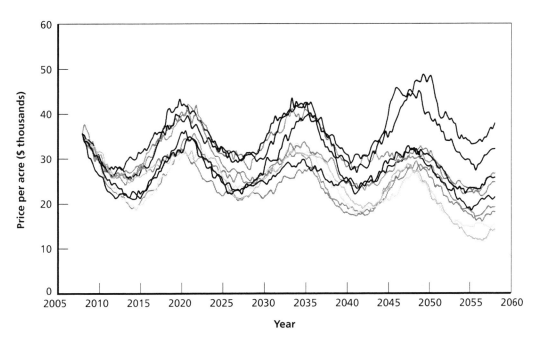

Revenue Sources for Existing Habitat-Conservation Plans

To inform our exploration in Chapter Seven of potential sources for additional revenue for the MSHCP, we examined the revenue sources of 19 existing HCPs of at least 1,000 acres each. Table C.1 summarizes the findings.

Table C.1
HCP Revenue Sources

HCP	Area (acres)	Percentage of Revenue (%)				
		Government Grants	Mitigation Fees	Timber Sales	Water Sales	Interest Earnings
East Contra Costa County Habitat Conservancy (Calif.)[a]	175,435	x	58.0			
Coachella Valley Multiple Species HCP (Calif.)[b]	240,000	x	32.4			x
San Joaquin County Multi-Species Habitat-Conservation and Open Space Plan (Calif.)	896,000		100			
Solano Multi-Species HCP (Calif.)	587,000		100			
West Mojave Coordinated Management Plan (Calif.)	1,523,936	x	x			
Clark County Multiple Species HCP (Nev.)	145,000	x	x			
Salt River Project Roosevelt Lake HCP (Ariz.)	2,250				100	
Cedar River Watershed HCP (Wash.)	90,546				100	
Wash. Department of Natural Resources HCP (Wash.)	1,600,000			100		
Elliott State Forest HCP (Oreg.)	93,000			100		
Mendocino Redwood Company HCP and NCCP (Calif.)	232,500			100		
Plum Creek HCP (Mont.)	1,700,000			100		
Yuba-Sutter NCCP/HCP[c] (Calif.)	200,078	100				
Douglas County HCP[c] (Wash.)	729,934	100				

Table C.1—Continued

HCP	Area (acres)	Percentage of Revenue (%)				
		Government Grants	Mitigation Fees	Timber Sales	Water Sales	Interest Earnings
Encinitas Subarea Plan[d] (Calif.)	12,080		x			
Clark County Regional Parks, Recreation and Open Space Plan (Wash.)[e]	7,400		x			
San Bruno Mountain HCP (Calif.)[f]	3,500		x			
Southern Subregion NCCP/Master Streambed Alteration Agreement/HCP (Calif.)[g]	132,000		x			x
Pima County Multi-Species Conservation Plan (Ariz.)[h]	607,700		x			

NOTE: x = This type of revenue is collected, but its share could not be determined because not all sources of revenue for the HCP could be identified.

[a] Mitigation fees include development fee (48 percent), wetland-impact fee (7 percent), and fees on rural infrastructure (3 percent).

[b] Mitigation fees include development fee (27.8 percent) and fees on rural infrastructure (4.6 percent).

[c] Supported by grants from USFWS (CESCF grant program).

[d] An open-space land-acquisition fee is a one-time fee paid to the city upon completion of new residential construction. Funds are used for land acquisition.

[e] The property seller pays a real-estate excise tax on the sale of real estate.

[f] The HCP assessment fee for all new developments on the mountain that are part of the HCP is a per-unit fee that must be paid until the purchaser moves in.

[g] Includes a benefit fee equal to 0.324 percent of the value of any developed residential parcel in the plan area on initial sale.

[h] Includes open-space bonds and flood-control tax.

Integrating Funding for Infrastructure Construction and Conservation

Thus far, our examination of potential funding sources has focused on funds that would be earmarked for conservation. But in considering potential financing mechanisms, much may be gained by considering both the construction of transportation projects and conservation as one integrated project. Such an integrated approach to funding in western Riverside County may increase flexibility in the timing of land-purchase decisions and ultimately reduce the cost of the integrated project. In this chapter, we investigate the extent to which existing institutions allow such integration.

Background

Currently, Riverside County bases decisions about construction and conservation largely on the availability of funding, with transportation projects handled by RCTC and conservation activities managed by RCA. The plan defines part of the relationship between the two activities, as many of the planned transportation projects are covered under the plan, and the plan provides for mitigating the planned projects' species impacts. From the perspective of planners in western Riverside County, acquisition of open space allows the county to comply with ESA's permit requirement and thus continue to implement its planned transportation enhancements.

When RCTC and RCA receive funding from the federal government, the funds flow either to RCA for conservation (CESCF grants) or to RCTC for transportation (Federal Highway Administration [FHWA] grants). An alternative approach is to pool funds and consider infrastructure development and conservation as one integrated project. As such, decisions about how to spend the funds could be based not simply on which type of funding was available, but instead on which activities were most cost-effective at that particular time.

Depending on the relative costs of transportation infrastructure and habitat acquisition, it may be more cost-effective in a particular year to spend more on conservation and less on infrastructure construction. For example, in the current economic downturn, home prices in the county have decreased from their 2007 levels, raising the prospect of lower near-term land-acquisition costs for the reserve. With an integrated funding source, planners could decide to spend more on habitat conservation to take advantage of the lower cost of land.[1] However, with the current framework, the availability of each type of federal aid might require a much different spending plan. If, as an example, most of the available federal grant money was for transportation and not conservation, then RCA would be unable to take advantage of the lower cost of land (on behalf of state and federal permittees).

With a predetermined amount of transportation infrastructure to construct and open space to preserve, there are various ways to reach those ends; some ways are more cost-effective than others. In this chapter, we investigate whether—under current laws and existing funding programs—it would be possible to envision highways and habitat to be conserved as a single, integrated form of infrastructure and whether that combined infrastructure could be funded through some sort of infrastructure bank or equivalent program, in which the funds could be used interchangeably for transportation infrastructure and conservation. Specifically, this chapter addresses the following questions:

- Which laws govern federal conservation grants, and which govern federal highway funds?
- What are the spending restrictions for each federal funding source?
- Does California have any infrastructure banks that could provide loans for transportation projects and conservation?

Federal Conservation Grants

The federal government provides funding to state agencies for species and habitat conservation through CESCF. The conservation actions must take place on nonfederal lands, and the state must either have—or enter into—a cooperative agreement with the secretary of the interior to be eligible for a grant. Groups—such as land conservancies—may work as subgrantees to state agencies that have cooperative agreements. Participating states must contribute at least 25 percent of the estimated program costs of approved projects, or 10 percent when two or more states undertake a joint project (USFWS, 2008). Four grant programs are available through CESCF:

- conservation grants
- HCP-assistance grants
- HCP land-acquisition grants
- recovery land-acquisition grants (USFWS, 2008).

---

[1]   If policymakers are concerned that project managers may allocate money in undesirable ways when given discretion to use funds for multiple purposes, it may be sensible to segregate (or fence) funds.

The first is considered a traditional grant, and the latter are considered nontraditional grants. State and local agencies must use each grant only for its specific purpose related to habitat conservation, as outlined here:

Conservation grants assist states in implementing conservation projects for listed and at-risk species. The activities that these grants may fund include habitat restoration, species status surveys, public education and outreach, captive propagation and reintroduction, nesting surveys, genetic studies, and development of management plans (USFWS, 2008).

HCP-assistance grants support the development of HCPs. Eligible planning activities include document preparation, outreach, and baseline surveys and inventories (USFWS, 2008).

HCP land-acquisition grants help states acquire land associated with approved HCPs. According to federal guidelines, the program has three primary purposes:

> (1) to fund land acquisitions that complement, but do not replace, private mitigation responsibilities contained in HCPs, (2) to fund land acquisitions that have important benefits for listed, proposed, and candidate species, and (3) to fund land acquisitions that have important benefits for ecosystems that support listed, proposed and candidate species. (USFWS, 2008)

Recovery land-acquisition grants provide funds to states and other nonfederal entities to acquire habitats from willing sellers in support of approved species-recovery plans (not permitted HCPs) (USFWS, 2008).

The Wildlife and Sport Fish Restoration Program Toolkit gives guidance on federal aid and includes information on CESCF grants. A section on eligibility standards clarifies specifically how state and local agencies may use the funds:

> Endangered species grants must have the purposes of conserving species of fish, wildlife, or plants included on Federal or State lists of endangered or threatened species, or those that are candidates for listing status [50 CFR 81.2, 43 CFR 12.50(b)(3)]. Activities may include: (A) Acquisition of endangered or threatened species habitat. (B) Introduction of species into suitable habitats within their historic range. (C) Enhancement of habitat. (D) Surveys and inventories of habitats or populations. (E) Research on endangered species. (F) Propagation of animals and plants for introduction or protection of the species. (G) Protection of listed or candidate species, or their habitat (e.g., mitigation of threats). (USFWS, 2008)

CESCF grants are limited in their applicability to conservation-related activities. State and local agencies may not use them for anything outside of their limited purpose—including transportation infrastructure.

Federal Highway Administration Grants for Mitigation

The federal government supports investment in surface-transportation projects in part through a grant-based funding strategy known as the federal aid program (FHWA, 2002). Title 23 of the U.S. Code regulates highways in the United States, including the use of federal-aid highway funds—also called FHWA grants. These funds may be used to mitigate the negative effects on habitat from highway projects in order to comply with the requirements of Section 404 of CWA and ESA, subject to the requirements of Title 23. Mitigation is usually considered to include the following three steps:

1. Avoid a project's potential effects.
2. Minimize a project's unavoidable effects.
3. Provide compensatory mitigation for the unavoidable effects (USDOT and FHWA, 2006; EPA, undated).

Once the first two steps are complete, the compensatory mitigation measures may take one of several forms:

- *Project-specific mitigation:* State agencies have traditionally undertaken compensatory mitigation on a project-by-project basis, with the mitigation activities occurring adjacent to the transportation project (on site) on land with a similar ecological function (in kind) (USDOT and FHWA, 2006). In doing so, agencies have typically assessed the effects from each project and mitigated nearby—not in conjunction with other projects.
- *Multiple-project mitigation:* This method combines the individual mitigation activities for multiple projects into one larger mitigation project. When the multiple transportation projects are small, one large mitigation project can be more successful ecologically by eliminating the fragmentation of the project-by-project approach (USDOT and FHWA, 2006). Three types of multiple-project mitigation are permitted:
  - *Mitigation banking:* Mitigation banks are wetlands that have been restored and protected to mitigate for development projects (EPA, undated). Government agencies, corporations, nonprofit organizations, or other sponsors may establish them by selling mitigation credits to developers who wish to mitigate a particular project (EPA, undated). Mitigation banks are aimed specifically at compensating for unavoidable effects to aquatic resources, thus addressing the mitigation needs of Section 404 of CWA (USDOT and FHWA, 2006). As such, they fall under the jurisdiction of USACE, which bases wetland-mitigation policy on a "no net loss" rule (FHWA, 1994; USDOT and FHWA, 2006). The bank sponsor typically establishes the bank prior to construction of the infrastructure project.

- *In-lieu fee (ILF):* If neither on-site compensation nor mitigation banking is appropriate for the project needing mitigation, then, in some cases, the agency may use an ILF arrangement. With an ILF arrangement, an agency pays the ILF sponsor to provide for a future mitigation project instead of putting the funds into an existing mitigation bank. The compensatory mitigation is provided after, and not in advance of, a project's effects (USACE et al., 2000).
- *Conservation banking:* Conservation banks are conceptually similar to mitigation banks but are aimed at ESA's mitigation needs and the authorizing agency is USFWS. The land conserved in a conservation bank is habitat for endangered species in general and not limited to a particular type, which is the case with wetlands in a mitigation bank (USFWS, 2003).

Regulatory Framework for Using Federal Aid to Mitigate Transportation-Project Effects

The Intermodal Surface Transportation Efficiency Act of 1991 (ISTEA) (Pub. L. 102-240) first included provisions for the use of federal aid to mitigate effects on wetlands, and guidance for doing so was provided in a 1994 FHWA memorandum (FHWA, 1994, 2005). Under TEA-21, which authorized federal surface-transportation programs from 1998 to 2003, Congress expanded the funding-eligibility provisions to include other habitat besides wetlands. Under 23 CFR 710.513 and 23 CFR 777, compensatory mitigation activities are eligible for federal aid funds from either National Highway System or Surface Transportation Program projects (FHWA, 2005). Under 23 CFR 710.513, acquiring and maintaining land for mitigation are eligible project costs for federal aid. A more comprehensive provision, 23 CFR 777, governs FHWA participation in wetland and habitat mitigation activities.

One important federal aid–eligibility requirement for mitigation spending is that it be a "reasonable public expenditure." Part 777.7(a) of Title 23 states that reasonableness must be directly related to the importance of the affected habitat, the extent of highway effects as determined by an impact assessment, and actions necessary to comply with Section 404 of CWA, ESA, and other relevant federal statutes (23 CFR 777.7[a]). Provided that this and other requirements are met, state and local agencies may use a certain portion of their federal aid funds to mitigate highway projects' effects. Resource and transportation agencies work together to determine the appropriate amount of mitigation for each project, but final approval must be given by USACE, USFWS, or both—depending on whether the mitigation is being undertaken to comply with CWA or ESA.

Under Title 23, mitigation activities may occur before or during construction of the transportation project and even before the project-level environmental reviews are complete (FHWA, 2005). In addition, according to resurfacing, restoration, rehabilitation, and reconstruction provisions, agencies may mitigate past federal aid projects with funding from current federal aid projects (USDOT and FHWA, 2006).

Federal aid may come in more forms than grants. In 1998, Congress passed the Transportation Infrastructure Finance and Innovation Act (TIFIA), which was enacted as part of TEA-21. Through TIFIA, Congress authorized the U.S. Department of Transportation to provide credit assistance to surface-transportation projects of national or regional significance. The assistance may come in the form of secured loans, loan guarantees, or lines of credit and allows state and local transportation agencies to leverage limited federal resources instead of simply receiving the money as a grant (FHWA, 2002). These funds are still considered federal aid and thus governed by Title 23. The regulations for funding mitigation are therefore the same as for grants.

Federal and State Movement Toward Multiple-Project Mitigation

State and local agencies have typically mitigated transportation projects using on-site and in-kind mitigation, on a project-by-project basis (USDOT and FHWA, 2006; Venner, 2005). While tried and true when done correctly, this approach is not always the most practical or the most beneficial to the local ecosystem (USDOT and FHWA, 2006; NRC, 2001). Multiple-project mitigation has the advantage of bulk discounts on land and early acquisitions to avoid rising real-estate prices (Erickson, 2008).

There has been a recent push both nationally and within California toward more coordination among agencies in conjunction with multiple-project, ecosystem-based, advance mitigation. *Advance mitigation* refers to mitigation in advance of project effects (Venner, 2005). Caltrans has been focusing more on this approach, examining opportunities for mitigating future projects (Sollenberger, 2008; Erickson, 2008). But mitigating in advance can be risky for a state transportation agency without approval from the resource agency, as the amount of mitigation a project requires may ultimately be more or less than the amount completed in advance. In 2003, to reduce these risks and further early mitigation planning, Caltrans signed a memorandum of agreement with FHWA, USACE, EPA, USFWS, and CDFG (FHWA, 2003).

Since 1994, a series of federal-agency memos and executive orders (EOs) has provided guidance for using federal funds for different types of mitigation. For the past decade, the guidance has attempted to encourage more agency cooperation and an ecosystem-based approach to mitigation instead of the more narrowly focused project-by-project approach. In 2002, EO 13274 called for expedited reviews of high-priority transportation projects and greater agency coordination during the review process. Two years later, in 2004, President Bush signed EO 13352, Facilitation of Cooperative Conservation. Its purpose was

> to ensure that the Departments of the Interior, Agriculture, Commerce, and Defense and the Environmental Protection Agency implement laws relating to the environment and natural resources in a manner that promotes cooperative conservation, with an emphasis on appropriate inclusion of local participation in Federal

decisionmaking, in accordance with their respective agency missions, policies, and regulations.

In addition to greater agency coordination, the federal government has also been promoting the ecosystem-based approach to mitigation, which "extends existing compensatory mitigation options by offering a way to evaluate alternatives for off-site mitigation and/or out-of-kind mitigation in the ecologically most important areas" (USDOT and FHWA, 2006). In 1995, the Council on Environmental Quality (CEQ) and 13 federal agencies signed an interagency memorandum of understanding (MOU) encouraging an ecosystem approach to natural-resource management, protection, and assistance (FHWA, 1995). Eight of the agencies, along with departments of transportation from four states, wrote a framework for achieving an ecosystem approach, as well as the interagency cooperation as described in EO 13352, titled *Eco-Logical: An Ecosystem Approach to Developing Infrastructure Projects* (USDOT and FHWA, 2006). According to the report, some of the mutual benefits of an ecosystem approach to infrastructure include safer, improved infrastructure; improved watershed and ecosystem health; increased connectivity and conservation; efficient product development; and increased transparency (USDOT and FHWA, 2006).

Although mitigation methods are changing toward advance, multiple-project, ecosystem-based mitigation, federal funding for infrastructure and conservation is not integrated. State transportation agencies may not draw at will from federal aid for transportation to mitigate without explicit authorization from the gove agency that the mitigation is suitable for the project and is a reasonable public expenditure. While the mitigation may be for multiple projects, the financial accounting for mitigation spending is done on a project-by-project basis.

Linking Transportation and Mitigation at the Local Level

Besides federal aid, other sources of infrastructure funds in California have addressed mitigation. Though their funds are not interchangeable between conservation and infrastructure, both Riverside and San Diego counties have apportioned some of their sales-tax funding to pay for mitigation. Riverside County's Measure A sales tax is described in Chapter Six. In San Diego, the original infrastructure-funding measure appeared on the ballot in 1987, and its passage enacted a $0.005 sales tax in San Diego County to pay for transportation projects. The measure was set to expire in 2008, but the voters in San Diego County renewed the tax in 2004 for an additional 40 years. A unique feature of the measure was that it designated $850 million of the $14 billion in projected revenues to establish the Environmental Mitigation Program (EMP) (SANDAG, 2005). The EMP funds were partially allocated for direct mitigation of major transportation infrastructure–improvement projects and partially for acquisition, maintenance, and monitoring to implement the Multiple Species Conservation Program and Multiple Habitat Conservation Program. The EMP's goal was to mitigate for priority projects comprehensively and not on a project-by-project basis, in order to take advantage of early land-acquisition opportunities (SANDAG, 2005).

Infrastructure Banks in California

Infrastructure banks offer a mechanism to enable greater integration of transportation and conservation financing. Loans could be made up front that allowed flexibility in allocating funds for transportation and conservation and then paid as the funds targeting mitigation and conservation become available.

We investigated whether infrastructure banks exist in California that could be used for these purposes. We identified two such banks: the Infrastructure and Economic Development Bank (I-Bank) and the Transportation Finance Bank (TFB). In this section, we describe these banks and the ability to use them to finance conservation and transportation infrastructure.

I-Bank was established in 1994 as an initiative of the Business, Transportation, and Housing Agency. It is governed by a five-member board and has authority to issue tax-exempt and taxable revenue bonds, provide financing to public agencies, provide credit enhancements, acquire or lease facilities, and leverage state and federal funds (CIEDB, undated). One of its major programs is the Infrastructure State Revolving Fund (ISRF) program, which provides financing to public agencies for a wide variety of infrastructure projects. Funding from the program is available in amounts ranging from $250,000 to $10 million (CIEDB, 2008). Activities to mitigate the effects of infrastructure projects must comply with the Title 23 requirements discussed earlier. The scale of highway development being planned and constructed in western Riverside County is more expensive than this amount of funding could support.

In 1995, the National Highway System Designation Act (Pub. L. 104-59) created TFB as part of the federal State Infrastructure Bank (SIB) pilot program (TFB, undated). The purpose of the SIB program was to leverage federal funds to finance state and local transportation projects through loans and other credit assistance. California was selected as one of 10 states to participate in the initial pilot program, and, in 1995, TFB was capitalized with $3 million in federal funds and $100 million in state funds (Lewis, 2007). However, the state funds were withdrawn several years later due to lack of use, as other financing sources were plentiful at the time (Lewis, 2007). Currently, TFB has about $2 million and administers a small revolving-loan program (Ingles, 2007). Local public agencies—such as transportation planning agencies and county transportation commissions—are eligible to apply for loans. Title 23 governs the eligibility of highway construction (and mitigation) project costs, and the project must be included in a Federal State Transportation Improvement Program.

Assessment

No current funding source exists that may be used to build transportation infrastructure and conserve habitat on a completely integrated basis. Federal CESCF conservation grants are limited strictly to conservation activities. State and local agencies may use federal aid in the form of FHWA grants, or even the innovative finance mechanisms under TIFIA, to mitigate effects of transportation-infrastructure projects. While this mitigation has typically been planned and completed on site and in kind on a project-by-project basis, there is a national push for multiple-project advance mitigation with more agency coordination and an ecosystem-based approach. Even when this new approach is used, mitigation expenditures are subject to Title 23 and accounted for on a project-by-project basis. Any new source of county funding from the federal government that could pay for both infrastructure and conservation would require its own authorizing legislation and could not take the form of a CESCF or FHWA grant.

The Effect of the MSHCP on Mobility in Western Riverside County

The MSHCP was developed in part to speed the placement of transportation infrastructure in western Riverside County. Faster completion of transportation-infrastructure projects will presumably improve mobility in the county, benefiting both residents and businesses. This appendix quantifies the mobility effects of the faster placement of four major transportation corridors that resulted from CETAP. While, as described in Chapter Eight, the MSHCP is perceived to have positive effects on a wide variety of road construction and safety and maintenance projects, the CETAP projects are by far the largest transportation projects planned for western Riverside County and the focus of our analysis. This analysis can be viewed on one hand as quantifying one part of the MSHCP's benefits and, on the other, as measuring the deterioration in mobility that would result if the MSHCP were abandoned.

The next section describes the relationship of CETAP and the MSHCP and then details the four major corridors included in CETAP. The following section discusses the model (the Southern California Planning Model, or SCPM) used to derive estimated effects of delaying CETAP corridor development. Findings on the mobility effects of delaying the CETAP projects are then presented, followed by an estimate of the dollar value of the reduction in mobility.

The Plan and the CETAP Corridors

The MSHCP and CETAP are two related branches of RCIP. The most important part of the relationship is that the MSHCP, by responding to the dangers that development poses to species preservation and by meeting ESA requirements, can accelerate the construction of the CETAP corridors. These corridors, in turn, can relieve congestion in what is expected to continue to be a rapidly growing Riverside County.

RCTC selected the four priority CETAP corridors from an initial field of 13 proposed by an advisory committee of 30 members (RCIP, undated). The four corridors include two entirely inside Riverside County and two linking Riverside County to Orange County and San Bernardino County (see Figure E.1). The two internal corridors

Figure E.1
Locations of the CETAP Corridors

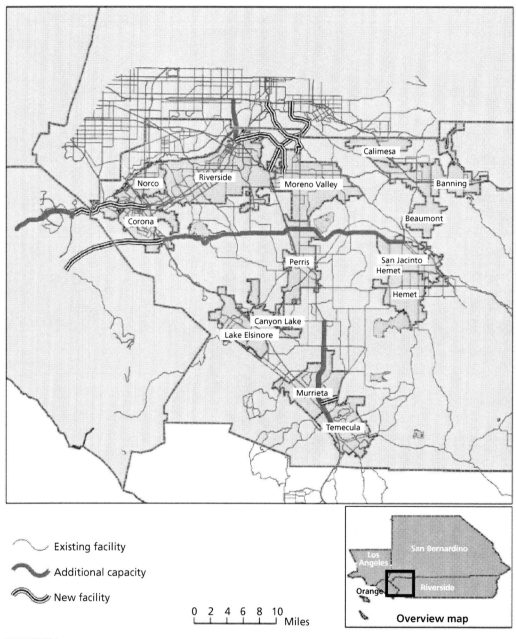

Existing facility

Additional capacity

New facility

0 2 4 6 8 10
Miles

Overview map

San Bernardino

Los Angeles

Orange

Riverside

are the Mid County Parkway, originally known as the Hemet-to-Corona/Lake Elsinore corridor (east-west), and the Winchester-to-Temecula corridor (north-south). The two intercounty corridors are the Riverside County–to–Orange County corridor and the Moreno Valley–to–San Bernardino County corridor.

The CETAP project was recognized under EO 13274, signed September 18, 2002, which requires the federal secretary of transportation to designate high-priority projects for expedited environmental reviews. Once environmental reviews are completed, the project is moved from a priority list to a transition list. As of December 2006, there were eight transportation-infrastructure projects on the priority-project list and 12 on the transition list (USDOT, 2008a, 2008b).

Environmental documentation and planning for roads can take place through a number of different processes. RCTC can first prepare a draft environmental-impact statement (DEIS) or draft environmental-impact report (DEIR) to fulfill tier 1 NEPA requirements of FHWA.[1] The tier 1 process provides environmental documentation to select the proposed route and to support the commitment of federal funds to CETAP planning. It also allows for the preservation of right-of-way. The DEIS or DEIR would then be followed by a final environmental-impact statement (FEIS) or final environmental-impact report (FEIR), which the federal government would then accept through a record of decision. However, going through tier 1 is not mandatory and sometimes is not desirable.

RCTC can go straight to tier 2, in which the documentation addresses FHWA's NEPA requirements for approving connections to interstates and approving federal funds for construction. In addition, tier 2 planning and engineering determine exact right-of-way width, analyze alternatives at the construction level of detail, and identify specific mitigation measures (Riverside County, 2002). Again, there is a draft and final process with a record of decision signifying federal acceptance. In addition, in some cases, an EIR or EIS is not required, though other environmental clearances may be.

RCTC has chosen to use different processes for different corridors. The rest of this section will describe these corridors in more depth and provide current estimates of the construction start date or completion date.

The Mid County Parkway

The Mid County Parkway is a proposed 32-mile east-west limited-access route for western Riverside County connecting the San Jacinto area with the Corona area. The project began with eight proposed alternatives. It has since been narrowed, though no specific route has been selected. However, it likely will start near the junction of Ramona Boulevard, Sanderson Avenue, and SR-79 in San Jacinto. It will then go west, skirting south of Lake Perris to I-215 in Perris. From I-215 in Perris, it will run west to the south

---

[1] The EIS is a federal requirement, and the EIR is a California requirement. They overlap in content, and one or both may be required.

of Cajalco Road, skirting south of Lake Mathews, then hitting I-15 in Corona. The project will also include connections to SR-79 in the east, I-215 in the center, and I-15 to the west. It will use some existing roads as well as new expressways.

RCTC started the environmental approvals for this project by going through the tier 1 process. An initial DEIS/DEIR was released for public review on July 19, 2002. Public hearings and a comment period followed. However, when disagreements about the route emerged among different levels of government, RCTC abandoned the tier 1 process and moved directly into the tier 2 project-level DEIS/DEIR. Following hearings and public comments, RCTC will then create the FEIS/FEIR, which is expected to be completed at the end of 2008. Following that, RCTC can gain final permits, and final engineering design can begin. If that schedule is adhered to, construction could begin in 2011, provided funding is available.

Winchester-to-Temecula Corridor

The Winchester-to-Temecula corridor involves the widening of I-15 and I-215 in the south part of western Riverside County, along with upgrading Date Street in Temecula to become the four-lane French Valley Parkway connecting Winchester Road to I-15. This preferred alternative was selected on February 12, 2003.

As with the Mid County Parkway, an initial tier 1 DEIS/DEIR for the Winchester-to-Temecula corridor was released for public review on July 19, 2002. The process was completed, and the final action, a record of decision from the federal government, occurred on September 17, 2003 (USDOT, 2008b).

The preferred alternative calls for widening I-15 from the I-215 junction to south of Winchester Road; widening I-215 south of Newport Road; and constructing the four-lane French Valley Parkway, currently Date Street, as a connection from Winchester Road to I-15, with a new interchange at I-15 (RCTC, 2003b; RCIP, undated).

The corridor has already received some funding. On February 28, 2007, the California Transportation Commission approved $38.6 million worth of funding for widening I-215 from I-15 to Scott Road (CTC, 2007). The money came from the state's Corridor Mobility Improvement Account, funded by the nearly $20 billion Proposition 1B transportation bond approved by California voters in November 2006. The project is estimated to cost $62.3 million, of which construction should cost $55.1 million. The contract award date is expected to be November 2010.

Riverside County–to–Orange County Corridor

The Riverside County–Orange County connection was studied as part of an 18-month major investment study (MIS) from June 2004 to December 2005 (Jacobs Engineering Group, 2006). The study defined a locally preferred strategy that was approved by both the RCTC and the Orange County Transportation Authority (OCTA) in December 2005. In June 2006, RCTC, OCTA, and the Foothill/Eastern Transportation Corridor Agency formed the Riverside Orange Corridor Authority (ROCA) to develop and manage the geotechnical studies for corridor improvements between the two counties. The CETAP Riverside County–to–Orange County corridor includes the following four elements:

- widening SR-91 beyond what improvements have already been planned
- building a corridor dubbed corridor A, to run from I-15 to SR-241, either as an elevated roadway in the middle of SR-91 or as a corridor north of SR-91. Discussion currently is for this to have two or three lanes in each direction.
- building a corridor dubbed corridor B, which is to be a limited-access road with two or three lanes in each direction from I-15 at Cajalco Road to Orange County ending near the junction of SR-241 and SR-133. Plans call for corridor B to be either completely a tunnel or part surface and part tunnel.
- adding operational improvements to SR-74 (the Ortega Highway), also known as corridor D.

Since the strategy was developed, further plans have been proposed to extend the SR-91 toll road from the Riverside County line to I-15, with two lanes in each direction. However, that improvement is not part of the MIS.

Based on a start date of the beginning of 2006, the MIS envisioned SR-91 being completed in 2011, corridor A being completed in 2015, corridor B being completed in 2022, and corridor D improvements being completed in 2013. In specific actions, in December 2006, RCTC agreed to a 10-year delivery plan for the western Riverside County Measure A freeway program that included as a priority extending the 91 Express Lanes toll road from Orange County to I-15 (RCTC, 2003a).

In addition, the U.S. Congress has authorized expenditures for the Riverside County–to–Orange County corridor. For FYs 2005 to 2009, Congress authorized $3.2 million for high-priority highway project 1176 and $12.6 million for high-priority highway project 3339, both identified as highway alternatives between Orange and Riverside counties, directed by ROCA and guided by the MIS (Pub. L. 109-59, §1702).

Riverside County–to–San Bernardino County Corridor

This final CETAP corridor may be the most complicated and has experienced the least progress. The main purpose is to improve mobility between SR-60 in Riverside County and I-10 in San Bernardino County. In the fall of 2000, a study was initiated of the Moreno Valley–to–San Bernardino County corridor, with a policy committee and a technical committee considering eight routes. They then focused on one for which to conduct an EIR (SANBAG, undated).

The alternative selected includes a core facility and two arterials (RCTC and SANBAG, 2003). The proposed core facility is a limited-access, four-lane expressway starting at the SR-60/I-215 interchange in Riverside County, then following Morton Road north to the Box Springs Mountain Reserve. It would continue as a four-lane tunnel under Box Springs Mountain, and then run east, cross the San Bernardino County line, and then head north to Barton Road through Loma Linda. At Barton Road, it is to head north to I-10 along the planned, six-lane California Street.

The two arterials will intersect with the core facility and will also run between Riverside and San Bernardino counties. They have the following routes:

- The first will include Pigeon Pass Road starting from SR-60. It is to be widened into a four-lane arterial and paved, and then to connect to the core corridor. From there, it will connect to Riverside Avenue, and then to Main Street, which runs along the Riverside–San Bernardino county line, then cross I-215, connect to Riverside Avenue, and then follow Riverside Avenue north to I-10.
- The second will include Reche Vista Drive where it starts at the confluence of Heacock Street and Perris Boulevard in Riverside County. Reche Vista will be widened and realigned into a four-lane road to Reche Canyon Road, which will also be widened into a four-lane road. Reche Canyon Road will then connect to the core corridor, head northwest to the county line, then head north to Barton Road in Colton. The arterial will then continue north on Hunts Lane to I-10.

So far there has been little activity regarding the core corridor from SR-60/I-215 to I-15. However, actions have been taken on the arterials. RCTC, the San Bernardino Associated Governments, and a number of local governments have negotiated an MOU for the development of much of the two arterials. In addition, Riverside County has programmed funds for project development and environmental work for the arterials (RCTC, 2006). It is expected that Riverside County and Colton will start on the environmental documents for the Reche Canyon arterial in 2007. In addition, work was expected to start on the Riverside County portion of the Pigeon Pass–Riverside Avenue arterial in 2007.

Modeling Alternative Development Scenarios

We model the travel effects of the four CETAP corridors under a range of development scenarios. The increased mobility afforded by these traffic improvements will be modeled with SCPM. SCPM has three primary components:

- *Input-output (I/O) model:* The SCPM I/O model is an interindustry model of the five-county (Los Angeles, Orange, San Bernardino, Riverside, and Ventura) metropolitan area. The model represents economic activity in 47 sectors. The main outputs of the I/O model are estimates of production and employment by sector. These estimates vary endogenously with outputs from the other two models described here.

- *Transportation-network model:* SCPM links a model of the Southern California transportation network to the I/O model. The network includes 3,191 TAZs plus 12 regional highway entry-exit points (treated like TAZs) and 89,356 highway links, including 647 high-occupancy vehicle (HOV) lane–miles. This model forecasts traffic flows and travel times throughout the network. To model different CETAP corridor-development scenarios, we modify the transportation network to represent improvements finished at different points in time.
- *Spatial-allocation model:* SCPM spatially allocates business activity and residences to the TAZs through an iterative process that takes into account transportation costs forecast by the transportation-network model.

SCPM has been used to model the economic effects of earthquakes on the Southern California transportation network (Cho, Gordon, Richardson, et al., 2000; Cho, Gordon, Moore, et al., 2001), the economic effects of a limited interruption of electric power in the Los Angeles region (Moore et al., 2006), and the economic effects of terrorist attacks (Gordon et al., 2005, 2006). A more complete description of the current version of SCPM can be obtained from the University of Southern California's National Center for Risk and Economic Analysis of Terrorism Events (CREATE) (USC Homeland Security Center, undated).

Using SCPM to Model Alternative Development Schedules for the CETAP Corridors

The SCPM model allows us to predict and compare population, employment, and travel outcomes in many years under a variety of infrastructure scenarios. To simulate the dynamic effects of MSHCP-related infrastructure construction, we utilize forecasts of population and employment for 2015, 2020, 2025, and 2030 based on projections prepared by SCAG for the 2004 Regional Transportation Plan.[2] As a result, SCPM generates predictions for these four points in time.

The spatial distribution of households and firms implied by the SCAG estimates is assumed to represent those that would occur without any CETAP improvements made to the current transportation network. We then add various combinations of corridor improvements in future years to the model to simulate alternative development scenarios. The model spatially reallocates households and firms and recomputes economic activity as well as travel activity and conditions under the alternative network scenarios.

A number of ambiguities should be noted. In particular, the routes, the timing, and even whether the corridors will be built under the CETAP process or another process are not known with certainty. In addition, there is some question as to whether

---

[2]   Data for the more recent 2007 Regional Transportation Plan could not be used due to changes in TAZ definitions and other aspects of the data from earlier releases.

all environmental clearances will be gained quickly because of differences of opinion among federal agencies.

We model the corridors as if the MSHCP expedited all of them by the same amount of time. Therefore, actual results may differ, depending on the evolution of road funding and administrative and legal procedures. Keeping that in mind, we developed the model runs under the following development scenarios:

- As our base case (scenario 1), we develop model runs assuming the likely development phasing described in Table E.1.
- We then model the various elements of the CETAP corridors delayed by five years (scenario 2), and then with a delay of 10 years (scenario 3).
- As an extreme bound, we run the model with no CETAP corridors ever built (scenario 4).

Table E.1
Development Assumptions for the Base Case (scenario 1)

Corridor	Year Completed in Base Case	Description
Mid County Parkway		
I	2020	This 32-mile, limited-access, freeway-level facility from SR-79 to I-15 starts from the junction of Ramona Blvd., Sanderson Ave., and SR-79 in San Jacinto and has 10 lanes to I-215. West of I-215, it will have four lanes all the way. It will have connections to SR-79, I-215, and I-15. All other roads will remain the same.
Winchester-to-Temecula corridor		
II-A	2015	This project adds one lane in each direction on I-215 from I-15 to Scott Road.
II-B	2025	This project widens I-15 from the I-215 junction to Winchester Road to seven lanes in each direction (six lanes plus one HOV lane; currently five lanes in each direction) and south of Winchester Road to six lanes in each direction (five lanes plus one HOV lane; currently four lanes in each direction); widens I-215 south of Newport Road to five lanes in each direction (four lanes plus one HOV lane; currently two lanes in each direction); and builds the four-lane French Valley Parkway, currently Date Street, as a connection from Winchester Road to I-15, with a new interchange at I-15.
Riverside County–to–Orange County corridor		
II-A	2015	This project creates one eastbound auxiliary lane from SR-241 in Orange County to SR-71 in Riverside County and one additional lane in each direction from SR-241 in Orange County to I-15 in Riverside County.

Table E.1—Continued

Corridor	Year Completed in Base Case	Description
II-B	2015	This project creates one general-purpose westbound lane from SR-55 to SR-241, one general-purpose lane in each direction from SR-71 to I-15, one new general-purpose eastbound lane from SR-55 to Lakeview Avenue, and two general-purpose eastbound lanes from Lakeview Avenue to SR-241.
II-C	2020	This grade-separated facility would run roughly parallel to SR-91 or in the median of SR-91 and link to SR-241, SR-91, and I-15. Both four- and six-lane roads have been discussed, and we model a road with two lanes in each direction.
II-D	After 2030	This tunnel would run from I-15 at Cajalco Road in Riverside County to the intersection of SR-241 and SR-133 in Orange County. Again, both four- and six-lane roads have been discussed, and we model a road with two lanes in each direction.
Riverside County–to–San Bernardino County corridor		
IV-A	2015	A new four-lane road (two lanes in each direction) along the route of the current Pigeon Pass Road starting from SR-60 would head north to Center Street just south of the San Bernardino County line. We then continue to model it as a new four-lane road running parallel to the county line and connecting with Main Street/Riverside Avenue. There, add one lane in each direction to Main Street/Riverside Avenue north to I-10. This arterial will have connections to SR-60, I-215, and I-10. It will also have connections to the core element when the two are modeled together.
IV-B	2015	This new four-lane road, running the route of Reche Vista Drive where it starts at the confluence of Heacock Street and Perris Boulevard in Riverside County, would continue as a four-lane road running the route of Reche Canyon Road to the county line. From there, it would run as a new four-lane road to the intersection of Barton Road and Hunts Lane. We then add one more lane in each direction to Hunts Lane north to I-10. This arterial will connect to I-10. It will also connect to the core element when the two are modeled together.
IV-C	After 2030	This is proposed as a limited-access, four-lane expressway starting at the SR-60/I-215 interchange in Riverside County, then following Morton Road north to the Box Springs Mountain Reserve. It would continue as a four-lane tunnel under Box Springs Mountain, and then run east, cross the San Bernardino County line, and then head north to Barton Road through Loma Linda. At Barton Road, it is to head north to I-10 along a new arterial with three lanes in each direction.

The base case uses the current estimates of when the projects will come online and thus implicitly factors in the MSHCP's effects on the project-approval process. Comparing the base case with scenarios 2 and 3 may be viewed as estimates of the effect of rescinding the MSHCP if the MSHCP reduces project completion time by five and 10 years, respectively. Alternatively, the difference between the base case and scenarios 2 and 3 can be viewed as a measure of the benefits of the MSHCP relative to outcomes had the MSHCP never been adopted if the MSHCP reduces project completion time by five and 10 years, respectively.

As reported in Chapter Eight, a number of stakeholders believe that the MSHCP speeds project-approval time by two to five years, and these estimates may not fully reflect time savings due to reduced litigation. Some interview respondents also believe that the MSHCP has increased the probability that projects will be built at all. We thus view the results of the various scenarios as relevant for assessing the potential mobility effects of the MSHCP. Given the uncertainty in both the MSHCP's effect on the permitting process and the effect that delaying projects has on mobility, however, the results should be viewed as providing a general sense of the potential magnitude of the MSHCP's effects on mobility rather than as precise estimates.

Predicted Effects That Project Delays May Have on Mobility

In this section, we compare travel conditions in western Riverside County under the alternative development scenarios.[3] The model predicts travel conditions for both personal and freight vehicles during the three-hour morning peak period. In this section, we describe how the following dimensions of travel change for both personal and freight vehicles originating from western Riverside County during the morning peak period:

- average travel times per trip
- average speeds
- average trip distances
- average total trips.

Travel Times

Table E.2 presents the average travel times forecast by SCPM for personal and freight vehicles originating out of western Riverside County during the morning peak period. The general time trend is that travel times per trip increase until 2025. In 2030, however, this trend reverses for some scenarios, perhaps due to new improvements or perhaps due to employers and households opting to locate closer to one another.

Across scenarios in a given year, SCPM results suggest that delaying CETAP corridor development leads to longer average travel times for trips originating in western Riverside County. Put differently, if the MSHCP speeds infrastructure development, we expect to see improvements in travel times. The effect of development timing can be

---

[3]   Our analysis also looked at population and employment effects. In general, the effect of delayed development on population was small, accounting for no more than a 0.6-percent (less than 15,000 persons) difference from the baseline population estimates in any model year. Effects on employment were also modest, resulting in employment changes of no more than 1.0 percent (7,000 workers).

Table E.2
Average Travel Times for Trips Originating in Western Riverside County During the Morning Peak Period (minutes)

Trip Type	Scenario						
	1: Scheduled Improvements (base case)	2: Improvements Delayed by 5 Years		3: Improvements Delayed by 10 Years		4: No Improvements	
	Time	Time	Difference (%)	Time	Difference (%)	Time	Difference (%)
Personal							
2015	34.29	36.46	6.33	36.46	6.33	36.46	6.33
2020	37.07	38.77	4.59	39.22	5.80	39.22	5.80
2025	40.73	41.78	2.58	43.15	5.96	41.50	1.91
2030	38.34	38.34	0.00	40.33	5.19	41.79	9.01
Freight							
2015	340.10	350.38	3.02	350.38	3.02	350.38	3.02
2020	335.91	357.22	6.34	340.56	1.38	340.56	1.38
2025	352.04	358.25	1.76	360.03	2.27	351.82	−0.06
2030	358.83	358.83	0.00	352.73	−1.70	372.23	3.73

large, reducing travel time by up to 3.5 minutes for personal vehicles (scenario 4, 2030) and nearly 15 minutes for freight vehicles (scenario 4, 2030).

Average Speeds

Over time, trips originating in western Riverside County will see a steady decline in speeds as more people move into the region. Investment in the CETAP corridors can, in most cases, provide marginal improvements, though they cannot reverse the general trend toward greater congestion and slower travel. Table E.3 reports the forecast average speeds for trips originating in the county during the morning peak period. It shows that delaying the CETAP projects will lead to a faster decline in travel speeds.

In a few cases, we observe slower speeds in our base-case scenario when compared with delayed-development scenarios. This can occur for a variety of reasons. For instance, the introduction of a new route might divert some traffic onto shorter but slower-moving arterials. Additionally, during intermediate years, only portions of CETAP have been improved, which can lead to increasing traffic at bottleneck points that are slated for later improvement.

Table E.3
Average Speeds for Trips Originating in Western Riverside County During the Morning Peak Period (miles per hour)

	Scenario						
	1: Scheduled Improvements (base case)	2: Improvements Delayed by 5 Years		3: Improvements Delayed by 10 Years		4: No Improvements	
Trip Type	mph	mph	Difference (%)	mph	Difference (%)	mph	Difference (%)
Personal							
2015	19.35	18.13	−6.31	18.13	−6.31	18.13	−6.31
2020	17.78	16.62	−6.54	17.78	−0.02	17.78	−0.02
2025	15.68	15.91	1.46	14.88	−5.11	14.54	−7.23
2030	14.12	14.12	0.00	13.85	−1.93	12.69	−10.17
Freight							
2015	15.73	15.11	−3.99	15.11	−3.99	15.11	−3.99
2020	15.14	14.25	−5.85	16.39	8.26	16.39	8.26
2025	14.17	14.24	0.46	14.01	−1.16	13.99	−1.29
2030	13.06	13.06	0.00	13.60	4.09	12.48	−4.48

Trip Distance

Trip makers facing greater congestion can respond by taking shorter trips when they have discretion over their destination. Commuters generally do not have this freedom, though they might respond by relocating closer to their employers or switching to jobs located closer to home. Furthermore, increases in congestion might cause firms that ship their products to move closer to ports or other shipment-receiving points.

Table E.4 presents the estimates of average trip distances for personal and freight trips originating in western Riverside County during the morning peak period. The figures suggest that, as congestion mounts over time, travelers and freight vehicles will respond by taking shorter trips. When comparing among scenarios in a given year, the results can be ambiguous.

Number of Trips

In addition to having some discretion over where they choose to travel, work, and reside, residents have some choice over when and how many trips they take. In general, as travel conditions worsen, people will tend to forgo low-value trips. Similarly, investments in infrastructure that lead to improved travel conditions may spur additional trips. Table E.5 presents the predicted number of personal and freight trips

Table E.4
Trip Distance for Trips Originating in Western Riverside County During the Morning Peak Period (miles)

	Scenario						
	1: Scheduled Improvements (base case)	2: Improvements Delayed by 5 Years		3: Improvements Delayed by 10 Years		4: No Improvements	
Trip Type	Miles	Miles	Difference (%)	Miles	Difference (%)	Miles	Difference (%)
Personal							
2015	11.16	11.11	−0.45	11.11	−0.45	11.11	−0.45
2020	10.99	10.74	−2.25	11.62	5.78	11.62	5.78
2025	10.75	11.18	4.06	10.81	0.56	10.16	−5.46
2030	9.11	9.11	0.00	9.39	3.11	8.91	−2.18
Freight							
2015	89.18	88.21	−1.08	88.21	−1.08	88.21	−1.08
2020	84.76	84.87	0.12	93.03	9.76	93.03	9.76
2025	83.17	85.02	2.23	84.06	1.08	82.04	−1.35
2030	78.12	78.12	0.00	79.93	2.32	77.41	−0.92

originating in western Riverside County. The results on trips are ambiguous—in some instances, delayed development leads to fewer trips, while, in others, more trips are forecast.

Quantifying the Travel Costs of Delaying CETAP Corridor Development

In this section, we estimate the dollar value of the direct mobility benefits forecast for each of the various delayed-development scenarios. The analysis characterizes these effects relative to the base-case scenario in each year so that the estimates represent the cost of delaying expansion under the assumptions of each of scenario.

The methodology has been adapted from the updated American Association of State Highway and Transportation Officials (AASHTO) Redbook (2003) which is a manual designed specifically for evaluating the benefits of highway-improvement projects. The benefit calculations utilize output from SCPM and other assumptions, which are described next. The approach is applied to both western Riverside County and the five-county metro region to obtain information on local and regional effects.

Table E.5
Forecast Number of Trips Originating in Western Riverside County During the Morning Peak Period

Trip Type	Scenario						
	1: Scheduled Improvements (base case)	2: Improvements Delayed by 5 Years		3: Improvements Delayed by 10 Years		4: No Improvements	
	Trips	Trips	Difference (%)	Trips	Difference (%)	Trips	Difference (%)
Personal							
2015	665,399	666,298	0.14	666,298	0.14	666,298	0.14
2020	752,246	752,154	−0.01	752,008	−0.03	752,008	−0.03
2025	843,219	842,636	−0.07	843,891	0.08	843,341	0.01
2030	901,906	901,906	0.00	898,921	−0.33	901,244	−0.07
Freight							
2015	6,621	6,779	2.38	6,779	2.38	6,779	2.38
2020	8,354	8,381	0.31	8,492	1.65	8,492	1.65
2025	10,245	10,277	0.32	10,090	−1.51	10,003	−2.36
2030	13,324	13,324	0.00	12,889	−3.27	13,013	−2.33

Analytic Approach

Figure E.2 depicts the economic cost implications of delaying expansion to a congested highway network. The curves $AC_0(Q)$ and $AC_1(Q)$ provide a stylized representation of how the average cost of travel per user varies as we vary the amount (here called *quantity*) of travel that occurs in the network under the base case and under a delayed-development scenario, respectively. The average cost of travel per user increases as more users travel, since this increased use creates additional congestion and delay for motorists.

The curve $AC_1(Q)$ lies above the curve $AC_0(Q)$ because it represents a build scenario in which less capacity is available. As a result, for a given quantity of travel (Q), congestion will be worse under the delayed-development scenario, leading to longer travel times than in the undelayed-expansion plan represented in the base case. The two curves diverge as Q increases because congestion's relative effect on travel times becomes more pronounced as Q increases.

The demand for travel is represented with the downward-sloping line. An equilibrium in this stylized setting is obtained where the average-cost curve intersects with the curve representing the demand for travel. That is, all individuals who value an additional trip more than they value the cost of making that trip will opt to make that trip (see Small, 1992). Figure E.2 therefore represents two equilibriums: In the

Figure E.2
Direct Costs of Delaying Transportation Enhancement

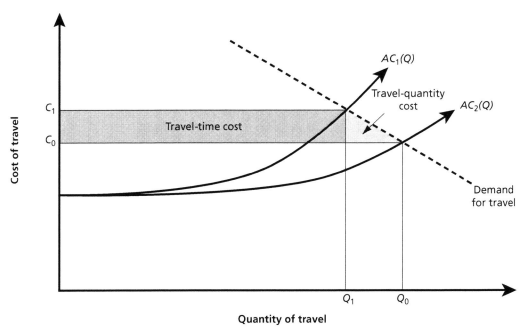

undelayed-build scenario, Q_0 trips are taken, and the average cost of those trips is C_0. The delayed-expansion scenario is depicted with the subscript 1 instead of 0. As Figure E.2 suggests, in the delayed-construction scenario, fewer trips are taken and the average cost of travel is higher at equilibrium.

In practice, the equilibrium cost of travel is calculated by multiplying the average value of time by the average amount of time it takes to make a trip, and the quantity of travel can be represented by the number of trips made in aggregate. Small (1992) summarized studies that reported estimates of the average value of travel time relative to the average wage rate. He found that the estimates suggest that, on average, motorists value travel time saving that is 50 percent of the gross wage rate. The U.S. Department of Labor reported average gross wage rate in the Los Angeles–Riverside–Orange County metropolitan area in 2006 as $21.21 per hour, implying an average value of travel time of $10.60 per hour for personal-vehicle trips in the region. For freight vehicles, estimates of the average value of travel time are more difficult to come by and vary more by source. For our analysis, we adopt an average value of travel time for freight vehicles of $40.00 per hour.

With this information for the base case and the delayed-development scenario, the rectangle (travel-time cost) and triangle (travel-quantity cost) areas in Figure E.2 can be calculated to obtain estimates of the cost of delaying expansion during the morning peak period. These costs can be broken into two elements:

- *Travel-time costs:* The travel-time costs represent the cost of additional delay imposed on trips that occur in both the base-case and delayed-development scenarios. It is calculated as the change in the average cost of travel multiplied by the number of trips taken in the delayed-development scenario:

$$\left(C_1 - C_0\right) \times Q_1.$$

- *Travel-quantity costs:* The travel-quantity costs represent the cost of fewer trips being accommodated at equilibrium under the delayed-development scenario. Under the assumption that demand is linear, this component of cost is calculated as

$$\left(C_1 - C_0\right) \times \left(Q_0 - Q_1\right) \times \frac{1}{2}.$$

The total cost of delaying development during the morning peak period is therefore calculated as the sum of the travel time and quantity components,

$$\begin{aligned}
\Delta_{\text{morning peak}} &= \left(C_1 - C_0\right)Q_1 + \left(C_1 - C_0\right)\left(Q_0 - Q_1\right) \times \frac{1}{2} \\
&= \left(C_1 - C_0\right)\left(Q_0 + Q_1\right) \times \frac{1}{2}.
\end{aligned}$$

The extrapolation of annual benefits from morning peak benefits was performed using techniques outlined in the AASHTO Redbook (AASHTO, 2003).[4]

Estimates of the Annual Mobility Costs of Delaying Development of the CETAP Corridors

The results of applying the approach described in the preceding section to trips originating in western Riverside County are presented in Table E.6.[5] Note that these estimates do not account for safety, environmental, or other effects that might be attributed to the various scenarios. Furthermore, we have considered the timing of improvements only to the CETAP corridors; this analysis does not capture effects on the timing of arterial and other infrastructure improvements.

---

[4] Specifically, we calculate benefit-expansion factors using the K-factor approach described in the AASHTO Redbook (AASHTO, 2003).

[5] The MSHCP's effect spills over into other counties. We estimated the aggregate cost of delaying the MSHCP for each scenario in the five-county region, and there was no consistent pattern in the magnitude or direction of effects.

Table E.6
Estimates of the Annual Costs of Delayed CETAP-Corridor Development for Trips Originating in Western Riverside County (millions of 2007 dollars)

	Scenario		
Trip Type	2: Improvements Delayed by 5 Years	3: Improvements Delayed by 10 Years	4: No Improvements
2015			
Personal	291.7	291.7	291.7
Freight	51.8	51.8	51.8
Total	343.5	343.5	343.5
2020			
Personal	258.1	326.3	326.3
Freight	135.5	29.5	29.5
Total	393.6	355.9	355.9
2025			
Personal	178.6	413.1	132.4
Freight	48.4	62.3	−1.7
Total	227.0	475.4	130.6
2030			
Personal	0.0	361.7	628.7
Freight	0.0	−61.9	135.9
Total	0.0	299.8	764.6

As shown in the table, the cost to western Riverside County drivers of delaying the CETAP improvements by five years would total on the order of $350 million per year in 2015. The total rises to nearly $400 million in 2020. In 2030, it falls to 0 because the CETAP corridors that are currently scheduled to be completed by 2030 will be completed by that date even if there is a five-year delay.

Inevitably, some of the variation we observe when looking at the estimated annual cost of delaying development across scenarios and years is due to modeling imprecision. Quantifying exactly how much of this variation is due to modeling imprecision is difficult, although, due to the model's complexity, we would anticipate that it is greater than one might expect from estimates derived from traditional travel-demand models. As a result, one should interpret these finding with considerable caution.

Conclusion

Our analysis suggests that delaying construction of the four CETAP corridors will cause travel speeds in western Riverside County to decline more rapidly than they would otherwise. While drivers can be expected to respond by taking shorter trips, the net effect will still be that delaying construction of the CETAP corridors will increase the time needed to complete the average trip. The effects on individual trips may not be large, but they can add up when aggregated across all trips taken in a year. Average speeds do not change by more than 1 or 2 miles per hour, but the cost to drivers as a group can total hundreds of millions of dollars annually.

Our analysis has considered only part of the potential benefits of the MSHCP on mobility. It has not considered benefits that result from the faster improvement of the region's arterial roads or the faster completion of road safety and maintenance projects. It also has not examined the MSHCP's environmental benefits. This analysis does, however, provide a starting point for discussions of how large the mobility benefits of the MSHCP might be.

Future Changes in the Permitting Process

As noted in Chapter Eight, the MSHCP's effect on the time needed to complete the permitting process may change over time as the MSHCP's requirements are satisfied. To provide insight into how the MSHCP's effects may differ in the future, this appendix explores how the permitting process will change once the total 500,000-acre reserve is assembled and when the plan's species objectives are satisfied. Such an analysis will help inform assessment of the overall effects of the MSHCP on the permitting process, not just those effects (as examined in Chapter Eight) that have occurred to date or that are expected in the next 10 years.

We first examine how the permitting process will change in three subregions of the overall 1.28 million-acre plan area:

- the area outside the criteria area and the PQP lands (approximately 630,000 acres)[1]
- the 500,000 acres that will ultimately constitute the reserve
- the roughly 150,000 acres that are in the criteria area but are not ultimately needed for the reserve (also referred to in this appendix as the remaining criteria area).[2]

We conclude this appendix by discussing the ongoing need for wildlife agencies to monitor the populations of threatened and endangered species and implications for western Riverside County if a transportation or development project puts a species in jeopardy of extinction.

---

[1] The overall plan area, which covers western Riverside County, is approximately 1.28 million acres. The PQP lands total about 350,000 acres, and the criteria area covers approximately 300,000 acres. There is some overlap between the criteria area and the PQP lands, but it is ignored in this accounting.

[2] As discussed in Chapter One, 153,000 acres in the criteria area will ultimately be included in the reserve.

Changes in Permitting Requirements Outside the Criteria Area and PQP Lands When the Reserve Is Fully Assembled and Species Objectives Are Met

All roads and development projects are permitted under the MSHCP outside the criteria area, and PQP lands must comply with the requirements of the following plan components:

- protection of species associated with riparian/riverine areas and vernal pools
- guidelines pertaining to urban/wildlands interface
- protection of narrow endemic plant species
- other survey requirements (TLMA, 2003, p. 7-1).

In this section, we describe each component's requirements and how they may change over time. We then discuss requirements for other habitat-related permits that the MSHCP does not directly address and how assembling the reserve or satisfying the species objectives may affect them.

Protection of Species Associated with Riparian/Riverine Areas and Vernal Pools

Current Requirements. The MSHCP requires the potentially significant effects on riparian and riverine areas and vernal pools to be assessed for projects proposed anywhere in the plan area (the entire 1.28 million acres in western Riverside County) (TLMA, 2003, p. 6-21). Project applicants are required to develop project alternatives that avoid and then minimize direct and indirect effects to riparian and riverine areas and vernal pools. Applicants are directed to select an avoidance alternative if feasible. If avoidance is not possible, a practicable alternative that minimizes direct and indirect effects on wetland areas should be selected and unavoidable effects mitigated (TLMA, 2003, p. 6-24). In choosing mitigation, the applicant must make a DBESP. Prior to approval of the DBESP, the wildlife agencies must be notified and allowed a 60-day review and response period. DBESP review does not need to go through the JPR process (discussed more later), and the wildlife agencies do not need to be notified of the project if mitigation is not required.

Requirements When the Reserve Is Assembled or Species Objectives Are Met. The MSHCP provides no indication that riparian or riverine and wetland requirements end either when the reserve is assembled or when species objectives are met. The plan does say that requirements may be reviewed and modified with concurrence from the wildlife agencies in light of data assembled through USACE's SAMP analysis (TLMA, 2003, p. 6-23).[3] Thus, the requirements for this MSHCP component may

---

[3] A SAMP is analogous to an HCP but addresses CWA requirements for wetlands rather than ESA requirements.

change over time, but any such change is not tied to completing the reserve or satisfying the species objectives.

Guidelines Pertaining to Urban/Wildlands Interface

Current Requirements. These guidelines address the indirect effect associated with development near the reserve area. The plan requires projects to address potentially adverse effects on the reserve due to drainage, toxic substances, lighting, noise, unauthorized public access, and invasive species (TLMA, 2003, pp. 6-42–6-46). There is no requirement that the wildlife agencies be notified or allowed to respond to the urban and wildland interface plan.

Requirements When the Reserve Is Assembled or Species Objectives Are Met. The requirements of this provision of the plan do not change when the reserve is assembled or species objectives are met. Edge effects are an ongoing concern for the reserve, and it is thus sensible that the urban and wildland interface guidelines remain in force. Satisfying the requirements of these guidelines presumably adds some time to the project-approval process, but the absence of wildlife-agency review may limit its burden.

Protection of Narrow Endemic Plant Species

The previous two plan components do not change when the reserve is assembled or species objectives are met. In contrast, requirements related to protecting narrow endemic plant species and other surveys do end when species objectives for the relevant species are satisfied.

Current Requirements. The data collected in developing the MSHCP did not provide sufficient information on some endemic plant species in the plan area (TLMA, 2003, p. 6-28). Thus, the MSHCP requires surveying for specified narrow endemic plant species in specified areas. If narrow endemic plant species populations are identified, effects on 90 percent of those portions of the property that provide for long-term conservation value of the species should be avoided. If the 90-percent goal cannot be met, the applicant must undertake mitigation that meets the DBESP requirements discussed earlier.

Requirements When the Reserve Is Assembled or Species Objectives Are Met. The survey requirements for narrow endemic plant species may be discontinued when the objectives for the relevant species are met. The objectives for these species typically require that a certain number of acres of the habitat suitable for the species be included in the reserve and can specify particular areas that must be included in the reserve (see, for example, requirements for California Orcutt grass, TLMA, 2003, p. 9-109). Once the species objectives are met and surveys are no longer required, neither DBESP mitigation plans nor wildlife-agency review of the DBESP plan would be required.

Other Survey Requirements

Current Requirements. The MSHCP identifies 20 plant and animal species for which there was inadequate information when the plan was adopted to satisfy the criteria for issuing a take permit under the federal ESA. The plan thus sets up survey, avoidance, and mitigation requirements similar to those described earlier with regard to the narrow endemic plant species. As with the narrow endemic plant species, wildlife-agency review of the DBESP proposals is required (TLMA, 2003, pp. 6-63–6-71).

Requirements When Reserve Assembled or Species Objectives Met. The survey requirements for these other species may be discontinued when the objectives for the relevant species are met. Note that, as for narrow endemic plant species, discontinuing the survey requirements is conditional on satisfaction of the species objectives. A 500,000-acre reserve would thus not trigger an end to the survey requirements if it did not satisfy the habitat-acquisition objectives for the species. Thus, simply acquiring the total amount of land called for in the plan is not enough in itself. The reserve must satisfy the species objectives.

Ongoing Requirements for Other Habitat-Related Permits

Projects outside the criteria area and PQP lands must do more than comply with the MSHCP to obtain the required habitat-related permits. If it affects wetlands or streams, a proposed project will be required to obtain a dredge-and-fill permit from USACE, a streambed-alteration permit from CDFG, and a discharge permit from the Regional Water Quality Control Board. Assembling the reserve or satisfying MSHCP species objectives will not eliminate the need to obtain these permits, but it could streamline the permitting process to some extent.

Dredge-and-Fill Permit. CWA requires projects that dredge or fill U.S. waters to obtain a permit from USACE. In evaluating the permit application, USACE must consult with USFWS concerning the project's effect on threatened or endangered species (so-called Section 7 consultations, referring to Section 7 of the federal ESA). Under the terms of the MSHCP, USFWS is not to impose measures in excess of those required by the MSHCP (RCA, 2004, p. 51). Some of those interviewed for this study believe, however, that USFWS does make demands that, in their view, go beyond MSHCP requirements.[4]

The requirements for a dredge-and-fill permit and a Section 7 consultation with USFWS will not terminate when either the reserve is fully assembled or the objectives for the 146 species covered by the MSHCP are met. Presumably, however, USFWS will raise few if any issues with the dredge-and-fill permit if the species objectives have been

---

[4]   Short of revoking the take permit for the species of concern, USFWS does not have the authority to stop a project that it finds inconsistent with the MSHCP. However, USFWS can, through the Section 7 consultation, impede the issuance of a dredge-and-fill permit for a project that affects streams or wetlands in ways that, in its view, are not consistent with the MSHCP.

met. Nevertheless, a potential source of friction is disagreement between USFWS and the MSHCP permittees on whether the species objectives have actually been met.

When the MSHCP was adopted, it was hoped that a SAMP would also be established that addressed CWA permitting requirements on a regional basis for projects in western Riverside County. The establishment of a SAMP could help to further streamline the permitting process for road and development projects. It is expected that, with a SAMP in place, USFWS would no longer be required to consult with USACE during the dredge-and-fill permitting process, given that this permit would be issued upon agreement over the SAMP just as the take permit was issued upon adoption of the MSHCP. However, a SAMP has not yet been created, and, according to those we interviewed, prospects are not good that one will be adopted in the near term.

Streambed-Alteration Permit. CDFG must issue a streambed-alteration permit. A project that proposes to modify a stream's physical characteristics must obtain a streambed-alteration permit (also referred to as a 1600 permit[5]) from the CDFG. The MSHCP requirements for protecting riparian and riverine areas and vernal pools address most of the concerns that are at issue in a streambed-alteration permit, and, according to an interviewee at CDFG, projects that are consistent with the MSHCP will easily receive a 1600 permit. Streambed-alteration permit requirements will not change when the reserve is fully assembled or species objectives are met; however, as long as projects continue to show consistency with the MSHCP's riparian and riverine and vernal-pool requirements, obtaining these permits should not be burdensome.

Summary of Changes for MSHCP Requirements Outside the Criteria Area and PQP Lands

Once the species objectives are met, the MSHCP's requirements outside the criteria areas and PQP lands will diminish. The survey and protection requirements for narrow endemic plants and 20 other species will expire, reducing, to some extent, the MSHCP burden in these areas. The only MSHCP requirements that will remain outside the criteria areas and the PQP lands will be those associated with riparian or riverine areas, vernal pools, or the urban/wildland interface. The requirements for the urban/wildland interface will continue for the duration of the plan. The requirements associated with riparian and riverine areas will continue for the duration of the plan unless modified with concurrence of the wildlife agencies in light of data assembled through USACE's SAMP analysis.

Unless a SAMP is created, USACE will need to issue dredge-and-fill permits on a project-by-project basis regardless of whether the reserve is fully assembled or the species criteria satisfied. USFWS will be consulted during the permitting process. Presum-

---

[5] This refers to section 1600 of California's Fish and Game Code, in which the terms of this permit are specified.

ably, fewer issues will come up during consultation once the reserve is assembled and species objectives are met.

Changes in Permitting Requirments in the Reserve Area Once the Reserve Is Fully Assembled and Species Objectives Are Met

Construction of projects inside the reserve, both now and once the approximately 500,000 acres are fully assembled, is restricted. No residential, commercial, or industrial projects will be allowed. Only those roads that were included in the western Riverside County circulation element when the MSHCP was adopted can be built or expanded in the reserve. Adding or expanding roads will require that the MSHCP be amended.

The MSHCP includes guidelines for siting and designing planned roads in the criteria area and the PQP lands. Siting criteria are detailed for individual transportation facilities.[6] Noting that the locations for the roads planned in the circulation element are not exact, the MSHCP establishes the following overarching guidelines for project siting, design, and construction:

- Planned roads will be located in the least environmentally sensitive location.
- Planned roads will avoid, to the greatest extent feasible, affecting covered species and wetlands.
- Design of planned roads will consider wildlife movement requirements.
- Narrow endemic plant species will be avoided or, when avoidance is impossible, mitigation as described earlier for narrow endemic plant species will be implemented.
- Natural vegetation will be cleared outside the active breeding season.
- Vegetation mapping and biological survey will be conducted within the project study area. Based on these studies, a qualified biologist will recommend methods to minimize the facility's effect on the reserve area, and the project biologist will work with facility designers during the design and construction phases to ensure implementation of feasible recommendations (TLMA, 2003, pp. 7-80–7-81).[7]

Disputes over a project's consistency with these guidelines are to be resolved through the JPR process (TLMA, 2003, p. 7-80). The project-specific siting criteria and the guidelines just described must be satisfied in the reserve regardless of whether the reserve is fully assembled and whether species objectives are met.

---

[6] For examples of such specific considerations, see TLMA (2003, pp. 7-27–7-30).

[7] Project effects on PQP lands must be mitigated by purchasing land and dedicating it the reserve at not less than a 1:1 ratio. The land cannot count toward the reserve acreage goal (TLMA, 2003, p. 7-15).

The permitting requirements detailed in the preceding discussion of the areas outside the criteria area and PQP lands apply throughout the plan area and thus also apply to projects in the reserve. As discussed, survey requirements for narrow endemic plant species and the 20 other named species will end when the objectives for these species are met. These reductions in survey requirements may benefit projects in the reserve area. However, the MSHCP does not specify which surveys will be required for projects in the reserve, so some surveys may still be required for some species, including those whose objectives have been met. Overall, this review of permitting requirements in the reserve suggests that these permitting requirements are not likely to change much once the reserve is fully assembled and the species objectives are met.

Changes in Permitting Requirements in the Remaining Criteria Area

Permitting requirements may change substantially in the approximately 150,000 acres that are in the criteria area but not ultimately needed for the reserve (the remaining criteria area) when the reserve is assembled and species objectives are met. There is considerable ambiguity about how large the difference will be, however, because the plan is silent on several points key to understanding whether the permitting requirements in the remaining criteria area will become much like those in areas outside the criteria area and PQP lands or whether the restrictions and procedural requirements of the criteria area will continue to apply.

Perhaps first in importance among these ambiguities is whether roads not in the circulation element will be allowed in the remaining criteria area without amendment to the plan. To the extent that they are, economic development in the remaining criteria area may proceed similarly to that in areas outside the criteria area and PQP lands. The MSHCP does not address whether additional roads will be allowed in the remaining criteria area once the reserve is assembled and species objectives are met. Strictly interpreted, the MSHCP limits roads in the criteria area to those in the circulation element, and nothing changes those limitations once the reserve is fully assembled and species objectives are met. It may thus be that an amendment to the plan will be required to authorize additional roads in the remaining criteria area.

There are also no provisions in the MSHCP that suspend the siting or design requirements, construction guidelines, or project-specific considerations that are required for roads in the criteria area once the reserve is assembled and species objectives are met. Thus, it would appear that circulation-element roads in the remaining criteria area will have to comply with the requirements just discussed for transportation projects in the reserve area. Changes discussed to permitting requirements that occur in the reserve area would also apply to the circulation elements in the remaining criteria area.

Completion of the reserve and achievement of the species objectives will presumably remove one component of the permitting process for development projects under the MSHCP in the remaining criteria area and potentially simplify another: The HANS process should no longer be necessary, and there should be fewer issues to address during JPR.

The HANS process specifies the procedures that are used to determine whether part or all of the land proposed for a commercial, industrial, or residential development is needed for the reserve and to acquire the needed acreage (see TLMA, 2003, pp. 6-2–6-11). Applications for proposed projects in the criteria area are reviewed within 45 days to determine whether any portion of the land is required for the reserve. If part or all of the property is required, then a negotiation process begins over what monetary or other incentives are available to induce the property owner to transfer the land to the reserve. Once the reserve is fully assembled and the species objectives are met, there should be no need for the HANS process.

The MSHCP requires RCA and appropriate permittee staff to review proposed transportation and development projects in the criteria area. This JPR process evaluates whether the proposed project is consistent with MSHCP requirements. A multistep dispute-resolution process is set forth to resolve disagreements between RCA and applicants over whether the project is consistent with those requirements (see TLMA, 2003, pp. 6-82–6-85).

There is no indication in the MSHCP that the JPR process will be suspended once the reserve is assembled and species objectives are met. There is reason to expect, however, that the review will become more straightforward and fewer disputes will arise. A central point of contention in the JPR process is what part of the land proposed for development is needed for the reserve. When the reserve is assembled and the species objectives are met, this issue will not need to be addressed. The JPR process will then focus primarily on consistency with the MSHCP requirements just discussed for areas outside the criteria area and PQP lands.

In summary, once the reserve is assembled and species objectives met, the MSHCP requirements pertaining to lands in the remaining criteria area will diminish, but how closely the permitting process in this area will follow that outside the criteria area and PQP lands is uncertain. Roads in the circulation element that have not been built by the time the reserve has been assembled and species objectives met will still have to meet the siting, design, and construction guidelines for roads in the criteria area. These guidelines do not apply to roads outside the criteria area or to PQP lands. The fundamental issue for roads is whether additional roads can be built in the remaining criteria areas. Strictly interpreted, an amendment to the MSHCP would be required to build such roads, and it remains to be seen how difficult it would be to adopt such an amendment. The permitting process for development projects will look much more like that outside the criteria area and PQP lands once the reserve is assembled. There will no longer be negotiations over what part of the property must be conserved. In contrast to development projects outside the criteria area and PQP lands, the remaining criteria area will still formally require JPR, but it will presumably focus on compliance with the requirements that all projects in the plan area must meet.

USFWS Responsibilities If a Species Is in Jeopardy of Extinction

The MSHCP was created to minimize and mitigate the effects of development on species and habitats in western Riverside County. While the measures in the MSHCP minimize "identified impacts [of development] to the maximum extent practicable" (TLMA, 2003, p. 9-1), it is important to note that they do not necessarily ensure the survival of threatened or endangered species. Under ESA, USFWS is charged with protecting threatened and endangered species and must act if a species is in jeopardy of becoming extinct.

Under the federal no-surprises rule, USFWS is limited in what it can require of permittees in the face of significant, unanticipated, adverse change in the status of a species covered by an adopted HCP. Modifications in the management of the reserve area can be requested under such circumstances (TLMA, 2003, p. 6-98). According to one of the stakeholders we interviewed, such modifications could potentially include swapping land in the reserve for habitat elsewhere that is critical to the threatened species. Consistent with the no-surprises rule, however, USFWS cannot require the permittees to provide additional financial compensation, land, or land restrictions beyond those required when the plan was adopted (TLMA, 2003, p. 6-100). Nevertheless, if a project puts a species at risk of extinction, USFWS must revoke the take permit for the species, resulting in a potential stalemate: USFWS cannot require addition mitigation for the project to ensure species survival but cannot allow the take permit to remain in place. In such an instance, USFWS might draw on federal resources—for example, by dedicating available federal lands or acquiring or restoring appropriate habitat for the species—but the authority or funds required to do so might not be available without an act of Congress.

USFWS's mission requires it to monitor the health of threatened and endangered species in western Riverside County, especially to guard against species-jeopardy situations, regardless of whether a multispecies HCP is in place. The MSHCP reduces USFWS's role in the day-to-day approval of projects in western Riverside County, and its role will be further reduced once the reserve is fully assembled and species objectives are met. However, absent changes to ESA, USFWS must continue to monitor species in western Riverside County and scrutinize closely any development that threatens to put species in jeopardy of extinction.

References

AASHTO—*see* American Association of State Highway and Transportation Officials.

American Association of State Highway and Transportation Officials, *User Benefit Analysis for Highways Manual*, Washington, D.C., AE-UBA-2-P, August 2003.

Bechtel, Cathy, project delivery director, Riverside County Transportation Commission, "Memorandum of Understanding No. 07-65-087-00 on Improvement of Transportation Facilities: Pigeon Pass and Reche Canyon Road Corridors," memorandum to Riverside County Transportation Commission, January 10, 2007. As of September 28, 2008:
http://www.rctc.org/downloads/7E.CB-RCTC-Pigeon%20Pass-Reche%20Cyn%20MOU.pdf

California Constitution, Article 1, Declaration of Rights, Section 2(a), declaring right of free speech.

———, Article 13, Taxation.

———, Article 13A, Tax Limitation.

———, Article 13D, Assessment and Property-Related Fee Reform.

———, Article 19, Motor Vehicle Revenues, Section 2(a), stating the purposes for which revenues can be used.

California Department of Finance, "California Statistical Abstract," January 2007. As of May 20, 2008:
http://www.dof.ca.gov/HTML/FS_DATA/STAT-ABS/Statistical_Abstract.php

California Department of Industrial Relations, Consumer Price Index for Los Angeles–Anaheim–Riverside, late 2007.

California Fish and Game Code sections 2800–2835, codifying the Natural Community Conservation Planning Act of 1991.

California Franchise Tax Board, "Are Mello-Roos Taxes Deductible on Your Personal Income Tax Return?" undated Web page. As of September 4, 2008:
http://www.ftb.ca.gov/individuals/faq/net/909.shtml

California Government Code section 43600, defining *issue of bonds*.

California Government Code sections 53311–53368.3, codifying the Mello-Roos Community Facilities Act of 1982.

California Infrastructure and Economic Development Bank, "About Us," undated Web page. As of April 21, 2008:
http://www.ibank.ca.gov/AboutUs/

———, *Criteria, Priorities, and Guidelines for the Infrastructure State Revolving Fund (ISRF) Program*, January 29, 2008.

California Public Resources Code sections 21000–21177, codifying the California Environmental Quality Act.

California Revenue and Taxation Code, sections 10752–10752.1.

———, sections 11911–11929.

California Transportation Commission, "CMIA Adopted Program of Projects," February 28, 2007. As of June 24, 2007:
http://www.catc.ca.gov/CMIA_action_0228.pdf

California Vehicle Code sections 9250.2, 9250.7, 9250.11, 9250.14, and 9250.16.

Capozza, Dennis R., and Robert W. Helsley, "The Stochastic City," *Journal of Urban Economics*, Vol. 28, No. 2, September 1990, pp. 187–203.

Case, Karl E., and Christopher J. Mayer, *Housing Price Dynamics Within a Metropolitan Area*, Boston, Mass.: Federal Reserve Bank of Boston, working paper 95-3, April 1995.

Center for Natural Lands Management, *Natural Lands Management Cost: 28 Case Studies*, Fallbrook, Calif., October 2004. As of September 11, 2008:
http://www.cnlm.org/images/28CaseStudiesPart1.pdf

Cho, Sungbin, Peter Gordon, James E. Moore II, Harry W. Richardson, Masanobu Shinozuka, and Stephanie Chang, "Integrating Transportation Network and Regional Economic Models to Estimate the Costs of a Large Urban Earthquake," *Journal of Regional Science*, Vol. 41, No. 1, 2001, pp. 39–65.

Cho, Sungbin, Peter Gordon, Harry W. Richardson, James E. Moore II, and Masanobu Shinozuka, "Analyzing Transportation Reconstruction Network Strategies: A Full Cost Approach," *Review of Urban and Regional Development Studies*, Vol. 12, No. 3, November 2000, pp. 212–227.

CIEDB—*see* California Infrastructure and Economic Development Bank.

City of Davis, California, Municipal Code, Chapter 15, Section 15.17.040, Open Space Protection Tax. As of September 28, 2008:
http://www.city.davis.ca.us/cmo/citycode/detail.cfm?p=15&q=2342

Clapp, John M., Mauricio Rodriguez, and R. Kelley Pace, "Residential Land Values and the Decentralization of Jobs," *Journal of Real Estate Finance and Economics*, Vol. 22, No. 1, January 2001, pp. 43–61.

CNLM—*see* Center for Natural Lands Management.

Code of Federal Regulations, Title 23, Section 710.513, Environmental Mitigation, *Federal Register*, Vol. 64, December 21, 1999, p. 71290.

———, Title 23, Part 777, Mitigation of Impacts to Wetlands and Natural Habitat, *Federal Register*, Vol. 65, December 29, 2000, p. 82924.

———, Title 43, Part 12, Section 12.50, Forms for Applying for Grants.

———, Title 50, Part 81, Section 81.2, Cooperation with the States.

Crabbe, Amber E., Rachel Hiatt, Susan D. Poliwka, and Martin Wachs, "Local Transportation Sales Taxes: California's Experiment in Transportation Finance," *Public Budgeting and Finance*, Vol. 25, No. 3, Fall 2005, pp. 91–121.

CTC—*see* California Transportation Commission.

DataQuick Information Systems, "Monthly Vacant Land Sale Data for Riverside County," data provided to authors, June 2008.

Dill, Jennifer, and Asha Weinstein, "How to Pay for Transportation? A Survey of Public Preferences in California," *Transport Policy*, Vol. 14, No. 4, July 2007, pp. 346–356.

DOF—*see* California Department of Finance.

EO—*see* Executive Order.

EPA—*see* U.S. Environmental Protection Agency.

Erickson, Gregg, California Department of Transportation, telephone communication with author, January 31, 2008.

Executive Order 13274, Environmental Stewardship and Transportation Infrastructure Project Reviews, September 18, 2002. As of September 16, 2008:
http://edocket.access.gpo.gov/cfr_2003/3CFR13274.htm

Executive Order 13352, Facilitation of Cooperative Conservation, August 26, 2004. As of September 16, 2008:
http://edocket.access.gpo.gov/cfr_2005/janqtr/3CFR13352.htm

Federal Highway Administration, "Reasons for EIS Project Delays," undated Web page. As of September 28, 2008:
http://www.environment.fhwa.dot.gov/strmlng/eisdelay.asp

———, *Guidelines for Federal-Aid Participation in the Establishment and Support of Wetland Mitigation Banks*, policy memorandum, Office of Environment and Planning, October 24, 1994.

———, *Memorandum of Understanding to Foster the Ecosystem Approach*, December 15, 1995.

———, *Innovative Finance Primer*, Washington, D.C., FHW-AD-02-004, 2002. As of April 21, 2008:
http://www.fhwa.dot.gov/innovativeFinance/ifp/

———, *Early Mitigation Planning for Transportation Improvements in California*, memorandum of agreement, November 12, 2003.

———, *Federal-Aid Eligibility of Wetland and Natural Habitat Mitigation*, memorandum, Office of Chief Counsel, March 10, 2005.

FHWA—*see* Federal Highway Administration.

Gordon, Peter, James E. Moore II, Harry W. Richardson, and Qisheng Pan, "The Economic Impact of a Terrorist Attack on the Twin Ports of Los Angeles–Long Beach," in Harry W. Richardson, Peter Gordon, and James E. Moore II, eds., *The Economic Impacts of Terrorist Attacks*, Cheltenham, UK, and Northampton, Mass.: Edward Elgar, 2005, pp. 262–286.

———, "The Costs of a Terrorist Attack on Terminal Island at the Twin Ports of Los Angeles and Long Beach," in Jon D. Haveman and Howard J. Shatz, eds., *Protecting the Nation's Seaports: Balancing Security and Cost*, San Francisco, Calif.: Public Policy Institute of California, 2006, pp. 71–90.

Hannay, Robert, and Martin Wachs, "Factors Influencing Support for Local Transportation Sales Tax Measures," *Transportation*, Vol. 34, No. 1, January 2007, pp. 17–35.

Hoyt, Homer, "The Effect of Cyclical Fluctuations Upon Real Estate Finance," *Journal of Finance*, Vol. 2, No. 1, April 1947, pp. 51–60.

ILG—*see* Institute for Local Government.

Ingles, Jeffrey, Transportation Finance Bank, telephone communication with author, May 2007.

Institute for Local Government, "Funding Open Space Acquisition Programs," last updated July 15, 2008. As of May 19, 2008:
http://www.ca-ilg.org/
index.jsp?displaytype=11&zone=ilsg&section=land&sub_sec=land_conserv&tert=&story=23902

Jacobs Engineering Group, *Riverside County–Orange County Major Investment Study, Executive Summary, Final Project Report: Locally Preferred Strategy Report*, prepared for Orange County Transportation Authority in cooperation with Riverside County Transportation Commission and Foothill-Eastern Transportation Corridor Agency, Pasadena, California, January 2006.

King, Rhonda, and Katherine Gifford, Riverside County Executive Office, "Funding the Western Riverside and Coachella MSHCPs and County Implementation of MSHCP Programs," memorandum to Multiple Species Habitat Conservation Plan Implementation Committee, March 8, 2005.

Kline, Jeffrey D., "Public Demand for Preserving Local Open Space," *Society and Natural Resources*, Vol. 19, No. 7, 2006, pp. 645–659.

Kotchen, Matthew J., and Shawn M. Powers, "Explaining the Appearance and Success of Voter Referenda for Open-Space Conservation, *Journal of Environmental Economics and Management*, Vol. 52, No. 1, July 2006, pp. 373–390.

Landis, John David, and Michael Reilly, *How We Will Grow: Baseline Projections of the Growth of California's Urban Footprint Through the Year 2100*, Berkeley, Calif.: Institute of Urban and Regional Development, University of California, Berkeley, working paper 2003-04, August 2003.

Landry, Charles, executive director, Western Riverside County Regional Conservation Authority, telephone communication with author, September 2, 2008.

Lewis, Barbara, telephone communication with author, May 2007.

Misczynski, Dean, director, California Research Bureau, California State Library, telephone communication with author, May 2008.

Moore, James E. II, Richard G. Little, Sungbin Cho, and Shin Lee, "Using Regional Economic Models to Estimate the Costs of Infrastructure Failures: The Cost of a Limited Interruption in Electric Power in the Los Angeles Region," *Public Works Management and Policy*, Vol. 10, No. 3, January 2006, pp. 256–274.

Mountains Recreation and Conservation Authority, "Frequently Asked Questions," undated Web page. As of September 28, 2008:
http://www.preserveopenspace.org/faqs.html

MRCA—*see* Mountains Recreation and Conservation Authority.

National Research Council Committee on Mitigating Wetland Losses, *Compensating for Wetland Losses Under the Clean Water Act*, Washington, D.C.: National Academies Press, 2001. As of September 16, 2008:
http://www.nap.edu/books/0309074320/html/

NRC—*see* National Research Council Committee on Mitigating Wetland Losses.

Office of Management and Budget, *Guidelines and Discount Rates for Benefit-Cost Analysis of Federal Programs*, Washington, D.C.: Executive Office of the President, Office of Management and Budget, circular A-94, 1992.

————, "Discount Rates for Cost-Effectiveness, Lease Purchase, and Related Analyses," *Guidelines and Discount Rates for Benefit-Cost Analysis of Federal Programs*, Appendix C, Washington, D.C.: Executive Office of the President, Office of Management and Budget, circular A-94, January 2008. As of September 11, 2008:
http://www.whitehouse.gov/omb/circulars/a094/a94_appx-c.html

OMB—*see* Office of Management and Budget.

OSA—*see* Santa Clara County Open Space Authority.

Porr, Robert, vice president, Fieldman, Rolapp and Associates, pricing of recent Riverside County bonds, personal communication, 2008.

Public Law 845, Federal Water Pollution Control Act, June 30, 1948, as amended through Public Law 107-303, November 27, 2002.

Public Law 91-190, National Environmental Policy Act, January 1, 1970.

Public Law 93-205, Endangered Species Act, December 28, 1973, as amended through Public Law 107-136, January 24, 2002.

Public Law 102-240, Intermodal Surface Transportation Efficiency Act, December 18, 1991.

Public Law 104-59, National Highway System Designation Act, November 28, 1995.

Public Law 105-178, Transportation Equity Act for the 21st Century, June 9, 1998.

Public Law 109-59, Safe, Accountable, Flexible, Efficient Transportation Equity Act: A Legacy for Users, August 10, 2005.

RCA—*see* Western Riverside County Regional Conservation Authority.

RCIP—*see* Riverside County Integrated Project.

RCTC—*see* Riverside County Transportation Commission.

Riverside County, *Winchester to Temecula Corridor: Draft Environmental Impact Statement/Draft Environmental Impact Report, CETAP Hearing Draft*, Riverside, Calif., 2002.

————, Amending Ordinance 810 to Establish the Western Riverside County Multiple Species Habitat Conservation Plan Mitigation Fee, ordinance 810.2, effective September 19, 2003. As of September 28, 2008:
http://www.clerkoftheboard.co.riverside.ca.us/ords/800/810.htm

Riverside County Economic Development Agency, "Riverside County 2008 Average Home Price," January 2008. As of March 11, 2008:
http://www.rivcoeda.org/Portals/0/demographicReports/
Average%20Home%20Prices%20-%20January%202008.pdf

Riverside County EDA—*see* Riverside County Economic Development Agency.

Riverside County Integrated Project, "The Riverside County Integrated Project (RCIP)," undated. As of September 28, 2008:
http://www.rcip.org/Documents/RCIP%20overview_REV.pdf

Riverside County Transportation and Land Management Agency, *MSHCP*, Vol. 1: *The Plan*, Riverside County, Calif., 2003. As of January 30, 2008:
http://www.wrc-rca.org/Permit_Docs/mshcp_vol1.html

Riverside County Transportation Commission, "CETAP Internal Corridors Recommendations," February 12, 2003a.

———, "Frequently Asked Questions for CETAP," April 14, 2003b. As of September 28, 2008:
http://www.rcip.org/pdf_files/CETAP_FAQ_04_14_03.pdf

———, "Minutes, Wednesday, December 13, 2006," December 13, 2006.

Riverside County Transportation Commission, and San Bernardino Associated Governments, "Notice of Preparation of an Environmental Impact Report (EIR) for the Moreno Valley to San Bernardino County Corridor in Riverside and San Bernardino Counties, California," May 2003. As of September 28, 2008:
http://www.rcip.org/Documents/Final_NOP_05_08.pdf

San Bernardino Associated Governments, "Moreno Valley to San Bernardino Valley Corridor Study," undated Web page. As of June 24, 2007:
http://www.sanbag.ca.gov/planning/subr_corridor_moval.html

San Diego Association of Governments, "TransNet: Environmental Mitigation Program Fact Sheet," September 2005. As of February 5, 2008:
http://www.sandag.org/uploads/publicationid/publicationid_1138_4880.pdf

SANBAG—*see* San Bernardino Associated Governments.

SANDAG—*see* San Diego Association of Governments.

Santa Clara County Civil Grand Jury, *2005–2006 Santa Clara County Civil Grand Jury Report: Exploring Open Space Special Districts in Santa Clara County*, 2006. As of September 15, 2008:
http://www.sccsuperiorcourt.org/jury/GJreports/2006/ExploringOpenSpaceSpecialDistricts.pdf

Santa Clara County Open Space Authority, *Engineer's Report, District No. 1: Fiscal Year 2007–2008*, 2007a.

———, *Engineer's Report, District No. 2: Fiscal Year 2007–2008*, 2007b.

SCAG—*see* Southern California Association of Governments.

Shoup, Donald C., *New Funds for Old Neighborhoods: California's Deferred Special Assessments*, Berkeley, Calif.: University of California, Berkeley, California Policy Seminar, 1990.

Silicon Valley Taxpayers Assn., Inc. v Santa Clara County Open Space Authority, Cal. App. 6 Dist., case H026759, July 6, 2005.

Small, Kenneth A., *Urban Transportation Economics*, Chur, Switzerland, and Reading, Pa: Harwood Academic Publishers, 1992.

Sollenberger, Joan, California Department of Transportation, telephone communication with author, January 29, 2008.

Southern California Association of Governments, *2004 Regional Transportation Plan*, Los Angeles, Calif., 2004.

"Southland Home Sales Drag Along Bottom," *DQNews.com*, La Jolla, Calif., July 16, 2008. As of July 29, 2008:
http://www.dqnews.com/News/California/Southern-CA/RRSCA080716.aspx

Stein, Bruce A., Lynn S. Kutner, and Jonathan S. Adams, *Precious Heritage: The Status of Biodiversity in the United States*, Oxford and New York: Oxford University Press, 2000.

TCA—*see* Transportation Corridor Agencies.

TFB—*see* Transportation Finance Bank.

Titman, Sheridan, "Urban Land Prices Under Uncertainty," *American Economic Review*, Vol. 75, No. 3, June 1985, pp. 505–514.

TLMA—*see* Riverside County Transportation and Land Management Agency.

TPL—*see* Trust for Public Land.

Transportation Corridor Agencies, "The Foothill (241) and Eastern (241, 261, and 133) Toll Roads: Environmental Mitigation," undated fact sheet. As of May 20, 2008:
http://tollroad.com/home/images/fe_mitigation.pdf

———, *Foothill/Eastern Transportation Corridor Agency FY 2008 Proposed Budget*, June 14, 2007a. As of May 20, 2008:
http://tollroad.com/home/images/publications/08_FE_BUDGET.pdf

———, *San Joaquin Hills Transportation Corridor Agency FY 2008 Proposed Budget*, June 14, 2007b. As of May 20, 2008:
http://tollroad.com/home/images/publications/08_SJH_BUDGET.pdf

———, *Foothill/Eastern Transportation Corridor Financial Statements*, June 30, 2007c. As of May 20, 2008:
http://tollroad.com/home/images/publications/2007_fe_audit.pdf

———, *San Joaquin Hills Transportation Corridor Agency Financial Statements*, June 30, 2007d. As of May 20, 2008:
http://tollroad.com/home/images/publications/2007_sjh_audit.pdf

Transportation Finance Bank, "Transportation Finance Bank: Fact Sheet," undated fact sheet. As of February 5, 2008:
http://www.dot.ca.gov/hq/innovfinance/t_f/tfb_facts.pdf

Trevino, Theresa, chief financial officer, Riverside County Transportation Commission, undated email to the authors.

Trust for Public Land, "Welcome to the LandVote Database!" undated Web page. As of May 20, 2008:
http://www.conservationalmanac.org/landvote/cgi-bin/nph-landvote.cgi/000000A/https/www.quickbase.com/db/bbqna2qct

University of Southern California Homeland Security Center, "Our Research," undated Web page. As of July 4, 2007:
http://www.usc.edu/dept/create/research/economics.htm

U.S. Army Corps of Engineers, U.S. Environmental Protection Agency, U.S. Fish and Wildlife Service, and National Oceanic and Atmospheric Administration, "Federal Guidance on the Use of In-Lieu-Fee Arrangements for Compensatory Mitigation Under Section 404 of the Clean Water Act and Section 10 of the Rivers and Harbors Act," *Federal Register*, Vol. 65, No. 216, November 7, 2000, pp. 66913–66917. As of September 16, 2008:
http://frwebgate.access.gpo.gov/cgi-bin/getdoc.cgi?dbname=2000_register&docid=00-28516-filed.pdf

U.S. Department of Transportation, "Department of Transportation Priority Project List," last modified August 15, 2008a. As of September 28, 2008:
http://www.dot.gov/execorder/13274/projects/pplist/

———, "Priority Project Transition List," last modified August 15, 2008b. As of September 28, 2008:
http://www.dot.gov/execorder/13274/projects/pptranslist/

U.S. Department of Transportation Research and Innovative Technology Administration, and Federal Highway Administration, *Eco-Logical: An Ecosystem Approach to Developing Infrastructure Projects*, Washington, D.C., April 2006.

U.S. Environmental Protection Agency, "Wetland Regulatory Authority," fact sheet, EPA843-F-04-001, undated. As of February 5, 2008:
http://www.epa.gov/owow/wetlands/pdf/reg_authority_pr.pdf

U.S. Fish and Wildlife Service, "Guidance for the Establishment, Use, and Operation of Conservation Banks," *Federal Register*, Vol. 68, No. 89, May 8, 2003, p. 24753. As of September 16, 2008:
http://www.fws.gov/policy/library/03-11458.pdf

⸻, *USFWS Conceptual Reserve Design of the Western Riverside County MSHCP Conservation Area*, Carlsbad, Calif.: Carlsbad Fish and Wildlife Office, May 26, 2004.

⸻, "Cooperative Endangered Species Conservation Fund," Web page, last updated July 28, 2008. As of February 5, 2008:
http://www.fws.gov/midwest/endangered/grants/S6_grants.html

USACE et al.—*see* U.S. Army Corps of Engineers, U.S. Environmental Protection Agency, U.S. Fish and Wildlife Service, and National Oceanic and Atmospheric Administration.

USC Homeland Security Center—*see* University of Southern California Homeland Security Center.

USDOT—*see* U.S. Department of Transportation.

USDOT and FHWA—*see* U.S. Department of Transportation Research and Innovative Technology Administration and Federal Highway Administration.

Venner, Marie, *Early Mitigation for Net Environmental Benefit: Meaningful Off-Setting Measures for Unavoidable Impacts*, American Association of State Highway and Transportation Officials, September 2005. As of September 16, 2008:
http://www.trb.org/NotesDocs/25-25(10)_FR.pdf

Wachs, Martin, "Local Option Transportation Taxes: Devolution as Revolution," *Access*, Vol. 22, Spring 2003, pp. 9–15.

Western Riverside Council of Governments, *Transportation Uniform Mitigation Fee Program Annual Report: 2006*, Riverside, Calif., c. 2007.

Western Riverside County Regional Conservation Authority, *Implementing Agreement for the Western Riverside County Multiple Species Habitat Conservation Plan/Natural Community Conservation Plan*, Riverside County, Calif., 2004.

⸻, "Resolution of the Board of Directors of the Western Riverside County Regional Conservation Authority Revising Its Fee Collection and Remittance Policy," Resolution 07-04, September 10, 2007a. As of September 28, 2008:
http://www.wrc-rca.org/Forms/RCA_Resolution_07-04.pdf

⸻, *Staff Report: Recommendation Regarding MSHCP Minor Amendment*, Riverside County, Calif., November 5, 2007b. As of February 6, 2008:
http://www.wrc-rca.org/2007_BD/071105/Agenda_Item_8.2_STAFF_Report.pdf

⸻, personal communication with the authors, February 2008.

WRCOG—*see* Western Riverside Council of Governments.